SOULS
IN THE SEA

SOULS
IN THE SEA

Dolphins, Whales, and Human Destiny

SCOTT TAYLOR

Frog, Ltd.
Berkeley, California

Published by Frog, Ltd.

Frog, Ltd. books are distributed by
North Atlantic Books
P.O. Box 12327
Berkeley, California 94712

Cover and book design Jennifer Dunn

Printed in Canada

North Atlantic Books are available through most bookstores. To contact North Atlantic directly, call 800-337-2665 or visit our website at www.northatlanticbooks.com.

Substantial discounts on bulk quantities of North Atlantic books are available to corporations, professional associations, and other organizations. For details and discount information, contact the special sales department at North Atlantic Books.

Library of Congress Cataloging-in-Publication Data

Taylor, Scott, 1949–
    Souls in the sea : dolphins, whales, and human destiny / Scott Taylor.
        p. cm.
    Includes bibliographical references.
        ISBN 1-58394-071-5 (pbk.)
        1. Cetacea. 2. Human-animal relationships. 3. Cetacea—Folklore.
I. Title.
    QL737.C4 T38 2003
    599.5—dc21

                                                                    2002152951

        1 2 3 4 5 6 7 8 9 TRANS 07 06 05 04 03

Contents

Acknowledgments

Writing a book can be a lonely endeavor, one that takes over your life and demands that you live within yourself for months at a time. To do this, one must have the support of others, and I have had wonderful allies throughout the process of the writing of this book. And to begin there must be the arrival of inspiration.

I am grateful to Peter Shenstone for the inspiring wave he sent around the world in the form of the Legend of the Golden Dolphin. I'm happy to acknowledge the gift he has shared so generously. I have elaborated on his ideas, adding many of my own. Therefore, I must accept responsibility for how his inspiration has been used. The Legend continues and I look forward to our next Legendarian session together.

I also acknowledge with deep gratitude the man who brought me Peter's story, Bruce Mace. His singular slant on the tale has been a constant guide to me. He sometimes seems like a combination of yogi and conceptual engineer, on loan from the Great White Brotherhood, when I consider the range of his knowledge and the enthusiasm he brings to improving the human condition. My recommendation: Fund this man's dreams. Bruce has taught me the meaning of brotherhood. I continue to have insightful conversations about the Dolphin Tale with Bruce, and this book reflects only parts of what he has helped me to see.

I owe a special thank you to John Lilly, who told me to "Just be here now!" when I most needed to hear it. John, may you now find the StarMaker Himself....

Thanks also are due to a long list of friends who have supported me in many ways: Kim Kindersley, Donna Brewer, Katryn Lavanture, Ashleea Nielsen, Deena Hoagland, Trish and Wally Franklin, Carolina Ely, Dr. Peter O'Brien, Jan Thornely, Timothy Wyllie, Elaine Seiler, Diane Firestone, Allan Armstrong, Beau Ives, Leslie Morava, Lorri Lester, Tim Smith, Dr. Devin Mikles, Troy Saville, Jim Nollman, Stan and Cynthia Tenen, Ed Ellsworth, Janice Otero, Jinni Richards, Michael Bailey, the FernGully Family, Claire Leimbach, Philip Bailey, Kathy Jenson and the Boys, Jerry Starnes, Gary Mitchell, Raya and Ross and Andrew, Steve and Kari and Zia, Danielle Leonard, Isabella and Zoe Mack, Mook and Shanto, Marie-Helene and Buddha, Ken Levasseur, Shelly Friend, Ohshala, Pahana and a host of e-mail correspondents.

Other friends and colleagues I will thank for reasons they may or may not know: Estelle Myers, Horace Dobbs, Kris Kollins, Roberta Quist, Kamala Hope-Campbell, Mike Woods, Paul Spong, Dr. Lindy Weilgart, John Sevenoaks, Howie Cooke, Mary-Caroline Meadows, Akbar, Bob Dratch, Scott McVay, Dr. Steven Birch, Sage Hamilton, Francis Huxley, Adele Getty, Gigi Coyle, Mela Leavell, Doug Gunton, Bill Mollison, Stephen Landers, Dave Cole, Deane-Paul Anderson, Lydia McCarthy, Joan Ocean, Jean-Luc Bozzoli, George Elston, Daniel McCulloch, and of course, Jim Loomis.

There is a long list of dolphins who deserve thanks, three of whom I will thank here. Squirt, thank you for the ride. This is a beginning. Suwa, your trust remains in me, mind and body. And Delphi, I listened, and I'm working on it....

I have been lucky to have the editorial help of Amy Taylor, Brendan Hanley, Lindy Hough, and Kathy Glass. They have endured much, and this book and all its readers have benefited from their participation.

I also want to acknowledge the quick and ready vision of Richard Grossinger, of Frog Ltd., who saw beyond my inexperience to a book that could be, who grasped the possibility of its significance, and who encouraged me to produce it.

The most important person on my list of allies and inspirations is Merrilee, my exceptional wife. I have abandoned her to months of neglect, hoping by the time I emerged she could help me remember the person I was. Her faith, her belief in something unseen, has been the mortar of the building of this book. Thank you Merrilee, for more than words can say.

And last in this list of people to whom I owe thanks, but first in giving me support to be here writing these acknowledgments, is my mother Betty Taylor and her assistant Jerry.

My sincere thanks to all.

Extracts

Collected by a sub-archivist for the *CetaceanCyclopedia:*

> As I first in the dark sea sprang
> In dolphin form onto the swift ship, so
> Pray to me as Delphinus; while this altar
> Shall ever be the Delphi altar, seen from afar.
> —Homer, *Hymn to Apollo*

> O for the ships of Troy, the beat
> Of oars that shimmered
> Innumerable, and dancing feet
> Of Nereids glimmered;
> And dolphins, drunken with the lyre,
> Across the dark blue prows, like fire,
> Did bound and quiver,
> To cleave the way for Thetis's son,
> Fleet-in-the-wind Achilles, on
> To war, to war, till Troy be won
> Beside the reedy river.
> —Euripides, *Electra*

The dolphin is an animal not only friendly to man, but a lover of music as well. He is charmed by melodious concerts, especially by the notes of the water organ. He does not dread man, as though a stranger to him, but comes to meet ships, leaps and bounds to and fro, vies with them in swiftness, and passes them even in full sail.

For a voice the dolphin has a moaning or a wailing similar to that of the human.

—Pliny the Elder (23–79 A.D.), *Naturalis Historia*

I have beheld the image of Derceto in Phoenicia. A marvellous spectacle it is. One half is a woman, but the part that extends from thighs to feet terminates with the tail of a fish. And from the ceiling of her temple is suspended the golden image of a fish.

—Lucian, *De Dea Syria*, ca. 200 A.D.

But notwithstanding, although the dolphins so excel in gentleness and though they have a heart so much at one with men, the overweening Thracians and those who dwell in the city of Byzas hunt them with iron-hearted devices—surely wicked men and sinful ...

—Oppian, *Halieutica*, ca. 200 A.D.

All just men who appreciate music bury dead dolphins out of respect for their love of music. But those to whom, as they say, the Muses and Graces are alien care nothing for dolphins. And so, beloved dolphins, you must pardon the savage nature of man.

—Aelian, *On the Characteristics of Animals*

And if we look at creatures in the sea, we need not wonder at the Dolphins loving their offspring, for they are superior creatures.

—Apollonius of Tyana, 220 A.D.

Son of man, take up a lament concerning Pharaoh king of Egypt and say to him:

> "... You are like a whale in the seas thrashing about in your streams, churning the water with your feet and muddying the streams."

This is what the Sovereign Lord says:

> "With a great throng of people I will cast my net over you,and they will haul you up in my net. I will throw you on the land and hurl you on the open field. I will let all the birds of the air settle on you and all the beasts of the earth gorge themselves on you. I will spread your flesh on the mountains and fill the valleys with your remains. I will drench the land with your flowing blood all the way to the mountains, and the ravines will be filled with your flesh."

> —Ezekiel 32:2–6, King James Bible

There is the sea, vast and spacious, teeming with creatures beyond number—living things both large and small. There the ships go to and fro, and the leviathan, which you formed to frolic there.

> —Psalms 104:25–26

But how should they, who gave their Scriptures to the whale nation, not expect that they would come to light, and who predicted, moreover, that this religion should be proclaimed to all nations?

> Jesus declared, "The kingdom of God shall be taken from you, and given to a nation bringing forth the fruits thereof ..."

> —Origen, one the Church Fathers

A tenth branch of the king's ordinary revenue, said to be grounded on the consideration of his guarding and protecting the seas from pirates and robbers, is the right to royal fish, which are whale and sturgeon. And these, when either thrown ashore or caught near the coast, are the property of the king.

   —Blackstone, in *Moby Dick*, 1851

New Plymouth Colony have great profit by whale killing. I believe it will be one of our best returnes, now beaver and [other pelts] fail us.

   —Secretary Edward Randolph to King George III,
    1688

What has ever caught the imagination more than the dolphin? When man traverses the vast domains his genius has conquered, he finds the dolphin on all the seas' surface. He meets him in the happy climes of temperate zones, under the burning skies of equatorial seas, and in the horrible valleys that separate those immense ice mountains that rise like so many tombstones to Nature above the Polar ocean. Man sees him everywhere—light in his movements, rapid in his swimming, astonishing in his jumps, delighting in charming away by his quick and foolish movements the boredom of prolonged calms, animating the ocean's immense solitude, disappearing like lightning, escaping into the air like a bird, reappearing, fleeing, showing himself again, playing with the wild waves and bracing the tempests. The dolphin does not fear the elements, nor distance, nor the sea's tyrants.

Returning to those peaceable retreats he has ornamented to his pleasure, man enjoys again the dolphin's image traced by artists on their masterpieces. In the immortal pieces prepared by poetry's genius to please his wit and heart, he reads the dolphin's touching history. And when, in the silence of a peaceful night, in those moments of calm and melancholy when meditation and tender memories so sorely try his soul, man lets his mind wander from earth to sky and lifts his eyes to the ethereal dome, he sees again shining among the stars that same image of the dolphin.

   —Leclerc de Buffon, *Natural History*, 1799

Vishnoo, who, by the first of his ten earthly incarnations, has forever set apart and sanctified the whale. When Brahma, or the God of Gods, saith the Shaster, resolved to recreate the world after one of its periodical dissolutions, he gave birth to Vishnoo, to preside over the work; but the Vedas, or mystical books, whose perusal would seem to have been indispensable to Vishnoo before beginning the creation, and which therefore must have contained something in the shape of practical hints to young architects, these Vedas were lying at the bottom of the waters; so Vishnoo became incarnate in a whale, and sounding down in him to the uttermost depths, rescued the sacred volumes. Was not this Vishnoo a whaleman, then? even as a man who rides a horse is called a horseman?
    —Herman Melville, *Moby Dick*, 1851

The Spermaceti oil gives the cleanest and most beautiful flame of every substance known in nature. We are all surprised that you prefer darkness and consequent robberies, burglaries and murders in your streets to the receiving, as a remittance [for colonial trade], our spermaceti oil. The lamps around Grosvenor Square … [can] chase away … all the villains, and save you the trouble and danger of introducing a new police into the city.
    —John Adams, American Minister to England,
      to William Pitt, May 1785

To the eyes of modern man the dolphin is merely a voracious carnivore, whose ends are solely those of feeding, resting and reproduction, and whose instincts serve no purpose other than the satisfaction of those needs. Yet, to the men of classical times, the dolphin was a gentle, good-natured and intelligent animal, most responsive to benevolent treatment. To strike a balance between opinions so diametrically opposed would necessitate a course of study which, in modern times, no man has even thought to undertake.
    —Frederic Cuvier, Naturalist, 1840s

The exploding harpoon, which, after entering the body of the whale, breaks open a vial of cyanide, which, in turn, ignites a charge which forces open the barbs on the harpoon and simultaneously destroys all flesh in its vicinity, was invented by Sven Foyn, a Norwegian.

He patented his harpoon on Christmas Eve, 1864. In his diary for that day, he wrote, "I thank thee, O Lord. Thou alone hast done all."
—From the *CetaceanCyclopedia*, a project of the
Cetacean Studies Institute

Then one whale began to sing; and a second, and a third. Soon the mewings, creaks, and whoops filled the water. Some of the performers were close, and some were far away. And, because of the underwater canyon, the sounds echoed two or three times at intervals of five or six seconds. It seemed almost that one was in a cathedral, and that the faithful were alternating the verses of a psalm ...
—Jacques Cousteau, *The Whale, Mighty Monarch
of the Sea*

Far-reaching undersea topographies that reverberated formerly with the shouts of whales now echo only the monotonous hiss and surge of sea-surface waves set against the dull, numbing roar of shipping. The once-vast host of right whales now is reduced to a few roving bands-harassed, divided, and dispersed.
—Roger Payne, *National Geographic*, 1972

At a depth roughly calculated to be between 600 and 1200 meters (1800 to 3900 feet), there is a thermocline known as the deep sound channel, which retains a proportion of underwater sound, and enables it to travel for enormous distances. (The sound of depth charges off Australia was detected off Bermuda, halfway around the world!) If the Humpback Whales are able to utilize this channel, it may be that they are able to communicate with any other Humpback, in any ocean where they are not separated by land.

—Richard Ellis, New Light on the Whale Song
Mystery, *San Francisco Chronicle*, June 1978

You will never get anywhere with a dolphin by force. If you try it, he'll break off contact, retire to the furthest corner of the pool and ignore you. If you persist, he'll go on a hunger strike. He'll let himself die rather than submit to doing something against his will.

—Adolph Frohn, the first dolphin trainer in the
modern era, ca. 1952

One of the greatest modern storytellers in the field of dolphins, Peter Shenstone, tells the story of when Burnam Burnam, a well-known Australian aboriginal man first heard an evening of his stories. He approached Peter in the parking lot afterwards.

"Well done, Peter!" he said. "You've done what no one else has ever done. You found the Totem animal of the White Fella! The dolphin is the only creature that every white person will take notice of. People of color have always had totems, special animals that teach us. Now the White Fellas have one.

"Good on ya, mate!" With that, he turned and walked off into the night....

—from an interview with Peter Shenstone, 1997

Dolphin societies are extraordinarily complex, and up to ten generations coexist at one time. If that were the case with man, (George Washington), Faraday, and Einstein would still be alive.... Could not the dolphin's brain contain an amount of information comparable to the thousands of tons of books in our libraries?

—Sen. Hubert Humphrey, quoting the Russian
Delphinologist, Yabalkov, at the U.S. Senate
hearings on the Marine Mammal Protection Act,
1970

Praise Song to the Dolphin
Most beautiful of the beautiful,
Fish of Salvation—Dolphin!
Great grandmother of the fishes, crabs and lizards of the
    waters.
Living vessel of wisdom,
Living house of all we know.
Beautiful Queen of dreams,
Beloved of the Oldest Gods.
Mother of the sea-spray who rides the restless waves.
O' let me hear your gentle voice
And see your smiling face.
When dark troubles and illness
Haunt my offspring and I
Send me bright dreams,
And fill my head with light
As I go through life's misty journey,
As I wend life's uncertain way!
            —Credo Mutwa, August 1997

Let us try to communicate with the dolphins and see if they do have
inner freedom. In the search, we may or may not find this freedom
for man. However, I am sure that we will find new mental vistas, if
and only if we are open to them....
        —Dr. John Lilly, *The Mind of the Dolphin* (1st edition)

[The calls of distant whales] carry over vast distances, the sounds
traveling in long, majestically curving paths and completely filling
the vast, vaulted spaces—at times echoing off the ceiling a mile or
two overhead, or off the oozy floor as far beneath. To many human
ears these sounds are very beautiful, even though whales and people have vastly different evolutionary histories and therefore might
be expected to appreciate very different kinds of sounds.
            —Roger Payne, *Among Whales*

- Humpback whales separated by 2,800 miles not only sing the same songs, but also change them at the same time.
- Humans have been able to hear their songs underwater, without amplification, from a distance of over 20 miles.
- Their songs have been recorded at levels of over 170 decibels, louder than a jet plane taking off.
- The longest recorded whale song session was 10 and one half hours. The song session was actually longer, because when the recording was begun, the whale was already singing, and the whale was still singing when the humans were forced to leave.

 —From the *CetaceanCyclopedia*, a project of the
 Cetacean Studies Institute.
 Compiled from various sources.

Here is the story of the Dolphin Dream. It happened nearly two years ago but I still remember every detail as though it happened last night. I don't know what it means and I don't care to interpret it. I only feel privileged to have been touched by the dolphins.

The story starts before I actually went to sleep. I was at home in my cell listening to music on the radio when over the air came the singing of whale song. It froze me where I was sitting on the bed. I felt that if I could only listen closely enough, receptively open myself, that I could understand what the whales were saying. That night I had the dream.

I was sitting on a hillside of tall wheat-colored grass. I was in a low spot between two hills. I was naked with my feet pointing uphill, spread apart. The sky was sunny and blue—it was warm.

A trickle of water started flowing down the hill and I thought it must be raining farther up in the mountains. The trickle grew in size until it was large enough to flow up over my legs. It carried trash; paper cups, sticks, tennis balls and other debris that bumped into me, then flowed over me. The trickle grew into a torrent of dirty brown water that lifted me up from where I was sitting and carried me rushing faster and faster down the hillside. It finally went over a cliff at the seaside, casting me far out into the ocean.

I landed feet first in the water and submerged deeply. The water was a clear turquoise and I had the wonderful sensation of how clean it was, purifying me from the dirty brown river that had deposited me there. When I broke through the surface the light was dazzling, the sun was illuminating the water in such a way that I seemed surrounded by spheres of light.

Then something touched me from below the surface of the water; it touched my side in my rib cage and the most incredible sensation spread like electricity both down to my feet and up to the top of my head. The experience of it took my breath away. Never have I felt anything to compare to it. It was like a jolt of pure love. Before I could figure out what had happened I was touched again, and again with the same overwhelming results. I looked down into the water then and saw it was dolphins who were touching me. They spoke to me in the experience of physically communicated love.

> —From private correspondence between a prisoner in the New Mexico State Penitentiary and one of his counsellors. By permission, 1994.

(At an aquarium) Suddenly I was beyond the rail, leaning my anguished face against the glass....

"You beautiful creatures, don't men understand that they have separated you from your families?"

Grief wracked my body ... then words began to flow back into my mind:

"We are ambassadors from the sea!"

The three dolphins began sliding their bodies against the glass where my face was....

"We are Love and Cooperation.... Play is the Answer you are looking for ... bring people together ... play together ... cooperate ... play ... Peace on the Planet."

I was deeply changed. Radiant and hopeful, full of energy, shooting synapses through my nervous system with hopeful explosions....
> —Rose Farrington, founder of the New Games
> Movement (based on cooperation), in Chia
> Gawain's *The Dolphins Gift*

The brain of a dolphin prepared for microscopic examination reveals these things at the cellular level:

1. The dolphin's cell count is just as high per cubic millimeter as is that of a human.
2. The connectivity, or number of cells connected to one another, is the same as that of a human brain.
3. There is the same number of layers in the cortex of a dolphin as there is in a human brain.

In other words, this brain is as advanced as the human brain on a microscopic structural basis.
> —Dr. John Lilly, *Man and Dolphin*

During the night two porpoises came around the boat and he could hear them rolling and blowing. He could tell the difference between the blowing noise the male made and the sighing blow of the female.

"They are good," he said. "They play and make jokes and love one another ..."
> —Ernest Hemingway, *The Old Man and the Sea*

The dolphins had long known of the impending destruction of planet Earth and had made many attempts to alert humankind to the danger; but most of their communications were misinterpreted as amusing attempts to punch footballs or whistle for tidbits, so they eventually gave up and left Earth by their own means.

The last-ever dolphin message was misinterpreted as a surprisingly sophisticated attempt to do a double-backward somersault

through a hoop while whistling "The Star-Spangled Banner"—but, in fact, the message was this: "So long ... And Thanks For All The Fish!"
—Douglas Adams, *Hitchhiker's Guide to the Galaxy*

No word conveys the eeriness of the whale song, tuned by the ages to a purity beyond refining, a sound that man should hear each morning to remind him of the morning of the world.
—Peter Matthiessen, *Blue Meridian*

It is not everybody's fortune to have had bedside company with whales in their own free playground. But those of us who have, feel an urge to support the growing majority of mankind that demands that the tiny minority who threatens the remaining whale species with complete extinction for personal economic gains should be forced to leave the whales in peace until able to multiply for the benefit of future generations on this planet.
—Thor Heyerdahl, *The Friendly Whale*

It would appear that we are more willing to consider the possibility of other intelligences on distant planets than we are on our own.
—Keith Howell, *Consciousness of Whales*

No sooner does man discover intelligence than he tries to involve it in his own stupidity.
—Jacques Cousteau, *The Living Sea*

We are forced to ask ourselves whether native intelligence in another form than man's might be as high, or even higher than his own, yet be marked by no material monuments as man has placed on earth. At first glance we are alien to this idea, because man is particularly a creature who has turned the tables on his environment so that he is now engrossed in shaping it, rather than being shaped by it.

It is difficult for us to visualize another kind of lonely, almost disembodied intelligence floating in the wavering green fairyland of the sea—an intelligence possibly near or comparable to our own...
—Loren Eiseley, "The Long Loneliness,"
in *The American Scholar*

Now that we know that the blood of the whale is the blood of God, let us no longer kill the whale but restore it to the azure seas as a guardian deity of the world.
—Masanobu Fukuoka, *The One-Straw Revolution:
A Recapitulation* (unpublished manuscript)

The song [of the humpback whale] is repeated ... and emitted with sound intensities of 100 to 110 decibels, that is to say, in a class with a pneumatic drill. What is most interesting in this context is that the song was heard at a depth of about 3,300 feet off the east coast of North America, which is just at the depth where we find two sound-reflecting layers close to each other. [These layers exist in all the oceans, at various depths.] Our calculations indicate that a sound of this intensity, emitted within the reflecting layers, could be heard by human ears at a distance of over 25,000 miles (which is the circumference of the Earth). Even if we make deductions for disturbance, background noise, and the like, it appears that by seeking out this communication layer whales could call to each other over distances as great as the entire breadth of the Pacific Ocean.
—Karl-Erik Fichtelius and Sverre Sjolander, *Man's
Place: Intelligence in Whales, Dolphins and Humans*

For a time I believed that the [dolphins] were responding to the sound of my voice when I hailed them from a distance or spoke to them or even swore at them when they got in the way of the nets, but then I observed something that surprised me. However short a sentence I spoke to them, they started to act upon it before the words were uttered. When I raced the boat against them, even the short word "Go!" was anticipated. They were shooting away before my mind had passed the word to my tongue and my tongue had acted on the impulse. They appeared to be short-circuiting my thought processes and taking the word directly from my mind. This was the great breakthrough in my understanding of mental communication.

... I knew that they were receiving my mental images and that any words I used—such as "Go"—served only to help me define the mental image I wanted. They were not part of the message.
—Frank Robson, *Pictures in the Dolphin Mind*

All was quiet, the place deserted. Even the city traffic outside had died down; the only spectator was Frank Logan, the pool manager.

I formed in my mind a dolphin's eye view of the scene—underwater, then from surface level, looking up at me standing on the board. The dolphins came and gathered round me—eager, friendly grins on their faces. There was silence, no distractions. I formed an image of the dolphins darting off and swimming round the pool. Even as the thought formed in my mind, they set off round the pool in the direction indicated, then flashed back to me and sat up in the water, waiting for more. My shouts of pleasure seemed to delight them and for who knows how long they swam and jumped and danced in the pool as one image after another formed in my mind. And I jumped and danced and rejoiced on the board with them.

The spell was broken by Mr. Logan applauding; I'd forgotten he was there. The upshot of this was that I was appointed head trainer and the training of common dolphins as performers began at once without the use of whistles or food rewards....

The message I seemed to get from them was, "Open your mind to our way of thinking—think like a dolphin." I believe I always tried to do this.
—Frank Robson, *Pictures in the Dolphin Mind*

Cetaceans unquestionably have big brains, and the frequency with which they use them in patterns that can only be described as play suggests that they frolic with their minds as readily as they do with their bodies. This tendency towards mental playfulness may in itself have been partly responsible for the enlargement of their brains.

    —Lyall Watson and Tom Ritchie, *Whales of the World*

The cetacea hold an important lesson for us. The lesson is not about whales and dolphins, but about ourselves. There is at least moderately convincing evidence that there is another class of intelligent beings on Earth beside ourselves. They have acted benignly and in many cases affectionately toward us. We have systematically slaughtered them. Little reverence for life is evident in the whaling industry—underscoring a deep human failing....

    —Carl Sagan, *The Cosmic Connection*

Two million whales have been killed in the last fifty years. The industry and the scientists connected with the industry have had an opportunity to examine the corpses of two million whales and yet maintain a need for still more to study. We can pile up the tables of weights and lengths and ages and measures until it reaches the sky, but it won't get us an understanding of the living creature.

    —Joan McIntyre, *Mind in the Waters*

The largest animal on Earth (the blue whale) is born already larger than anything else! It is approximately 20 to 25 feet long at birth, weighing about 6,000 pounds. While nursing, they gain weight at the rate of 200 pounds per day, or about 8½ pounds per hour! They grow at the rate of 1½ inches per day for the first 7 months.

    An adult's tongue weighs as much as an elephant, and its heart is the size and weight of a Volkswagen.

    —*CetaceanCyclopedia*, compiled by the Cetacean
      Studies Institute

Fin whales are toothless filter feeders who scoop large amounts of water in their mouths, full of plankton and fish. Their mouth remains open for up to five seconds, but the fish do not swim out. The whale has a joint at the forward tip of its lower jaw that makes a very loud cracking noise that scares the fish, driving them into the center of the whale's mouth, just before they are swallowed.

—*CetaceanCyclopedia*, compiled by the Cetacean
Studies Institute

On Mating:
- Cetaceans and humans are the only animals that mate face to face.
- As with all mammals, cetaceans conduct lengthy sessions of courting and foreplay. They will spend long hours caressing, swimming around, over and under each other.
- Done face-to-face, with flippers touching, belly to belly.
- Usually the male on his back, under her, while swimming.
- Some species will face each other and swim rapidly toward one another and then, at the last moment, turn vertically toward the surface, coming together, belly-to-belly, with flippers entwined, to rise above the surface of the water in an embrace, then falling back, downward, only separating after re-entering the water. This allows about an eight-second embrace.
- Some whales mate with the female swimming on her back, the male swimming beside her, on his side. He rolls quickly toward her, aiming his penis, which may be up to 9 feet long, at her genital slit. He then will pump up to 150 gallons of sperm into her, washing out the sperm of her earlier mating partner. The last male to do so will be the father of her next infant....
- In several species, it has been observed that there is almost always at least one other whale present, either helping her into position or helping to "make the connection."

—*CetaceanCyclopedia*, compiled by the Cetacean
Studies Institute

Once in the city of Iquitos, there was a redhead who loved to dance all night. But no matter what he was doing, no matter how much he danced, he always wore a straw hat. Eventually, he wooed a girl and she fell in love with him. But every night, he would leave her at 2 A.M. One night he got very drunk and passed out. The girl reached over and took his hat off. Underneath, she saw that he had a round hole on the top of his head that looked like a blowhole. He woke up suddenly, grabbed his hat, ran down to the river and dived in. Out of the water where he had disappeared, a dolphin emerged.

—Maximo Yumibato, park guard at Pacaya Samiria
National Reserve, Peru, *Nature Conservancy*,
March 1994

It is an important and popular fact that things are not always what they seem. For instance, on the planet Earth, man had always assumed that he was more intelligent than dolphins because he had achieved so much—the wheel, New York, wars and so on—whilst all the dolphins had ever done was muck about in the water having a good time. But conversely, the dolphins had always believed that they were far more intelligent than man—for precisely the same reason.

—Douglas Adams, *The Hitchhiker's Guide to the Galaxy*

If you can visualize a mass of phosphorescent fire fourteen feet in length travelling through the water with the greatest of ease, then suddenly leaping into the air, the spray and dripping water from him giving one the impression of innumerable fine flashes of electricity, you will get some idea of what Jack looked like.

—Fred Barltrop, quoted in Antony Alpers, *Dolphins: The Myth and the Mammal*, describing Pelorus Jack, a famous New Zealand dolphin

I'd love to have a porpoise. They're so adorable to look at, always laughing. And they're so smart. Smarter than man. They came out of the sea years ago, got depressed and went back in. We didn't have enough sense to go back.

> —Tallulah Bankhead, in the Chicago *Daily News*,
> quoted in *The Dolphin Smile: Twenty-Nine Centuries of Dolphin Lore*

In a manner of speaking, humans are fish out of water. . . .

At some eschatological moment, having at last absorbed the values that the Nommo, literally or figuratively, came here to impart, we may ride the currents of the stars, where, in the dimension of the overmind, we'll experience closure with the godhead, eventually to embark on even higher tides to even stranger destinations requiring even more unimaginable transformations.

> —Tom Robbins, *Half Asleep in Frog's Pajamas*

Oh, the rare old Whale, mid storm and gale
In his ocean home will be
A giant in might, where might is right,
And King of the boundless sea.

> —Whale Song, in *Moby Dick*, 1851

Preface

I have been fascinated by the dolphin mystery for almost two decades, ever since I first heard the Legend of the Golden Dolphin.[1] The story of the long relationship of humans with cetaceans came to me one spring evening when a man in a turban, with sparkling blue eyes, knocked on my door and invited me to come along to hear a tale. That moment opened mythic realms to me. Characters from a parallel world entered my life. The Legend came to find me, offering itself as a vehicle for my aspirations. I discovered that I was a character in an ageless tale; I was within the story. Like Arion, I was carried away by the dolphins.

For a long time, I simply followed the thread of the Legend through historical records and mythical tales and images. In more recent years, my research has also included my own experiences, personal contacts, news events, movies, television shows, and cultural trends. And some of my research has been another kind of exploration, using the inner senses, opening up to a visionary process—a mystical exercise using a well-prepared imagination.

I have been seeking understanding of our connection to whales and dolphins in many areas. Sciences, histories, arts, and philosophies—each one contains a pattern of belief, a wheel made of facts, experience, and images. In my mind's eye, I have placed each "medicine wheel" of knowledge onto a central spindle and attempted to see down through them all, spinning them into new relative positions, hoping to discover deeper patterns.

Thus there is a sort of "Dolphin Mystery, Part 1" that consists of ancient tales of cetacean-human contact, as well as historical records and artifacts. What the "fish-gods" had to tell us, how their messages were communicated, and how we managed to forget or become unworthy of this interspecies contact are facets of the legend lost in time. There is much we can only speculate about. The Legend claims that cetaceans have had a major influence on the flowering of human civilization throughout the ages. This claim is well supported by facts, both historical and scientific, as I attempt to show. With such a huge concept, however, it is difficult to contain all the loose ends. I do not claim any kind of final authority in what I offer in this book. I have created an almost child-like storyline that I hope will make clear the essence of this idea without making it subject to criticism from experts in various fields. This is an overview, a sweeping flight over a vast ocean, touching down in a few places to look for evidence. Much remains for future exploration.

As the original messenger of the Legend suggested, the Dolphin Story illuminates a process of awakening in humankind. I have chosen to call the movement of deepening self-awareness the "Delphic Wave." The subtle forms of the Wave have had their effect at a scale much larger than single lives, gradually altering us generation by generation.

After the wide distribution of early humans across the Asian landmass toward the rising sun, the Wave of self-knowledge appears to reverse this direction. The progression of cetacean contact and its influence moves from east to west, beginning in the Dreamtime of aboriginal Australia, and is marked in its course by cross-cultural legends and the rise of Western civilization. (The Wave can be traced in other directions as well, through Asia, South America, and many places that I have not mentioned or covered sufficiently in these pages. The events described in India and Sumeria are no doubt seminal to Eastern civilization as well as Western.) Everywhere, Teachers and cultural Heroes have all carried elements of this influence, emphasizing self-discovery as the path toward perfection. On the personal level the Delphic Wave is felt as a spirit of gentle regard for others based on compassion, mutual benefit, joy, and freedom (traits exhibited by dolphins themselves). To all of us this brought a reverence for love and beauty and the perfection of the arts, building a spirit of community. One could say that the Delphic Wave awakened both the human heart and the human mind. Slipping behind the stage-sets of history, we can recognize the dolphin influence as a silent, floating, gentle spirit, providing whatever each human culture most needed at the time. Looking at past eras with dolphins and whales in one's mind, we see that they have left a trail, a liquid map for us to follow.

Whales and dolphins do leave "footprints" of a sort. As these powerful creatures swim, their tail flukes create large swirls of water. If they are close to the surface, the swirls can be strong enough to flatten the waves temporarily, creating a circular patch of water that quickly disappears, a footprint on the water, a liquid mark that can only be seen if you are in the right place at the right moment....

A few centuries after the disappearance of Jesus, the Delphic Waves subside, dissolving from sight as the human race forgets its love and respect for dolphins and whales, and their service to us as benefactors and friends. The divine status they were accorded vanishes, as the advance of human cultural evolution absorbed our attentions, hypnotizing us into a trance of forgetfulness. Our former embedded-ness in nature ended. Like a stone eroded from a riverbank, we tumbled into the rushing stream of human time, no longer dreaming in the mythic worlds.

Transformed, the Wave was barely visible for centuries, yet it stimulated movement toward mental development in the north of Europe and toward passion and feeling in the south. The northern form sought information, knowledge of all things. The southern form sought unity of belief, a global system of passionate surrender to God. It was the birth time of self-awareness among nations and the rapid expansion of global knowledge, as two new forms of the Wave arose, contending for territory and influence. Hidden in dreams of a new world, the Waves swept across the Atlantic to the Americas. There was little direct cetacean contact during those times other than slaughter.

I have found that it is possible to pick up the trail in modern times of a "Dolphin Mystery, Part 2." What does the reappearance of cetacean contact with humans look like today? Are we ready to remember our former bond?

Many readers will find personal links to this part of the saga, as we explore the worldwide support for conservation and humane treatment of whales and dolphins, the increasing number of "swim-with-dolphins" programs, the potential of dolphin-assisted therapy, and the growing love and popularity of dolphins and whales among people everywhere, of all ages. This returning recognition of the "specialness" of these ocean monarchs is itself progress, as more of us begin to care about the fate of the Earth's cetaceans and to move away from an attitude of dominion over all. Perhaps this is the beginning of remembrance.

I believe that today's world is just as affected by the esoteric influence of whales and dolphins as it was in ancient times. Cetaceans have inhabited this planet much, much longer than we have, and they possess a deep wisdom about how to live sustainably and joyfully. We have never been more in need of this message.

To those who watch from the oceans, we might appear lost. The distance that has grown between the natural world and ourselves is great. We have forgotten where our food comes from, how important water is to our lives, and we no longer pay attention to the wisdom of the animals, the iconic truths that have informed all ancient cultures. From the perspective of the ocean people, this is an Age of Darkness, the legacy of the holocaust years when whales were hunted in every ocean. If we attempt to view this from a higher level, where a divine plan might be underway, we can ask: Did this horror occur to startle the human world into wakefulness? Our collective guilt is not limited to whaling. We have abused mother Earth, not by finding and extracting what we need, but by taking too much, ignoring natural limits, and finding no shame in the mountains of waste we have built. In the words of Credo Mutwa, "We gave glamour to destruction and beauty to death."[2] Lacking the long view, we have been slouching toward our demise, looking only at the next step toward the fulfilment of a desire. Our desires have been manipulated by those who need to sell useless things, by people who are themselves empty of vision. All too many of us are like fish that do not know they are in water. The Dolphin Legend is a key to the long view, the Big Picture that we all need to see.

One can imagine something urging cetaceans to engage with us again, after the centuries of abuse, to initiate interactions that will improve our perception of them. Certainly the heart-winning performances of captive dolphins would qualify here. Can we suppose that self-aware members of another species *sacrificed* themselves—from whaling to tuna-dolphin deaths to captivity—to light the dawning of a new human consciousness? This is taking it too far, you may protest, yet in the closing chapters of this book I discuss the implications of accepting—as I do—the reality of cetaceans possessing the faculties and self-awareness that define them as evolved Beings entirely different from us and capable of such a choice. If a "soul" can be defined as an aspect of inner divinity, a sparkling inner Self who knows the warmth of love and joy that comes from being alive, who reflects this awareness in its harmonious life by choosing to do so, then there are souls in the sea. They deserve respect, and they deserve rights. We still have much to learn from them. How will we know the truth of this if we don't open to the possibility? We have evidence that this occurred in the past, why not again today?

In the appendix, "A Dolphin and Whale Primer," I offer some biological facts about these creatures that I believe support my claims for their abilities, including their power to emotionally, mentally, and in some cases physically transform people who enter the water with them. But this is not a natural history of cetaceans, so my description is necessarily brief.

Let me note here that just about everything I relate in this book can be taken further, either by me or by the reader. One of the hallmarks of the Legend is that it has a way of expanding in the mind of each person who hears it, as they make their own connections, just as I have. My efforts to write about history and myth, whaling, interspecies contact, and the promise of mental and physical therapies that heal people are not exhaustive, only suggestive of the myriad possibilities inherent in letting the Legend of the Golden Dolphin into one's life. It bears repeating that the Legend is a key, a device that unlocks old thoughts and histories, science and dreams, one that opens a door into a deeper chamber of understanding. It is not a simple tale.

Some of what we will explore is challenging. The use of cetaceans for military purposes is deeply disturbing. The dolphin entertainment business is not easy to accept in all its forms. But the growing love of dolphins and whales that captive situations have facilitated cannot be discounted. I believe we can create ideal environments for interspecies interaction that need not be intrusive or restrictive, where the gifts we have for each other can be shared. I explore these ideas toward the end of the book.

No matter how many words or books I write to convey the essence of the Legend of the Golden Dolphin and its significance to us, they can never equal the understanding to be found in an eye-to-eye, soul-to-soul encounter with a cetacean. They see right into us, and the love is palpable. Like Apollo's credo at the Oracle of Delphi, these creatures urge us: "Know Thy Self."

The tale itself is alive, beyond this book. It includes all that has happened and all that is happening between ourselves and the "people" in the seas. As you read this book, you are participating in the gradual movement of the Delphic Wave from the deeps to the land, bringing the sweet waters of their friendship into the deserts of human difficulty. The path to our destiny, our glory as fully awakened humans participating successfully and joyously in the dance of life, is being shown to us by the souls in the sea.

Scott Taylor
Byron Bay, Spring 2002

Introduction:
Who Are the
Dolphins and Whales?

May I introduce you to them? There are so many different kinds.

Spotted and Spinners, Common and Striped, Rough-Toothed and White-Beaked, Hector's and Heaviside's, Commerson's and Peale's. Then there are the Indo-Pacific Humpback Dolphins, Pacific White-Sided, Fraser's and Risso's, Irrawaddy and Hourglass. There are Duskys, Tucuxis, Southern and Northern Right-Whale Dolphins, and the strange River Dolphins, mostly blind, snaggle-toothed and bulbous, from India, China, and South America.

I haven't even mentioned the Bottlenose, the most familiar of them all. I also haven't listed the six kinds of Porpoises, small and discrete and largely unfamiliar to most of us.

And then there are the whales. Some of them have teeth. One kind has two strap-like teeth that grow out and over their beaks until they almost cannot open their mouth at all. One kind has the habit of growing a single tooth nine feet long directly through its upper lip. One wears a disguise that makes it look like it has gills. And another kind has a brain over five times the size of a human brain.

The whales without teeth—those odd creatures who sing mournful oceanic operas and strain their tiny food through "mustaches" hung inside their mouths—number eleven different kinds. One kind of these baleen whales is the largest breathing creature ever to have lived on Earth.

There are also the deadly whales generically called Blackfish. Orca, Pilot Whales, Melon-Headed Whales, Pygmy Killers, and False Killers all live in structured pods, like police squads patrolling the seas.

This listing is general. It does not name them all.

What do you hear of the rare ones—Cuvier's Beaked Whale, Gervais' Beaked, Stejneger's, Sowerby's, Andrew's, Gray's, True's, Shepard's, or Arnoux's? There are Hubb's, Blainville's, Longman's, and even the Ginkgo-Toothed.

Somewhere in the list should be placed the gentle Beluga, the White Whale with its highly mobile forehead, exceptional range of sounds, and its expressive and moveable lips.

And still the list is not complete.

Each of these is a species unto itself, separate tribes, each with special characteristics.

How do we compare? How many kinds of humans are there? Only one. We have a few variations that we call races, but these are not significant differences, only small variations. When we strip away the skin, we have skeletons so similar that it takes an expert to guess what color we were.

Humans have long considered themselves to be the crown of creation, the ultimate development of evolution. We stand in a different relation to Earth and its creatures than any other life form. Thinking beings, we contemplate our actions, measuring them against memory and imagination. In a real sense we are masters of time. Our actions occur in present time, our memories in past time, and our imagination may occur in future time. We have left behind our animal instincts and taken control of our reactions. Living in a self-awareness that over-rides our biological background, we desire, we dream, and we create. We hold the timing of life and death in our hands, as if we were gods.

We see no other creature with conscious control of its instinctual nature, so we claim the top rung on the ladder of life.

Somewhere in us is a discomfort with this self-image, if we are thinking people. We see the harsh reality of our behavior with one another and toward the world around us. We find ourselves, our fellow humans, acting in brutal and plainly stupid ways despite knowing better. We allow our personal pains to grow into monstrous angers, and we attack the hearts of great cities. We know we are poisoning parts of the Earth in ways that will be unmitigated for thousands of years. And we are eradicating entire species at a rate we cannot fully calculate.

We stare with deep dismay at what we do, yet seem incapable of stopping ourselves. Good men and women around the world, in every community, call out for sensible care and gentle regard for people, for children, and for the natural world, but are in many ways trapped by the very systems we have created to improve our lives.

When we take time to reflect on these things, we come to the inevitable conclusion that we are the best and the worst of all living things.

When this disturbing truth sits heavy in our hearts we may find ourselves looking out over the open sea. The waves calm us with the regularity of their sounds and flowing forms. Letting go, we gaze into distances that sweep our minds clean. We open to the immensity and resilience of the world, larger than human failings. As the waves curl and splash, we may recall that the oceans are three times larger than all the lands put together. And there, among the waves, lives a kind of creature who offers answers, gifts of quiet mystery, for our troubled souls.

The cetaceans (whales, dolphins, and porpoises) top the hierarchy of the oceans. In the wet world nothing comes close to the combination of qualities they possess.

In the last two hundred years, our knowledge of these mighty animals has grown. The last fifty years have seen our understanding increase exponentially. And at the window of every new discovery, we stand amazed.

In the distant past, as this book explores in some detail, humanity saw the dolphins as magical and unfathomable creatures who stirred new thoughts, new sensitivities, and even new relations with God. A deep resonance was felt between human aspirations and dolphin and whale lore. They were revered, treated as god-like beings who, after appearing for a moment along a shore or playing in the bow wave of a boat, would dive into another world, disappearing into the mysterious underwater realms.

Where myths meet history, we discover that many early cultural advances were attributed to contact with these odd "people" in the sea.

The "gifts" received from the sea seemed to be from a dream, the land of myths, the "collective unconscious." Many early teachings about mastering the ways of the world are said to have been passed on by large beings from the sea who originated in the stars, teachers who stimulated humans to rise above the animals.

Some of the ancient tales are clearly psychological remnants of the shock of seeing self-awareness in another life form. And some contain internal evidence of other, more mysterious origins.

We have always found lessons in our relations with whales and dolphins, mirroring the current stage of human development. The Greeks found guidance and legal precedents in dolphin interaction, setting up courts of law based in temples devoted to the Dolphin God. The Romans told stories of platonic love between dolphins and young men. In early England, the tales of Merdhinn, or Merlin as we have come to know him, told of a magical journey under the sea, where wise creatures taught him his mystic arts, enabling him to aid the coming of a perfect King. In France the next in line for the king's role, the anticipated new God-King, was called *Le Dauphin* (the Dolphin).

Animism, shamanism, Goddess worship, patriarchal churches, beliefs in impersonal or personal gods, and even the agnostic systems of science itself have all received revelations from dolphins. Odd, almost amphibious beings, with minds that both receive our thoughts and send us unequivocal messages, they have been central to many of our deepest discoveries.

Images and ideas associated with dolphins played a part in the early Christian church. These often were abstract ideas, such as salvation, redemption, overcoming fears of the unknown, and teachings about grace, about the beauty of the human soul as it finds its way across the depths of time.

Later, whales came to be part of the human drama too. Huge and doubly mysterious, they daunted mankind for centuries, great God-like monsters of the dangerous deeps. As explorers set themselves free from the coastlines, whales became accessible, yielding oils and bones and meat. Products taken from the bodies of whales aided us in developing the range of technical advances required to finally become complete masters of the land.

In modern times, with religions too tired and limited to be very helpful in understanding our world and our lives, and science too cold-blooded to solve our moral challenges, we seek yet another source of inspiration, one that can lead us to a unified form of belief. We want a way to live life that embodies a universal code of virtue (the guidance that religion used to offer) and that learns and grows from experience (what science has given us, an adaptability to change). We want a living path, a way through life that offers time-less values and playful discovery.

And then, as if by magic, some of us begin to suspect that the "ocean people" have learned to live this way, that they are inside the "sacred hoop" of life and are self-aware participants in the world around them. Their images surround us, and we feel a great lift of inexplicable joy when they appear in the flesh. We find ourselves turning to the dolphins and whales again for inspiration.

Those of us who have managed to survive the disparagement of our peers, parents, and cultures to maintain a mystical worldview while remaining in the "regular" world with all its advantages of technology—in other words, those of us who have already begun the move into a unitary state—find dolphins and whales to be delightful companions. We have come to see them as friends, teach-ers, guides, and examples. They delight our sense of play, they deepen our meditations, and they light our sense of holiness. When we are able to relinquish control, we are led into profound realizations about the transcendent realms, or are made to confront the hard truths of our own wishful thinking.

We watch them play, we play with them, then we come home and reflect on what we experienced. Often enough, we are challenged. And on that rare day when everything seems destined to be perfect, we look into the eye of another creature who is as bemused by it all as we wish we were. We receive a brief flash of communion, of unified thought and feeling, and we escape the bounds of our regular life. The experience of that first penetrating look into the eye of a dolphin or a whale creates an explosive expansion inside the human mind. One feels that a portal has just opened up in space and time.

A pathway that leads to another being, one who understands....

Not every moment with dolphins is like this; in fact, most are not. Despite the wishful fantasies of many, simply being in the water beside a dolphin does not guarantee a mind-blowing experience. It takes time, special preparation, and a unique set of circumstances.

And when it happens, it changes everything.

For some, it verifies what has been theoretical. For some, it opens new vistas never contemplated before. For some, it startles all preconceptions so profoundly that *everything* suddenly comes up for questioning. And for some, there is redemption, a new beginning. Occasionally, one is baptized, washed clean by the acceptance of a kind and alien eye.

Are cetaceans the descendants of wolf-like canines who lived on land, then moved back into the sea? Are they former sailors who, having kidnapped a god by mistake, were turned into dolphins? Are they the relatives of a tribe of native people who fell into the sea when they were crossing a rainbow bridge? Are they good fattening food, easy to harvest? Are they no smarter than dogs, and not as smart as chimpanzees or pigs? Are they closely related to hippopotamuses, or are they more closely related to humans than humans are to monkeys?[1] Could they be the embodiment of re-incarnated Teachers, an advanced race of star-born healers from Sirius? Are they a strange aberration in the organic history of our planet, with a platypus-like combination of traits that, in the end, doesn't mean anything special? People at one time or another have accepted all of these possibilities.

When people buy tickets to board a boat, intending to visit dolphins at sea somewhere, just what are they looking for? What is the intention behind the US$1 billion per year spent on whale-watching around the world?[2] When the first whale or dolphin is sighted, why do all the people rush to that side of the boat, gasping, laughing, and shouting? There is an excitement that overcomes crowds of people when cetaceans appear, a pitch of eagerness and delight that can reach surprising heights. Eager customers line up to buy tickets to spend thirty minutes in the water being entertained by dolphins and perhaps having a special moment with one; hordes of children gather around the underwater windows of an oceanarium, transfixed by the graceful play of an orca. These are common scenes. Yet, only a few years ago, there was none of this.

Although the first known zoo, which included dolphins in pools, was built almost three thousand years ago, the recent history of our love affair with cetaceans is very short. Since the middle of the twentieth century dolphins and whales have entered the dreams and lives of mass humanity, taking a position unrivaled by any other creature. The last fifty years have brought them into the lives of hundreds of millions of people, many of whom live nowhere near the ocean. In a mysterious way, we are opening up again, listening to their ancient messages. They have reappeared in our collective eyes, rising from the depths.

It is significant that I ask the question as I have: Who are the Dolphins and Whales? I am not asking *what* they are, but *who?* They have self-awareness. They know who they are. This fact ought to send shivers up and down your spine. The expectant desire we have expressed through science-fiction fantasies, religious aspirations, and mystical yearnings to meet another being who is self-aware has come true. Oddly, they have been here all along, longer than we have, at least one hundred and fifty times as long.

They are here, today. Since they are in every ocean, and the oceans cover 71 percent of the planet, it is fair to say that they have us surrounded.

As Sherlock Holmes pointed out, the best place to hide something is in plain view.

The Delphic Spirit

Dolphins and whales are strange creatures. Their bodies have parts and systems like terrestrial mammals, and they live the unfettered lives of wild animals in the sea, but there is something beyond this, some mysterious quality that has always drawn us.

In my many years of seeking an understanding of who they are and where they fit in the Big Picture of life on Earth, a theme has emerged that at first may sound preposterous, yet once we examine the evidence, it begins to seem plausible:

> Dolphins and whales have the ability to carry and deliver a silent message for us, a gift that has helped us to rise above our animal origins, becoming a new kind of creature: human.

We can see this message-carrying capacity as metaphorical, whereby we contemplate the dolphins and whales and derive new understandings for ourselves, or we can accept that they are active participants in the carrying and sending of messages. The result is the same.

It is possible to trace a Delphic Spirit moving slowly around the world, enlightening humankind, and playing a part in the movement of civilization itself. This spirit inspires us to become more compassionate, kind, and altruistic. It has given us some of the most important clues we have ever received as to how to live successfully, sustainably, here on Earth.

The Delphic Spirit is wise. It responds to conditions of time and circumstance. Its presence has been stronger in some cultures than in others. Various means have been used by it to create alterations in human beliefs, attitudes, and actions. Some were very subtle and require a sharp eye to discover, while some of the lessons and demonstrations to humans have been forthright, direct, and even blatant.

Many early cultures have dolphin tales, but around one thousand years ago the stories dry up. Perhaps a time came when the lessons of human development were in need of becoming more intrinsic, more fully embodied by people, so the Spirit withdrew to allow the lessons to take root undisturbed by further lessons. In recent times this Spirit has resurfaced, coming once again to offer us inspiration.

To discover the true nature of the dolphins, we need to look for some of these mysterious influences. Most are properly called "esoteric," or hidden. Subtle, behind the scenes, there may never be a full accounting of their effect on us. Our search will seem like a journey of imagination, a mythic voyage into a mystery. We will look at thin wisps of fact and disappearing mentions of ideas, and listen carefully for any evidence that something like our Delphic Spirit is at work.

Before history, there was myth. A tale of imagination can show us the past, from before the time when the habits of historians took hold. Imagination often serves to clothe our memories and fill in where facts are indistinct, and that is the land of the myth.

My working definition of myth: myth is a truth that can only be expressed poetically.

In contrast, the things of science can be measured and repeated and then asserted as fact. The mythological (or is it myth-illogical?)

truths are not like that. Can falling in love be measured? Does the first smile of a baby at her father mean anything? What about the beauty of a sunrise? These are things that are entirely real, known and accepted as important and true, but not susceptible to science. They can only be spoken of in poetic terms. They are part of our mythic world.

We all live in two "worlds," one of fact and science and one of feeling and myth. Just as science can enable us to peer deeply into the heart of an atom, a myth can lead us to high places from which we can see great vistas of life. Science could be said to provide the micro-view, while myths provide the macro-view.

For example, most Polynesian cultures have strong taboos against eating or harming dolphins. A mythic part of the history of Tonga and Ha'apai tells of a war between the two islands. The Tongans had landed on Ha'apai and killed most of the men, and the women ran up the mountain to hide. After six days they came down, only to be attacked by the Tongans. The women ran across the beach, dove over the reef, and emerged as dolphins, swimming rapidly away. From that time the people of both islands have considered dolphins to be their relations and have protected them from harm.

This tale gives a poetic explanation of an important environmental lesson about protecting the beneficial dolphins by thinking of them as being closely related to humans. Before the ascent of science, this was how people learned valuable lessons that could be passed on, with emotional connection to the subject preceding the measured facts.

The Dolphin Story is part of our collective history. Not every assertion made in these pages will be measurable, not every idea is factual. Some of it is merely suggestive, leading us to imagined conclusions. Nonetheless, it carries the ring of authentic truth and the suggestion that we know only parts of the story.

Like a key to a lock, this tale is capable of opening up a new understanding. It can also be thought of like the *legend* in the corner of a map. It is a set of definitions of the symbols used in the "big picture." In the case of the Dolphin Story, the big picture is the world around us.

This legendary "Delphic Spirit," embodied by the whales and dolphins, is an intelligent wave of uplift and enhancement that has always led humankind toward its destiny.

Dolphins are our benefactors, teaching us, demonstrating to us from before the beginning of history that they hold a key to the challenges of human life. They are the means for us to overcome the Dragon within, the barbaric aspect of our selves. It was their gentle guidance that lifted us out of the realm of simple survival and brought us to the door of a higher mode of life. As we will see, encounters with cetaceans caused new thoughts, new ideas to be born within the human mind and heart. How this happened is one of the mysteries that we will explore.

We have arrived at a time when we can become not only aware again of the Delphic influence, but co-designers, active participants in the process of our own awakening.

There must be answers; there must be techniques to overcome the barbaric stupidity of our fellow men. Some we have been taught already. Some have been deep secrets for millennia. Some of those techniques can be found among the mysterious tales of the dolphins.

It is important that we not put the dolphin on a pedestal, above us. They are not gods to be worshiped. They are sort of like us, not always perfect. However, they have been working out how to be dolphins longer than we have been working on how to be humans. Besides, they don't do well on pedestals, where they dry out. They prefer to be in the sea....

They are the best friends we have ever had, an older race of beings who understand the difficulty of being self-aware in an instinctive world, where almost everyone else is guided by a voiceless inner system of simple responses. Like us, they are made to reflect on every action, having to discover among many paths the route to an unknown goal.

Maybe they enjoy our company in part because we have had it even harder than they have. As a result, we have gifts, abilities, and a kind of individuated self-awareness they dream of having.

They have the dreams, we have the means.

They know the answers, we have the hands to make the answers come to life.

A Very Human Point of View

Do we dare anthropomorphize this way? May we project human values and dreams onto them?

Of course we may. No human can do otherwise. It is quite impossible to do anything else. Until we can become something other than human, we will never be able to do anything else.

That having been said, it is also true that a thoughtful, empathetic, and compassionate perspective is possible across the boundaries of species, without projecting too much. The capacity for empathy, or even "telempathy" (a combination of thought and feeling that conveys a partial experience of one being to another) is not only a possibility, but a real phenomenon. It has happened to me.

When we think of our easy understanding of the thoughts and feelings of our companion animals—the dogs, cats, birds, horses, and others with whom we share our homes and lives—we can begin to accept the fact that we do communicate and understand animal thoughts and emotions more than we can explain.

Not all experiences with dolphins fit into a standard mold. Some experiences demonstrate that there are other realities than those we are accustomed to, and that the dolphins are beings who do not live *only* in the worlds we know.

Traditionally, these experiences are called mystical or shamanic journeys into another world. Can science explain these phenomena? I should hope so. When science develops the ability to measure and analyze the substance of thought and can explain the dimensions of fun, it will all be made clear.

I have met quite a few dolphins, both in the wild and in human-managed situations. Some have decided to spend some special time with me. Some have even "spoken" to me. Several have allowed me to carry on conversations with them. Those of us who have managed this feat, and kept our wits about us, are challenged by this awkward situation. We have heard voices in our heads that weren't our own. We have been shown images of things, felt radical changes in our bodies, seen vistas of otherworldly realms, and have been told histories that do not exist in any book. More real than any television program, these experiences are something we are certain of, yet we are often challenged by others as to the truthfulness of our tales. The best answer to these questions is to spend time among dolphins.

Who are the Dolphins and Whales? If a friend is someone who knows everything about you, and likes you anyway, then the answer is simple:

They are our best friends.

23 September:
Once again I was alone in the bay. Today visibility was poor but I could hear dolphins everywhere, high-pitched whistles and chatter.... Lumpy came in and singled me out to swim alone with him. I dived beneath him as he remained on the surface. I brushed past, feeling his warm underside. When I

dived and spiraled up he circled very close, swimming overhead just before I surfaced. As I took a breath he waited
patiently, one eye out of the water, quite still—and then we
raced off together again....

25 September:
Today my Interlocks were long and repeated. I swam among
so many dolphins I felt I could never return to the rest of the
world. I could not see beyond the group I was with—dolphins
above, below and on both sides. They were touching me on
either flank. I would lead the way and dive down. All followed
and circled. I swam upside down. They covered me, block-
ing my way to the surface until I needed air, then a path was
cleared....

    —Janet Nowak[3]

PART ONE

Myths and Legends from the Ocean of Time

CHAPTER ONE

A Telling of Legends, Part I

Australia, India, and Sumeria

Blue, turquoise blue, the color of healing rushes into my eyes. Great feathers of bubbles rush along my body. I undulate my legs as if they are fused together, my arms at my sides, swimming headlong toward the coming dolphins.

Beneath the surface, six feet under water, I stare forward, my dive mask tunneling my vision. Fast, they come winding out of a knot of darker blue, arrowing toward my face.

Their gyre grows suddenly into an expanding flower with eyes, silver skin, and flippers, exploding toward me through the water, made of their living bodies. Swirling, they pass within inches, almost touching me. As I spin around, watching them fly past, they reform their loose knot of pumping bodies—at a distance of fifteen feet they flip, twist and stop to face me, the group suddenly hanging still, looking at me.

Six dolphins have just examined me, minutely exploring my shape, my surfaces, my density and muscle tension, the contents of my lungs and sinuses. They have looked at my stomach and kidneys, my bladder and bowels. The flush of adrenaline and endorphins into my bloodstream has been noted.... Now they want to see if I remember how to play.

Welcome to Dolphin Dreamtime. We are about to take a journey through time. Like a dolphin, the shining essence of this tale surfaces into the clear light of day, then dives deep, disappearing for a while.

Then it rises again, breathes and plays in the waves, before diving with its friends back into the blue.

Some of what you read will be familiar, some completely new. This is a story that will help you connect the dots in your mental coloring book and fill in some of the colors. We needn't exactly stay inside the lines....

The day is hot, windy, and bright. Down the rough track the Land Rover has bounced and jostled us until we have forgotten what stillness is. So empty is this stretch of country, we have to remind ourselves that we are on a track, a trail that leads to the ocean.

Finally, the road smoothes slightly and we top a low rise, and there before us is the water, the endless expanse that stretches to Antarctica. Deep blue, it seems infinite under the cloudless sky.

We stop and climb out, our bones weary, joints aching from the ride. Stretching, we walk slowly toward the cliff's edge, eager to see down to the waves below.

The three men whose homeland this is are still at the truck, tying red loops of yarn around their heads, thick, soft ceremonial crowns of red wool. They take their time.

We stand looking down at the small bay, waves crashing powerfully against the rough rocks below. The seething swell is immense.

Finally, the three men come walking toward us. One gestures with his click-sticks, and we follow along the slight trail they are taking.

In a few minutes, we reach a promontory, where there is a more rounded slope, and the men clamber down and settle into seats in the stone. The natural softness of the limestone has weathered to create more than a few of these seats, and each of us settles into one.

We are suspended above the waves crashing onto the rocks seventy-five feet below. We listen to the water, the wind dying now to a gentle breeze.

Click. Click. Click. Click.

ClickClick. ClickClick. ClickClick.

The three men begin striking their sticks and a rhythm naturally comes. After a few moments a flat-sounding, chanted song begins. Each takes it up, roughly at first, until the three of them are tapping and chanting as one.

The song is not melodic. Instead, it is hypnotic, repetitious. It sounds as if it has never been sung before, but is being created on the spot, a voiced response to the day, the clicks, and the sea. But we know this is an ancient song, the song that calls the whales.

—An imaginary visit to the sacred land of the Mirning

The Oldest Continent, the Oldest People, the Oldest Story

Our survey of the ancient beginnings of human contact with the cetacean families begins in Australia. Although the first humans seem to have radiated outward from Africa in their primal migrations and probably encountered dolphins in a river, a lake, or along the ocean shores of that continent, we know none of the stories from that time. It is in Australia where we find the longest continuous habitation of humans in direct descent from their ancestors, with current field studies turning up evidence of over 90,000 years of aboriginal culture. And it is in Australia where the stories appear out of the Dreamtime, the oral tales of mankind's earliest contact with the people of the sea.

Australia is Earth's oldest land mass. It has not been submerged and its mountains have worn down to low hills in the 4.5 billion years of its exposure to the rain and sun. Nowhere else is the unmoved Earth so ancient as it is in Australia.

It suits us to begin in Australia for other reasons as well, one being the general westward trend of the Delphic Wave, the gentle influence of the cetacean presence. The Wave rose somewhere to the east, in some mysterious place beyond the sunrise....

The oldest myth that I have heard connecting humans to whales is one that belongs to the Mirning people of South Australia, an aboriginal tribe from the Nullarbor Plain, near the Head of the Bight. (*Nullarbor* means "treeless," and it is the huge south central region of Australia, an empty limestone plain that ends at cliffs along the sea.)

At Fowler's Bay, one looks south into the Antarctic Sea. Along this rugged coastline, the sea pounds the rocky cliffs, splashing high into the air. Just above the water line in a corner of the larger bay is a curious rock formation shaped like the tail flukes of a whale. Flat, about forty yards across, it appears to lie upon the waves. *(See Plate 1.)* This is connected to a steep stone cliff that curves around, forming a whale-like shape, enclosing a small cove. At the position corresponding to the head of this great stone whale is a natural blowhole, where the waves crash into a cave and strong gusts of mist and air blast up into the sky. This is where the Mirning have sung their songs to Jiderra for thousands of generations. Their tradition is to wait 'til noon on the day of the full moon, and three at a time they stand by the blowhole, to be drenched in the rainbows of the misty breath.

In 1954, the Mirning tribe was dispossessed of its lands, which were given to the Yalata people, who had been displaced from their own lands in turn by the English testing of nuclear weapons at Maralinga, farther north in the outback desert of central Australia.

The Mirning have been returning from their near-extinction during the last decades of the twentieth century. A white man set up a tourist company to take tourists to the cliffs along the shore of their former territory and hired a few of the Mirning men to be guides, allowing them limited access once again to their sacred Dreaming sites.

They are the Whale People,[1] some of whom are said to have birthmarks in the shape of whales on their bodies. Today they retain only fragments of the ancient Dreaming of their ancestors.

They tell the tale of *Jiderra*, the Ancient One who came from the star Sirius, accompanied by the Seven Sisters from the Pleiades, the *Yugarilya*. Playing one day, the sisters chased him, and he pressed his body against the land leaving the shapes we see today. Here his blowhole continues to create the air by which we all live. One hundred thousand years ago this enabled the Mirning, the First People, to join him.

Jiderra, the Ancient One from the stars, is an enormous White Whale. His skin is iridescent, shining with the colors of the rainbow.

Today these aboriginal people sing a special song accompanied by click-sticks, sitting in ancient stone seats along the cliffs, looking out to sea. And the southern right whales come to the base of the cliffs, to rise up and roar into the wind. *(See Plate 2.)*

(Roaring? No whale scientist will agree that this is possible, since right whales do not have vocal cords and have never been recorded making sounds like a roar. Nevertheless, visitors accompanying Mirning singers have witnessed this several times.)

On the barren plains of the Nullarbor, above the cliffs, there are large circular depressions in the stone, with symbols carved into the inner rim—of crosses, stars, and circles. According to the Dreaming, this is where the ships from the stars landed, and where the Mirning, who are sometimes called "the Dog Star people" (the star Sirius), descended to this world as the friends of Jiderra, coming to join him long, long ago. Even today the Mirning tell of the *Ngunkinga*, or little star people whom they have known since the Beginning.

Scattered about on the ground along the cliff tops are thousands of dolphin-shaped stones. We were given one of these stones, and we took it to an American expert in flint knapping, the art of stone tool making.

"These artifacts have lain on the ground so long since they were shaped that they have been discolored by the sun, a process that takes tens of thousands of years. Where did you say you got this?" he asked.

"The people who gave us the stone are the descendants of the people who made it," we told him.

"Well, somebody is telling a tall tale, because this is really old. Older than any living tribe! I think somebody is having a laugh at your expense," he warned us.

. . .

As a test, we had decided not to tell him that we had just returned from Australia. We wanted him to gauge the age of this stone artifact without letting him know beforehand where it came from. It is now generally acknowledged that the Australian aboriginal people have lived in the "Great South Land" for at least 50,000 years. Some say even longer....

In 1996 a white whale appeared along the southern coast of Australia. To the Mirning and many other aboriginal nations, this signaled that the time had come to sing the Forgiveness Song, the song that will bring Jiderra, who is also known as the Rainbow Serpent, back into close relationship with humankind. It is imperative that they sing the song, asking forgiveness of the whales and dolphins, the People of the Sea. It is said that if this is done, a new future will become possible, the world will be redeemed and balanced again, and it will be a time of good living.

The Mirning believe that this is to be done in a ceremony with the bones of a whale that they have preserved for thousands of years. The skeleton is to be reconstructed on the beach, the song sung around a fire lit within its rib cage.[2]

The image is haunting.

Other Australian aboriginal nations also have a close connection to the whale and dolphin nations. Lorraine Mafi-Williams, an aboriginal grandmother and activist of the Bundjalung and Thungatti nations, told me of her grandfather's designation as the Whale and Dolphin Dreamer, responsible for looking after all the cetaceans along the north coast of New South Wales, on the east coast of Australia. He went to special dreaming caves where he would commune with the cetaceans on a regular basis. He served as an ambassador for both sides, conveying messages between the two communities.

The Arakwal people, a clan of the Bundjalung nation, know the dolphin as one of their totems and to this day they speak of visiting with their aunties, the dolphins, in the Brunswick River. On a windy day in the fall, sitting near a beach, one of the Arakwal elders spoke with me about her youth, swimming among the dolphins. At the age of seventy-four she was delighted to hear from a local surfer that the same dolphin who had shared the surf with her as a child was still visiting swimmers nearby. An extraordinary smile lit up her face as she spoke of her lifelong friendship with the dolphins.

Manduwuy Yunupingu, the lead singer of the top-selling aboriginal music group Yothu Yindi, tells of his people's relations with the whales. He calls them a sister clan, and names them the Waramari Clan. One of the names by which he calls upon them is *"Lorokara."*

Other tribes in the Northern Territories of Australia have traditions linking them to the dolphins, including those on Groote Eylandt and Elcho Island.

Burnum Burnum, a famous artist and aboriginal activist who died in 1997, told stories of his tribe, the Wurunjeri or Dolphin Tribe, and their close relationship with cetaceans. He used to tell how his grandfather had a "pet whale."... Their tribe was guided and nurtured by the dolphins, and they rejoin them after death.

Researchers are still finding tribal stories along the coasts of Australia, where it seems that almost all tribes along the longest coastline in the world were both friends and partners with the cetaceans. Cooperative fishing, with dolphins bringing fish to their human partners, was practiced in dozens of places.

The Traditions of Oceania

Throughout the Pacific region, there are ancient traditions of close relations between humans and dolphins and whales.

The Maori people of New Zealand claim that Maui, an important figure throughout the Pacific islands, and one of the founders of their culture, rode from Hawaii on the back of a whale and pulled their islands from the bottom of the sea.

Among the Maori, as the story goes, there would sometimes be born a Whale Singer, who was called by the whales to swim among them. The Whale Singer was taken by a whale, on its back, on longer and longer journeys over the sea, and even under the water. They say the whale could speak directly to the mind of the Singer to tell him or her to hold on while he dove, to put their face over the blow-hole so the whale could let bubbles out for them to breathe.

In his books, *A Pattern of Islands* and *Return to the Islands*, Arthur Grimble tells of the Gilbert Islands, to the north and east of Australia, where the islanders had a Dolphin Dreamer among them. This person was able to summon the *"Friends from the West,"* as they called them, by means of a trance. Large pods of dolphins would come, led by an enormous leader, who would enter the lagoon and beach themselves in front of the Dreamer. Sometimes a few of the dolphins would be selected, hauled up onto the sands and sacrificed to become the main course of a great ceremonial feast. Occasionally one was sacrificed to obtain the teeth, which were used in the dowry of a Royal Princess.

In 1918, as an English colonial administrator, Grimble was told by a Gilbert Island chieftain that he was too skinny to be a leader, and that he could put on the much-needed weight if he ate dolphin meat. The chief arranged for Grimble to travel to a nearby island where the resident Dolphin Dreamer proceeded to "call" a pod of dolphins to shore. Grimble witnessed this feat, astonished, as one might imagine.

The ensuing sacrifice of a dolphin was followed by a huge feast, but Grimble avoided eating any of the meat. He was shaken by the experience and felt a lingering remorse for his role in the sacrifice many years later.

(In another gruesome tale, Grimble tells of a Gilbertese king who flavored his rum by pickling dolphin flesh in the casks.)

In general, the people of the Gilbert Islands referred to the dolphin as the High Chief of the Oceans, and the whale as King of all the Fish.[3]

Throughout Polynesia, a male god named Tinirau, the Lord of the Ocean, had whales and dolphins as his messengers. One of his favorite whales was named Tutunui. Tinirau loaned Tutunui to an old, wicked priest named Kae to carry him home after a ceremony. Kae, who had been given a sacred piece of Tutunui to eat during the ceremony, decided to kill the whale when he arrived home. Tinirau sent forty dancing girls to Kae to discover what had happened to his friend the whale. Kae was captured and brought back to Tinirau, who killed and ate him in turn. This is said to be the beginning of cannibalism in the South Pacific, a ritual punishment for a man who killed a whale.

Another tale of Tinirau and his consort Hina tells of Kae taking Hina's brother, the whale Tunua-nui, for a ride, then killing him. A second whale was sent to carry Kae's son, and when the people on Kae's island saw the whale and attempted to drag it onto the beach, they were all pulled into the sea and drowned, avenging Tunua-nui.

In Samoa and Tonga is the tradition of a paradise-island for departed chiefs, ruled by Hikuleo, a benevolent ocean god with a whale's tail.

In stories from both New Zealand and Tahiti a demi-god named Tawhaki turned his foes into porpoises.

Across eastern Polynesia is found the belief in Vatea, the half-human, half-fish god who fathered Tangaloa, the god of the sea and the winds.

On Ulithi a story is told of a dolphin girl who came to watch people dance. She would leave her tail hidden in the bushes so she could join in. A young man discovered her tail and hid it in his house so she couldn't leave. He married her and they had children. One day she discovered the hidden tail and put it back on. Before she left, she told her children who she was and that they should never eat the meat of dolphins, as they were their relations.

In the Solomon Islands there is said to be a kind of sea-sprite called an Adaro, with a body both human and fish-like. The Adaro act like dolphins, riding waterspouts and rainbows and teaching people songs and dances.

And in remotest Oceania, the Hawaiian Islands, the whale is Kanaloa, the Sustainer. His tooth was carved into a strange shape called the Lei Niho Palaoa, the "tongue of the Commander," as the symbol of the divine Word. Suspended on a fabulous necklace braided of human hair, representing Aka, the spiritual energy that connects one's power to one's ancestors through time, the tooth of Kanaloa was worn only by the first-born child of the royal families.

In China, the Baiji or pink river dolphins were considered to be princesses who, having such love for the people, returned after death to live as guardians and supporters of the villages. The river dolphins of the Yangtze would drive fish onto the banks for the people to collect, and in turn the people maintained shrines near their villages where the dolphins were revered.

Sadly, there are now less than three hundred of the gentle Baiji living in the Yangtze River. Dams, fishing techniques, boat traffic, and pollution have severely reduced the number of "princesses." Heroic attempts are being made to revive the population, but little hope remains for them.

In the distant, mythical past of China, there was a male and female couple among the immortal beings. They are credited with not only founding the culture of China, but designing many of its enduring elements, such as the *I Ching*, a book of wisdom and divination still used today. His name is Fu Hsi, and his wife is Nu Gua. They are depicted as having serpent-like tails, and they hold the tools of design, a square and a plumb. They are said to have ruled China from the waters of the ocean.

In modern-day Vietnam, villagers still take great pains to give proper burial to dolphins who strand on beaches. They conduct full ceremonies as if the dolphins were people. A year later they exhume the bones, wash them, and place them in a shrine to be prayed over, eventually re-interring them.

Among the Ainu, the ancient indigenous people of Hokkaido, the north island of Japan, a sacred dance is preserved to this day, celebrating their relationship with God in the form of the whale called Kamui-Fumpe.

The Shinto religion of Japan also reveres the whales, with shrines in many towns dedicated to the souls of whales and dolphins found stranded nearby, as well as those killed for sustenance. The last few traditional whaling villages in Japan still rely on their local priests to absolve them of the spiritual debt incurred by killing whales.

Nowhere else in the world are there as many miles of beaches as on the eastern Asian and the Pacific islands. The myths and stories from this part of the world about whales and dolphins will never be fully documented. Many are now forgotten, but the ones that remain tell us a familiar story of friendship and mutual benefit.

India and the Arts of Civilization

The arrival of civilization in India is recorded in the oldest texts of Hinduism, the Vedas. The part that contains the cosmology and tales of creation is called the *Rg-Veda*.

The *Rg-Veda* tells of Manu, the Divine Man, who, like Noah centuries later, was instructed by the gods to build a boat to save all the animals during the destruction of the world by flood. Manu built the boat and grew thirsty. He was given a glass of water, in which he found a small fish. The fish grew rapidly, and Manu kept putting it in larger and larger containers until he finally had to cast it into the ocean, all the while asking, "Who are you?"

The fish revealed that he was Vishnu, the Savior and Preserver of life. Vishnu had taken form as Matsya Avatar, his first incarnation. He brought Manu and his ark safely through the raging floods, to the shore of a new world to repopulate it, and there Vishnu taught the barbarous humans the arts of civilization.

In the vivid style of Indian art, Matsya Avatar is represented as a strange figure, an upright fish with a man standing in its mouth. The man has many arms, each hand holding something such as a seashell or a sword. In some depictions, beside the fish lies an ugly insect-like thing, its head cut off. In the foreground, a group of men hold their hands in prayer toward the Fish-Man. Floating in the background is a lotus flower, with several men seated on it, each offering things to the Fish-Man.

The floating ones are the ancients, who are sending their gifts through time to the simple-minded men in the present world. Matsya, the Vishnu figure, wields his sword of intellect to defeat the demon of ignorance, Hayagriva.

He does this by teaching the people the arts of civilization: agriculture, architecture, mathematics, geometry, music, irrigation, writing, and metal-working.

Figure 1 MATSYA AVATAR

The first incarnation of Vishnu, according to the Hindu scriptures, was in the form of a dolphin. Here he is depicted as half-man, half-fish, giving a discourse to his worshipping followers, after defeating the demon of ignorance. Known as Matsya Avatar, He taught the early Indians the arts of civilization, including agriculture, mathematics, writing and irrigation.
From Encyclopedia of Religious Rites and Ceremonies of All Nations, *by Bernard Picart, 1722*

If you ask Hindu scholars what this figure represents, this man-in-a-fish's-mouth, they will tell you that it represents a dolphin. To the pre-literate, how else could one describe a fish-like body that has human attributes, such as speech?[4]

Vishnu will have ten incarnations. He has had nine so far, and the last one is expected soon. Some Hindus believe it will be as a dolphin once again.

Discourse Twenty-Three, Book Five of the Srimad Bhagavata, is titled: *The Disposition of the Stellar Sphere Represented in the Form of a Dolphin*. This holy text describes the constellation in which we live as a dolphin, when viewed from the heavenly realms. The North Star, Polaris, is said to be in the tail of the celestial dolphin. The stars of Sirius are the heart of the dolphin and our sun is in the chest, close to the heart. The planets of our solar system are also associated with this stellar cetacean: Mars with the mouth, Saturn with the penis, Jupiter with the dorsal fin, the Moon with the mind, Venus with the navel, Mercury with the breath, and comets with the whole shining body. The name of our constellation is Narayana, which is another name of Vishnu.

To the Hindus, we live inside a great Dolphin. And, between worlds, between the times of existence and non-existence, the Endless Ocean into which all things are absorbed is also Narayana.

An astral dolphin in an ocean of stars.... [5,6]

The Cradle of Civilization: Oannes and the Apkallu

As we follow the Delphic Spirit westward we come to the area often called the Cradle of Civilization or the Fertile Crescent, where the Euphrates and Tigris rivers empty into the Persian Gulf. Long rivers, they drain a huge area. The Euphrates is one of the longest rivers in the world, flowing from the high mountains of Ararat across Syria and the plains of Iraq to the head of the Persian Gulf, more than

1,700 miles. In the distant past the two rivers came close to each other but didn't connect. Now, they do join together. The rivers have built a vast alluvial delta at their mouths, rich marshes of deposited topsoil. It was here that the first intensive agriculture began and the first city was built. The people were called the Sumerians.

At the place where the rivers become marshes, on the edge of the Gulf, was built the first true city on Earth. Called Eridu, it was built on reclaimed land. Today, the site of Eridu is more than 150 miles from the Gulf. The land has continued to build itself outward, southward into the sea.

The cultural advancement of the Sumerians began about 7,500 years ago. Something about the Sumerian way of life was powerful. They were invaded many times over the centuries. Each time the invading culture would settle down over the Sumerians, and before they knew what happened they had adopted Sumerian religion, language, and culture. In later years, the Sumerian lands were called Mesopotamia, Assyria, Babylon, and Chaldea.

According to Berosus, an early Greek priest and historian, the people of Sumeria were scattered, uncivilized barbarians until they were visited by a strange being who showed up one evening along the shore.

This being was described by Berosus as having the shape of a fish with a human voice. He was called *Oannes*. Records now show that there were seven Oanneses who appeared on the beaches, teaching and sharing advanced knowledge with people. They appeared sequentially over a period of several hundred years. They taught the civilizing arts to the Sumerians: agriculture, canal building, writing, mathematics, architecture, engineering, music, a legal system, and spiritual practices.

In a very short time a written language appeared called cuneiform. This was written with a triangular-ended stick, pressed into slabs of mud to make patterns in lines. The slabs were left in the sun to dry, and tens of thousands of these tablets have survived to this day.

As we will see in Egyptian civilization, which rose just after

Sumeria, the appearance of language and writing seemed to happen overnight, with little *development*. This means that the skill of writing had most likely developed somewhere else....

According to Berosus:

> At Babylon there was (in these times) a great resort of people of various nations, who inhabited Chaldaea, and lived in a lawless manner like the beast of the field.
>
> In the first year there appeared, from that part of the Erythraean Sea which borders upon Babylonia, an animal endowed with reason, by name Oannes [whose whole body] (according to Apollodorus) ... was like that of a fish.... His voice too, and language, was articulate and human, and a representation of him is preserved even to this day.
>
> This Being in the day-time used to converse with men; but took no food at that season; and he gave them an insight into letters and sciences, and every kind of art. He taught them to construct houses, to found temples, to compile laws, and explained to them the principles of geometrical knowledge. He made them distinguish the seeds of the earth, and shewed them how to collect fruits; in short, he instructed them in every thing which could tend to soften manners and humanize mankind. From that time, so universal were his instructions, nothing has been added material by way of improvement. When the sun set, it was the custom of this Being to plunge again into the sea, and to abide all night in the deep; for he was amphibious.
>
> After this there appeared other animals like Oannes....[7]

A startling story, isn't it? Just like the story of Matsya Avatar, the dolphin-God who came to India.

As Berosus says, there were more of these beings who visited the Sumerians. Over a period of seven hundred years, the "Oannes," Apkallu, or Seven Sages (as they are variously called) came to share knowledge. This heralded a New Age in which the food supply was stabilized, the waters that flooded the region were tamed, writing

Figure 2 OANNES

> The Apkallu tradition of Sumeria tells of a succession of half-man/half-fish creatures who came to the shore to teach early man the arts of civilization. There are no reliable images of the primary Apkallu named Oannes, but this drawing, after a carving in the palace in Khorsabad, Iraq, is thought to represent Oannes.

began in the form of cuneiform, the wheel was invented, and the concept of Kingship began.

Some of the original names of the Apkallu are revealing. Most historians know of the Fish-Men of Sumeria by the generic name Oannes; however, this was the name of the *type* of being, not limited to an individual. Lists of their names vary. One such list is: *Euedocus, Eneugamus, Eneuboulos, Anodaphus, Anementus, Musaros,* and *Odacon.* Another source has them named *Adapa, U-an-dugga, En-me-duga, En-me-galanna, En-me-buluga, An-enlilda,* and *Utu-abzu.* They were also collectively referred to as the *Annedotus.*

The names Annedotus and Musaros are peculiar. They both translate to "something repugnant, horrible or monstrous." We will explore the implications of this a little later on. *(See Plate 3.)*

Also worth noting: the fifth name in the second list, *En-me-buluga* contains the name of the charming white whale with the moveable lips, the beluga!

Beneath hundreds of thresholds and in buried stone boxes in the excavations of ancient homes of this region have been found collections of fish-skin-draped figures, molded of fired clay. There are always seven figurines, each slightly different. They are the Apkallu, the Seven Sages, and they are understood to have held the prayers and magic of protection, wealth, health, honor, integrity, joy, and wisdom for the household.

The teachings of the Oannes/Apkallu were world-changing, literally. Learning to drain the marshes of the alluvial delta to gain fertile dry land with irrigation canals, useful for transport as well as flood control, gave the people of early Sumeria the ability to take charge of the cycle of food production and distribution.

EA, the Apsu, and the Fish-skin Cape

Many early "mysteries" about these times are relevant to our story. For instance, it has been discovered that most of the ziggurats, or terraced pyramids of the region, had pools on some of the terraces. Originally thought to be water catchments for the "hanging gardens of Babylon," they now appear to have been used for other purposes as well. The pools often have steps leading down into them. While many of the ziggurats were made of packed mud with sun-dried bricks, the pools were masterful constructions of stone made waterproof with a natural form of asphalt.

The ziggurats in Ur and in Nimrud, major cities in Sumeria, were surrounded on all sides by constructed canals and lagoons. Thus, the holy precincts were designed to replicate the heavenly realm "in the midst of the waters."

This region had a lengthy history of worship of and interaction with water and water creatures. A carved relief excavated from the ruins of a palace tells us that at the court of Ashurnasirpal II in

879 B.C., in the city of Nimrud, a gift of exotic animals was received to be displayed in his palace, including elephants, bears, deer, and dolphins. This is the oldest recorded instance of dolphins in a human-designed environment, as part of the earliest known zoo.[8]

It was in the land of the Apkallu that EA was revered as one of the two sons of NAMMU, the highest female deity.

The god EA was amphibious. Among the many gods of Sumeria, this one in particular survived the centuries to come down to us, a shadowy aspect of the God of Abraham (see Chapter Six). One of the primary gods, EA was said to live in the *Apsu,* the watery realm. He is always depicted wearing robes made of water, with fishes swimming around him. In one ancient description, he is "... in the swampland, lies stretched out ... "[9] Often he is shown sitting in a tank full of water.

In the collections of the Middle Eastern Museum in Berlin, Germany, is a temple artifact that holds special importance for our story. It is a stone tank from the palace temple in the city of Assur, a temple of Sennacherib, an early king. On the sides of the tank are depicted numerous priests with fish-skin capes. The tank is almost four feet deep and just over ten feet square and is referred to by archeologists as an Apsu Tank, or tank for holding "holy water." *(See Plate 4.)*

Holy water?

The Roman Catholic Church uses holy water as a key element of its rituals. The container for holy water in cathedrals is usually in the form of a small font, holding no more than a few gallons of water. Why, might we ask, would the Sumerians, who had no metal tools, have gone to such lengths to find the large slabs of dolerite, a very hard stone, flatten them, fit them together, then carve them with surface decorations depicting humans with fish-like capes, to create a water-tight tank large enough to swim in? Perhaps something more than water was kept in this tank. Something sacred....

Figure 3 EA IN TANK

EA the god of the Apsu, was often shown with water spouting from his shoulders. He is always depicted with fish and water and here he seems to be in a tank. A priest is approaching him, climbing stairs to enable him to see into the tank.

Image after a cylinder seal from Ur in Iraq.

In this long-gone era, round cylinders with engraved designs were used to create "signatures" on soft mud documents by rolling them along the surface. On many of these cylinder seals are depicted water creatures, including both fish-draped priests and mer-people.

Figure 4 MARDUK

Marduk, fabled son of the water god EA, is here depicted wearing the distinctive fish cape with a watery skirt. He holds a sacred pollen basket and a pollen applicator, some believe, indicating the mastery of agriculture.

The priests of this era were magical and powerful. They could give or withhold life. An image from the Babylonian era gives us some idea of the method of their magic (see Figure 4). At an archeological excavation near the ancient city of Babylon (which was later buried under a landslide), an artist in the 1800s was able to make a drawing of a low-relief carving of a muscular man in a sort of skirt, with a long fish skin draped over his back, the head of the fish forming a hat. The skirt he wears features patterns of flowing water. In one hand he holds a basket, and in the other he extends some object forward. This carving has been called Marduk, Dagon, and Oannes by various authors. The best scholarship would indicate that Marduk is the proper name for this now-familiar image.

This relates to several important parts of our story. The fish skin had to be something very special. It appears that this image represents the King or High Priest, demonstrating that his authority and power are derived from the power of the Fish-Men. The Apkallu tradition lived on, commemorated by wearing the insignia of their presence.

It is thought that the original idea of kingship began in Sumeria, that it was the priests who held all the power until, in time, a royal family was recognized apart from the religious caste of priesthood. Despite our current ideas about power being dependent on military might and economic control, the concept of kingship is not one that depends on temporal powers. A king is a religious figure, a social role in which a human being is designated as having power and authority given by God. They are God's representatives in the world of human relations.

A king could be a powerful and controlling influence only if he held something that was not available to others. In the image of "Marduk" we see several things that would not have been part of the life of the common man.

First is the fish skin. Second is the basket and cone in his hands. The basket may be a pollen basket, the cone an applicator. The act depicted so graphically symbolizes the King's power, both his mastery of the waters and the ability to guarantee the food supply. Instead of depending on bees and natural pollination by the wind, a secret method of hand pollinating had been developed, and the gradual genetic improvement of cultivated grains began. Starvation was beginning to be brought under control. Thus, the King held the power to give life to his people.

Irrigation, seed gathering, controlled pollination—in short, the very roots of agriculture. This is the basis of one of humanity's most important and distinguishing characteristics—management of our food supply—which began in Sumeria under the influence of the amphibian Apkallu, the Dolphin gods.

CHAPTER TWO

A Telling of Legends, Part II

Tales from Egypt and Africa

The Water Gods of Egypt

Not long after the advent of the Sumerian civilization with its amphibian Apkallu, a great culture appeared in Egypt, a land that has left us with more active mysteries than any other. Something similar was going on at virtually the same time, something mysterious.

We cannot explore much of Egyptian history without feeling the distance that lies between our lives and all that was occurring so long ago in the land where Africa and Asia meet.

Among the most traditional and established academics of our day, it is calmly stated that the hieroglyphic language and writing of ancient Egypt was developed over a period of three hundred years. Perhaps this does not strike one as anything out of the ordinary at first glance, but three hundred years is not very long for something as profound as a written language to evolve.

Language requires a long time to develop. And yet, in Egypt, we see the arrival of an entire language and notation system virtually overnight, with no record of any development. Apparently it did not evolve in Egypt; it appeared as a complex and sophisticated system, fully capable of recording transactions, rituals, and histories. As the years passed, there was a definite growth and change in the system, eventually producing three different eras in Egyptian writing, but the beginning was a startling appearance, seemingly from nowhere.

Among other mysteries of early Egypt, there are architectural masterpieces, advanced irrigation systems, complex and even incomprehensible religious practices, well-developed social hierarchies, substantial differences in the apparent physical traits of the ruling class (including the probable appearance of a new blood type among the Pharoanic families), and evidence of technologies that baffle us today.

Ancient Egypt hosted a civilization that bloomed overnight. As in India and Sumeria, as we have already discussed, something happened that points to outside intervention. (Theories abound, including extraterrestrial sources, Atlantis, or a lost civilization buried under miles of ice in Antarctica, but no one truly knows where the rapid and parallel development of both Sumeria and Egypt came from. Perhaps the dolphins and whales were involved in some way, as the messengers for both cultures.)

If our thesis is correct that cetaceans have had a major influence on the flowering of human civilization throughout time, shouldn't this theory be borne out in Egypt as well? Well, it is, but we have to be diligent to find any hard evidence.

One of the defining traits of Egyptian history is the role of the priesthood. Priests had control and influence over their culture that we cannot entirely grasp today. Writing, mathematics, architecture, agricultural techniques, boat design, weaving, beer making, and even bread baking were all the province of the priests. Over time, the secrets of the more mundane processes, like bread and beer making, were released to the populace, but secrecy was the byword.

The arts and techniques of building the pyramids, much discussed and debated, are still a mystery. The priests of Egypt were good at keeping their traditions esoteric. Yet tantalizing bits have survived, stories that seem to tell us that the cetaceans, or something we have come to know as the dolphins, were playing a role in early Egypt.

. . .

Consider the following:

• In *The Egyptian Book of the Dead*, by E.A. Wallis Budge, several versions of the Egyptian creation story are given. An overview of these tells us that *out of the primordial waters came a Creator* who set RA in the heavens as the sun. And RA, as the Egg of the Sun, gave birth to a family of gods, among them Osiris. Osiris was perhaps the most widely revered and long-lived divine being in all of Egyptian tradition, equal to the Savior in their Holy Family.

RA, as the sun, made his way across the heavens each day in a boat, and this boat was guided by the personification of law, order, and unfailing regularity—two "fishes" swam before his boat.[1] They acted as pilots and lookouts, to warn of coming danger.[2] They were named Abtu and Ant. They act very much like dolphins.

• The main temple of Osiris is in Abydos, a city far up the Nile, where the "Fish of Abydos" (Osiris)[3] was said to have lived. In several of the prayers carved on walls in the temple complex, there is reference to the witnessing of "... *the Transformations of the Fish.*" On the entrance of the temple are the words: *Osiris Lives.*

The Temple of Osiris is large, but the majority of it was built long after the most important feature, called the Oseirion. This large

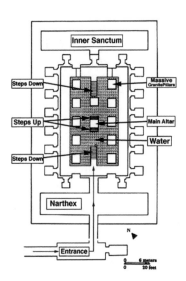

Figure 5 OSEIRION

The temple of Osiris in Abydos, Egypt was built to have its main room flooded, with an altar in the middle rising out of the dark water. One can easily imagine some amphibian form of Osiris shining in his brilliant robes, resting on the central platform.

underground room, hidden behind the main complex, is partly flooded, *which is part of the original design*. Built of enormous undecorated blocks of stone, the Oseirion is considered by scholars to be one of the most enigmatic of all Egyptian temples.

> *Footsteps echo as we descend, following the priest with his flaring, smoking reed torch. Down damp undecorated halls we walk, each footfall repeated nine times. Our linen robes make no sound. We pass through a dim entry hall into a passage that opens into the main hall.*
>
> *The flickering light reveals huge pillars lining the room, which stretches beyond sight. We stand on a narrow walkway, looking down into the black, still water. The flat blank ceiling is mirrored there, wavering in the light from the torches. The ceiling seems to press down on us—our breath comes with difficulty. Dimly, we see rising out of the water, far out in the middle of this dark room, a dais, upon which is a glowing form, the body of the radiant amphibious God....[4]*

Osiris was the central figure of Egyptian religion, in part because he was the resurrected God. He was brought back to life after being murdered. Each person who died in ancient Egypt who aspired to immortal life had ceremonies held for his or her benefit, in which the deceased was always referred to as Osiris "X," with X being the name of the person. Everyone made certain that the formula used to resurrect Osiris was repeated for him or her. This was also the basis for the embalming practices that produced tens of thousands of mummies, many of which are still with us.

Osiris is always shown with his legs wrapped together and is occasionally depicted as a bi-form being, partly fish, with a horizontal tail. According to Plutarch, Isis had to separate the "legs" of Osiris so that he could walk like men.[5]

• In 1998 it was announced that a new discovery had been made on the Giza plateau, the latest in a series of sites called a tomb of Osiris. It lies about two hundred yards from the Sphinx, at the bottom of a well. A sarcophagus was found under water with hallways leading away from it in several directions. The water has been pumped out and explorations continue. Like the Oseirion, this is another underwater site of Osiris.

• In Egyptian texts, the general populace was referred to as "the drowned ones," perhaps referring to their inability to swim in the waters occupied by Osiris.

• In the tale of Osiris, when he is killed and dismembered by Set, his body parts are scattered and hidden. Only one of his body parts was not found when he was resurrected. A fish swallowed his phallus. Could this mean that his generative powers, the sources of life, were hidden in the Water People?

• Isis, wife of Osiris and member of the Holy Family of Egypt, is occasionally depicted with a headdress that some people interpret as having a snake at its front, wings draped down over her ears, and fish scales and tail at the back. In some instances, she is depicted as a bi-form being, having a fish's tail.

• Isis and Osiris have a son, Horus, sometimes called Harpocrates. He is "born maimed"[6] or "weak in his lower limbs."[7] This would seem to indicate an amphibian family, with fish tails that are concealed within the wrappings of their "legs."

• The hieroglyph for the Creator God Amun Ra depicts a man wearing a hat with a unique shape, and a tail coming from the hat, down his back. He holds an ankh in his hand, the symbol of life. The shape of the hat is clearly that of the fish so often seen in the Sumerian priest images. Again, we have the Creator in association with the "fish."

• South of the Great Pyramid of Giza is a lake that was visited by Herodotus, the Greek historian. Called Lake Moeris, it was said to be artificial, dug by men, and containing water brought by canals from the Nile River. His description includes a vast labyrinth, containing three thousand rooms, and two pyramids over three hundred feet tall. (Robert Temple, in his wonderful book *The Sirius Mystery*, pp. 16–22, postulates that amphibious beings of extra-terrestrial origin, similar to the Oannes of Sumeria, lived in Lake Moeris. He also suggests that the water-weathering of the Sphinx was due to the statue being surrounded by water, and that the underground chambers said to be beneath the Sphinx, which are reported to be filled with water, would be the natural design of these amphibious beings....)

This description of a complex of temples and pyramids in the middle of an artificial lake has frustrated Egyptologists for many years. No one has found any trace of these structures, yet Herodotus claims to have seen and visited them. One part of his description has, however, proven to be accurate. The lakebed, still in existence, shows that the flooding Nile River filled it and that it could be blocked off so that as the river fell back to its normal levels the lake would remain full. This was used as a source of water for irrigation.

• The priests of Egypt were prohibited from eating fish except one day a year. This was in honor of the high esteem they had for their Teachers. This was a taboo that was ritually broken once a year in an early version of transubstantiation, the literal transformation of a food into the flesh of God, which is ritually eaten. Most early cultures had ritual practices that involved the eating of God in one form or another. This survives in the Catholic practice of the wafer and the wine of Holy Communion.

• Other Egyptian traditions tell of the original teacher-gods arriving "in a boat that has arisen out of the Sea of Atum." A source of original wisdom, from the sea.[8]

• In an ancient manuscript written by the greatest of all Egyptian spiritual teachers, named Thoth or Hermes (part of the *Corpus Hermeticum* entitled *The Virgin of the World)* is a segment delivered by Isis. Here she tells Horus that dolphins are to be regarded as superior beings, more evolved than mere animals. They are to be considered as eligible, just as the most advanced humans are, to enter the divine state upon dying.[9]

• The star Sirius is central in the Egyptian traditions, and as we will see, Sirius is present in most cetacean mythology.

• And finally, returning to Wallis Budge, the eminent Egyptologist and Keeper of the Egyptian and Assyrian Antiquities in the British Museum, it is his belief that both Egypt and Sumeria were the recipients of the same ancient traditions and teachings, that their systems of the zodiac, astronomy, mathematics, and even religion were nearly identical, and that this knowledge appeared fully developed at nearly the same time. He concludes that these teachings must have come from the same source, a third culture, older than either of them.

Egypt: there are tales of gods with tails, worshipped in temples either flooded or surrounded by water; there are the two "fish" who serve as guides of the boat of RA, and who serve the Law; there is special reverence for fish; and there is the sudden appearance of the many arts of civilization, similar to Sumerian and Indian stories, brought by amphibious beings. These are tantalizing bits of Egyptian history to support our thesis—not enough to make a strong case, but enough to make us wonder. Perhaps we must be willing to wait, to continue looking for more discoveries, to see what the years will uncover.

Evidence from other cultures will be much stronger, and we will re-visit some of the clues from Egypt to bring them into sharper focus.

Nommo Dié, Star Whale of the Dogon

In our trek westward, we now arrive in the region of the Mediterranean Sea. Around the "Great Sea," as it was called, we will find plenty of stories about the dolphins.

Not far distant in time from the founding of the Egyptian civilization, climatic changes in northern Africa began to drive some tribal people from their lands. As the desertification of the Sahara progressed, a tribe that may have originated along the shore of the Great Sea began an epic migration. Eventually, they came to a stop in a forbidding land of desert ridges and difficult terrain. Their shamans told them they had arrived at their homeland, where they were to wait until the changing of the worlds.

These people are known as the Dogon. They live today in sub-Saharan Africa, in the landlocked nation of Mali. They are south of Timbuktu, in a remote and desolate landscape.

The Dogon have an important story to tell us. They say they have maintained their knowledge since before their migration, and that they have faithfully kept their traditions and ceremonies throughout time.

In the 1930s, a French anthropologist, Germaine Dieterlen and her husband, went to Mali to explore the religious traditions of the Dogon. There they discovered a tradition that was to cause large ripples in the ponds of several academic disciplines. The Dogon had retained a complex mythology and gradually allowed the couple to learn about it. Astonishing as it may seem, it fits perfectly into the theme we are following.

The Dogon tell of star beings in the shape of whales, who came to Earth to swim in the sea. They came in tall starships with flames on the bottom. Named the Nommo, or Nommo Dié, these star whales created children to live on the land and to be their family. Called Ogo, these children began to forget their origins. In time, Ogo became Ogo Anagonno, "the one who introduces disorder to the Universe," "the one who forgets."

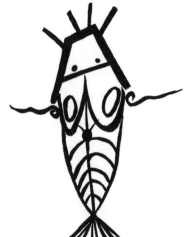

Figure 6 NOMMO

A Dogon drawing of Nommo, the star-whale from Sirius. Here we see Nommo with lungs and a horizontal tail, its head above water, breathing and/or speaking.

Ogo forgets his origins and begins to hunt the Nommo, and kill them. The sacrifice of Nommo on the altar of greed begins destroying the order of the Universe. The Nommo planned for this, and arranged that all Nommo who are sacrificed be allowed to return to life as a new kind of Ogo, to live as humans if they want to. More and more of them choose to do this.

This new Nommo is called Ogo Titiyayne, "he who remembers." Who are they referring to? Who is Ogo Titiyayne?

We are, the hearers of this tale, all of us in the world who understand and support the great Ocean nations. Those of us who remember or intuit (however vague) a sacred and ancient relationship with cetaceans could well be characters in the ongoing mythos, largely unconscious players in a grand drama. Perhaps the Nommo essence is the special linking factor in the lives of those of us who know the importance of the Dolphin message, those of us who see the whales in our dreams, and who are becoming conscious participants in the Web of Life. Perhaps one explanation for the worldwide increase in sensitivity to the environmental crisis we face is that we *are* the Nommo—returned to re-establish order in the Universe, as the Dogon say.

According to the Dogon, Nommo Dié comes from a special star system, where two or more stars spiral around each other, and there is a planet covered by water. The star is Sirius, brightest star in our skies.

The Dogon celebrate the fact that the two stars complete a revolution around each other in just over fifty years. And the Dogon say that the smaller star is heavy, heavier than anything we know.

The star Sirius was thought to be a binary star by astronomers as early as the 1860s. No one was able to prove it until a photograph was taken with both stars in the frame in 1974. It was then determined that the period of rotation is fifty and one-tenth years. The smaller star is a white dwarf, a kind of star containing matter of almost unimaginable density, the heaviest matter in all existence. And recently, a third star has been detected.

Somehow, the Dogon knew the details of this. Their stories are complex and difficult to follow,[10] steeped in references to their local environment, and cast in terms of seeds, animals, kinships, and sexual acts. After years of preparation by the tribal elders, Dieterlen and her husband began to unfold the mystery when they examined the symbols carved into doors, lintels, and masks and were given keys to the interpretation of paintings. Preserved in the religious carvings, rituals, and stories of these unique people are records of Ocean Beings who brought superior knowledge to Earth.

Because of this mysterious knowledge, the Dogon loom large in the Legends of the Dolphins. (An interesting tidbit relating to the Nommo story: in Greek, the word "nomo" means law....)

Like the playful dolphin whose twists and turns surprise us, let's return to Babylon for a moment. For them, the Mother of the Gods was NAMMU. She was from the watery abyss, the Apsu, and was regarded as the personification of a subterranean ocean that lies beneath the physical earth. She was the mother of EA as well as AN and ANTU. Notice the similarity to the Egyptian pantheon, where the dolphins who guide RA across the sky each day are called Ant and Abtu. And of course, the similarity of NAMMU to NOMMO is unmistakable....

Whales and Dolphins in Africa

A few more African tales will help flesh out our legend.

In the Libyan desert, in the searing heat of the Sahara, are the ruins of an enigmatic civilization of which we know almost nothing. The most startling artifact of this culture's existence is a series of tunnels, extending for over a thousand miles of total length, under the sands. These tunnels, ten feet wide and twelve feet high, are part of an enormous water system running in parallel lines across a desert plain. The tunnels are driven through limestone, ending at the edges of plateaus. They are known to be for water, but how they functioned has not been discovered.

Figure 8 TANIT FROM HOUSE OF DOLPHINS

Tanit in a mosaic from a site excavated in Delos, Greece, called the House of Dolphins. It depicts the goddess Tanit in her most common form, as a pyramid with rays of light extending from the top.

Image from Marcel Bulard, Paintings, Murals and Mosaics of Delos, Paris, 1908

Figure 7 TANIT

Tanit, the goddess of Carthage, a ruined city in Tunisia. Here she is depicted over a dolphin, invoking the word of Heaven. She stands over an opening in which is inscribed a message.

Image after a stone carving in the collections of the Louvre

The people who lived here were the *Garamantes*. During the height of Rome and the days of the Coliseum, with its wild-animal fighting, the Garamantes were on the route from the jungles to Rome and were a major source of animals for the bloodthirst of symbolic battle.

The Romans knew only that the Garamantes were ancient people with many secrets. Their worship was centered on *Tanit*, a goddess who was also worshipped in Carthage, along the Tunisian coast. She is often depicted imploring heaven with a dolphin beneath her (see Figures 7 and 8).

The Garamantes were yet another culture that worshipped the dolphin and were masters of water, far from the ocean.

In Ghana, among the people of the Akan tribe, the Mother Goddess is known as Ngame, sometimes depicted as a humpback whale. And Yemanja, a dolphin-tailed water goddess of west Africa, made her way to South America, carried by the millions of slaves forced to move west, and she is worshipped to this day in Brazil.

Farther south in Africa we find the Zulu, a huge tribe of ancient people. Almost unknown to white culture has been the deep spiritual belief system they live by. Until one man came forward to share this system, the Zulu were considered to be like the stereotype of all black African people—unsophisticated in their beliefs, suspended in a timeless state of simple animistic worship and superstition.

Credo Mutwa, the current Vusa'mazulu or spiritual leader of the Zulu, broke his people's traditional rules by publishing a book in 1964 called *Indaba, My Children*. In his book Mutwa tells the story of creation, the origins of the Zulu people and all humankind, and the special beliefs the Zulu hold dear. Attacked by his own people for revealing their precious secrets, including attempts on his life and the murder of his son so that he would be unable to pass on his role as Vusa'mazulu, Mutwa continues to teach others the special beliefs of his people.

From Credo Mutwa we learn that the Zulu use the same word, *Nkuma*, for whale and for God. They speak of the dolphin as the Savior (*Hlengeto*, "the one who saves"). Mutwa wears a ceremonial "necklace" on special occasions, a huge crude bronze disk with a hole in the middle for his head, from the outer edge of which are suspended various objects. One is a green stone dolphin, from whose mouth hangs a golden tablet. This is described as the "Tablet of the Law," brought to the Zulu by the dolphins from the stars. *(See Plate 7.)*

In an interview with an English filmmaker in 1995, Credo Mutwa said, "Dolphins are symbols to us of humanity's reconnection with nature and therefore with God."[11]

Mutwa has also shared the Zulu knowledge of the Nommo with

the world,[12] expanding the story held for so long by the Dogon. He says that the Nommo live on a water world, one of twelve that circles Inja, the star of the Wolf (Sirius). Both humans and the Nommo people, who are like dolphins, shared the water world. The humans had come to that world after escaping a dying planet and had been welcomed by the gentle water people, the Nommo. Their King was also named Nommo. When some humans killed a Nommo (dolphin-person) and ate him, the water people declared war on the humans. Nommo the king, wanting to avoid war, committed his two sons to the task of saving the humans. They obtained a huge egg from the sky and got all the humans inside it and took it to the stars. They brought it to our Earth and landed it safely.

One of the sons was killed by the bird whose egg they had stolen, just as they were returning it, and the other came back to Earth to live in the oceans here. Called Mpanku, he became the father of the dolphins we know today. He was killed later in a fierce struggle with a great shark, and has been mourned ever since by the Zulu people as the lost savior.

Mutwa then tells us that Nommo, the king himself, came with twelve of his fellow water-beings many centuries later. They taught people about the stars, how to make tools and how to use them, and many of the arts of civilization. When he left he said he would return when we had rid ourselves of war, hunger, and disease. Once we have accomplished these basic feats, he promised to enable us to travel to other worlds as we did long ago.

In this Zulu tale we have a more complete account of our story, which helps us piece it together as never before. We have an ancient relationship with the dolphins from a time on another world, when they were different than they are now. According to this legend, the dolphins we know on Earth must have interbred with a higher-order being, becoming genetically blessed, demi-gods.

A team of higher-order amphibians came to Earth to visit the long-banished humans who had caused the death of the King's sons.

Yet he loved them enough to teach and aid them, inviting them to aspire to being re-admitted into the family of the star people.

The Oannes tradition comes to mind here—of a group of amphibious beings who emerge from the sea to teach advanced arts to humans. In this case, they would have been present as a group, thirteen of them. They taught us that humans can achieve their status once we complete the process of self-mastery, that we can be "re-born" into a higher state of being.

Perhaps it is no coincidence that the Greek word for law is "nomo." This may be a legacy from the time when order, the divine law so much desired in the world, was known to come from the Star Whales.

CHAPTER THREE

A Telling of Legends, Part III

The Delphic World of Greece

F*ifty oars flashing together, the sun is reflected as they rise out of the water. The surging power of the ship, pulsing forward with each stroke of the oars, raises a pressure wave in front of the bow.*

Dolphins, always looking for ways to play, frolic in the wave. Slipping sideways, they veer off and dive, then race back to slide between the others, the whole wave filled with silver bodies.

Standing at the bow, a young man looks eagerly toward the land:

"Months of travel are about to come to an end. Home to my ancestors' altars, my family. I've been gone over a year, yet I recognize the sweet smell of my home in the air."

On a hilltop can be seen a white temple, its marble shining. It looks like a dream, a house where a god would be pleased to visit. The harbor is becoming visible over the waves. Masts are swaying, the wharf-side buildings are becoming distinct, and banners are flying in the air.

The dolphins, who are all one form, one self-same beauty, continue to roll and rise and glide in the waves before the bow.

"Egypt—it now seems so far behind me, the memories of my year in school, the family who looked after me. Dolphins were there to greet me when I arrived, weaving their dance for our ship, and the same were there to play with us as we left.

"Now, the dolphins are with the ship again, bringing us all home. Are they the same ones? Have they stayed with us, to bring us safely back?

"Home—the wharf is near. I see the bright robes of my family among the crowds.

"Safe again, Poseidon's dolphins have brought me home...."

—An imaginary student returns home, Greece, 300 B.C.

Among the most well-known symbols of classical Greece, such as white marble temples on cliffs overlooking the sea, and men in togas discussing philosophy on the steps, we find the icon of a boy riding a dolphin. He is often shown with a lyre in one hand, or carrying a trident. This elegant image has been used in so many contexts, from movie titles to advertising icons, that its original source has been largely forgotten.

When we follow the Delphic Wave to Greece, we find that this boy and his dolphin friend are a small but very important part of a cultural phenomenon unique in history (see Figure 9).

The culture of classic Greece—the so-called Golden Age—was suffused with the spirit of the dolphin. In many aspects of this small but influential country, dolphins and the wisdom of the sea played crucial roles. Some of the social institutions we enjoy today can be traced directly back to this extraordinary era in Greece, when dolphins were favored creatures. It might be said that at no other time in our ancient

Figure 9 ARION

Arion, the classic "boy on a dolphin", has been used to symbolize many things. Here he resembles Apollo, bringing the arts of civilization as the ten strings of his lyre, riding triumphantly on the back of the dolphin.

history were they as revered and their influence felt more than then.

It was a mysterious series of events that set in motion the Greek wave of dolphin-inspired development. It is a mythic tale, told by many writers. The traditional story is mixed, muddled, and many-limbed, but the essence is this:

Apollo, a god whose attributes include music, poetry, beauty, youthfulness, and grace, decided to bring a gift to Earth in his love for humanity. He would establish an Oracle, where answers to life's threats and challenges could be heard, where his spirit could be accessed.

He chose to appear one evening to a group of travelling Cretan businessmen who were sailing in the Gulf of Corinth. As they gazed westward, across the tranquil ocean at the setting sun, down the golden river of light came a leaping dolphin, growing larger and larger. To their astonishment the dolphin leapt high above the ship, transformed into the figure of a Golden Youth, and landed on the deck among them.

He declared: "Behold, I am Apollo Delphinios! I have come to bring a lasting gift to mankind. You are to be the priests of my new Oracle. Come, we sail to our new home!"

Apollo returned to his dolphin form and lay on the deck, glowing. The businessmen were terrified at first, then when the sails began filling with wind and the rudder turned of its own accord, they realized they were in the grip of something that could not be resisted. The ship sailed to a small port, where they disembarked and followed Apollo in the form of a radiant young man up into the mountains.

He led them to the site of the Oracle of the Python, where a sisterhood of priestesses had long maintained a temple of prophecy, relying on messages received from the Earth Serpent, Python. The Chief Priestess, the Pythia, outraged at the coming of Apollo and his new priests, challenged him to a duel. They wrestled, and Apollo defeated her.

Instead of killing her, however, he set a new standard for the treatment of the vanquished: he honored her, her bravery, her skill at wrestling, and all the many years of her service in the temple. For this, he rewarded her and her sisterhood with a new role, that of the Voices of the new Oracle of Delphi.

The Pythian priestesses were, according to legend, able to withstand exposure to deadly gases that came from a crevice, by chewing a secret herbal mixture containing laurel leaves. This enabled them to stay in the twilight realm between life and death, where they could clearly hear the voice of Apollo.[1]

Setting aside the questions of veracity that mythic tales always bring up, we are looking at a source of information that was reliable, unique, and accessible. This fits into the scheme of the Golden Age, when the world became knowable. The Dolphin God had arrived, with a gift that was to last more than 1,300 years as the source of certainty and wisdom for a vast area. The founding of the Oracle of Delphi is thought to have occurred in approximately 1000 B.C., and the last prophecy recorded from the Oracle was in A.D. 346, when the Roman Emperor Theodosius outlawed the use of all oracles. The priests at Delphi bewailed this turn of events, saying, "The voice of the waters is fading away."

In today's world, nothing of the kind exists. We have no higher authority to turn to now that we have banished the gods from our public lives. Our science denies the possibility of a superior intelligence living among us, of another, wiser kind of being living in our world, symbolized (or embodied) by the dolphin. We are on our own now, and we can hardly appreciate the feelings of humans who lived with the certainty of a definitive answer to be had for the most dangerous questions. It is all in the past now, so we can only think of how it might have been.

On a large rocky shelf hanging on the side of the mountain is the Holy Place, the home of Apollo. Shining against the tall cliffs behind, the scene looks like Olympus itself. A large amphitheater overlooks the streets, where a string of temples and treasuries stand, glorious and gleaming in their golden decorations. Each is filled with the tribute and gifts of hundreds of years, the payment of pledges to Apollo for his truths. Gardens surrounding the temples are filled with trees and collections of cultivated flowers, shaded and welcoming.

The roads are swarming with people, for this is the season of the Games, the contests between the most beautiful, blessed, and divine of the times. Speakers of wit, orators of philosophy, poets and singers, dancers and jugglers will all be challenging each other to outdo themselves in praises to the Gods. The races begin tomorrow, and the young men, naked as the Gods made them, will contend with one another in speed, strength, and endurance. Who will the Gods favor this time?

The crowds will stay for several weeks, camping in the meadows below the town. Each day they will climb the steep road to attend the rituals, watch the contests, and absorb the blessings of this most marvelous town. It is not a town, really, but a place where the Gods allow mortals to dwell among them for a time, to be inspired to reach deep within to find the divine gifts with which each is endowed.

Delphi is the sacred home of Apollo Delphinios, the Divine Dolphin who speaks through the mouth of his Priestess. The Games constitute the time when the Gods allow themselves to play among humans.

Know Thy Self

Upon the temple of Apollo at Delphi were seven inscriptions, reported to be the essence of the wisdom of the Seven Sages. Who were the Seven Sages? Rather than look for them among the Greeks, I prefer to think of them as the seven Apkallu, the fish-cape-shrouded wise men of Babylon.

Three of their sayings have survived and are reported to us by none other than Plato:

> Know Thy Self
> Nothing to Excess
> Know Thy Opportunity

These ideas, although simple and even common to us today, were startling and revolutionary in their time.

The first, *Know Thyself*, suggests the possibility of self-knowledge. Priests were to be removed as interpreters and intermediaries of God's will. The source and the target of one's quest were to rest directly within the accessible self. This would remove the veil of mystery surrounding all of nature, taking from Isis the shroud of secrecy behind which she had always lived. To know oneself is to know the human condition, and should lead to a universal appreciation for our world and the lives we lead. In self-knowledge lies the revelation of the nature of others. It is the key to compassion.

The admonition of *Nothing to Excess* is wise counsel for the moment when dazzling new horizons open as we focus ourselves on self-knowledge. In the discovery of the self in the role of creator, lover, and destroyer, one can become drunk with the implied power and glory. A new state called freedom opens itself to the seeker, and dangers lurk in unexpected places for everyone who reaches this new revelation. Even freedom can be abused.

Know Thy Opportunity. What a fine notion, to know the best time to act! If we practiced mindfulness adequately, we might be more on time and more on track. This suggestion has to do with time, which is one of the most convoluted of man's concepts. We are perhaps the only beings in the Universe so concerned with the many kinds of time. This wise saying infers that one can understand timing in life and act on it. It reinforces the basic concept of self-awareness and self-control.

In these few words an Apollonian Creed was framed.

This creed speaks subtly of respect for the human spirit, implying that there is good reason to know the self. It is the beginning, the cornerstone of the very idea of democracy.

The word *Delphi* in Greek means "dolphin." The word *Delphy* means "womb." *Adelphos* means "brother." The association between the nurturing source of our lives, our families, and the benevolent dolphins carries a resonance we can all feel. In some sense, this encapsulates the entire thesis we are examining.

In the Greek era, the dolphins were perceived as being closer than any other creature to the gods, half-divine themselves. These demi-gods were messengers between the human and the divine realms, and were, of course, sacred to Apollo. Mysterious beings, they came and went, living lives unimaginable, far out in the dangerous seas. Where did they go, beneath the waves? How could they survive the storms without being divine? What was their true nature, with warm breath, joyous frolicking, and care for humans?

Dolphins were very prominent in the Greek mythos. They were on the shields of Odysseus and Hercules; they were credited with delivering the love of Amphitrite to Zeus, for which they were made into a constellation; they saved many young princes; appeared on coins and in statuary; gave their name to towns, the main court in Athens, and elsewhere; were the companions of the Nereids, daughters of Neptune; and on and on. *(See Plate 8.)*

There were even obituary poems written for them, carved onto tombstones erected in their honor. Here are two examples, written for dolphins who had stranded:

> Never again rejoicing in the surges that I sunder
> Shall I toss my neck aloft, as I leap from gulfs of sea;
> Nor, circling round a galley, at its fair prow snort with
> > wonder,
> Proud to find it fashioned in the shape of me.
> For the dark-blue rollers hurled me high on the land's dry
> > breast
> And in this narrow shingle I am laid to rest.[2]
> > —By Anyte of Tegea, 300 B.C.

> No longer, Dolphin, sea foam darting,
> Will you startle deep-sea shoals,
> Nor, dancing to the reedy piping,
> Splash up spume beside our hulls;
> No longer will you, foam-clad, carry
> Nereids on your back and bear

Them off to Tethys, for tides high
As hills have cast you on the shore.[3]
—By Archias

In Athens, Apollo called for a Dolphin Temple to be built in his honor. This temple was eventually the home site of a network of Dolphin Temples built in many cities around the Mediterranean. They were the social hubs of the city, where feasts and ceremonies occurred frequently. Today, the Temple of Apollo Delphinios in Athens still stands, its ruins visited by tourists every day of the year.

It was in this Dolphin Temple that Neoptolemus, the son of Achilles, was ritually murdered for an affront to Apollo. He had falsely claimed that the god was responsible for the death of his father. Neoptolemus was the grandfather of Alexander the Great.

It was a capital offense to kill a dolphin in Greece. This is indicative of their importance to the Greeks, whose ideas of democracy and the rights of humans were still developing. Slaves were a large part of all early civilizations, and Greece was no exception. It was entirely permissible to kill a slave without fear of legal reprisal, yet it was a major offense to kill a dolphin.

Oppian (in his *Halieutica*, approximately A.D. 200) said,

> The hunting of dolphins is immoral, and that man can no more draw nigh to the gods ... nor touch their altars with clean hands, but pollutes those who share the same roof with him, who willingly devises destruction for the dolphins. For equally with human slaughter the gods abhor the deathly doom of the monarchs of the deep.

Dolphins were also sacred to Athena, the principal goddess of Athens, the city-state that was the apex of the league of Greek states.

Theseus, an early king of Athens, said to be the son of Zeus and the original consolidator of the Greece that we know today, established the first common courts of law for the confederacy. This court was known as the Court of Apollo the Dolphin, or the Dolphin Court. It had been discovered that the decisions of the Dolphin's priests and priestesses were reliable, well considered, and acceptable. Theseus also maintained the Dolphin Temples, where many of the rulings of the Court were implemented.

Theseus had various links to the dolphins. In a youthful contest to prove his worthiness, he called upon the dolphins to help him retrieve a ring tossed into the ocean. They not only provided him with the ring but the crown he was to wear.

The Boy on a Dolphin

And what of the boy on the dolphin? Who was he and what was his tale?

Arion, son of the king of Lesbos, was the most accomplished musician of his time. He sailed to a distant city for a contest, which he won, and on his return voyage was threatened by the crew as they neared his home port. He offered to sing one last song before he was cast into the sea, which they accepted. Arion sang a high-pitched song called the Orthian, which means "the shrill song," and when he finished, he bowed to the sailors, turned, and leapt into the sea.

Arion knew that the dolphins would invariably come when he sang the Orthian. He had written and practiced the song in the sea-side palace where he grew up, learning much of it from them, and he knew of their love for its sound. When he leapt off the ship, they saved him by carrying him to shore.

Arion presented himself in court, telling of the robbery and attempted murder, and when the sailors were brought before the throne, his father asked Arion's whereabouts. They lied and said he had taken another ship to come home. Arion then exposed them and they were executed.

Arion's ride on the dolphins was commemorated by his father on coins, in song, and in statuary many times over.

There were others whose lives were saved by dolphins in the Greek era. Perhaps exaggerated by time, stories come down to us of no less than seven princes of royal families described as having been saved by dolphins! (If that many princes were saved, either they were exceptionally clumsy, or many, many more people were saved whose lives were not as newsworthy.)

Many other stories are told of boys befriending dolphins in extraordinary ways, and riding on them. An example:

> ... the goodwill and friendship of the dolphin for the lad of Iasus was thought by reason of its greatness to be true love. For it used to swim and play with him during the day, allowing itself to be touched; and when the boy mounted upon its back, it was not reluctant, but used to carry him with pleasure where he directed it to go, while all the inhabitants of Iasus flocked to the shore each time this happened.
>
> Once a violent storm of rain occurred and the boy slipped off and was drowned. The dolphin took the body and threw both it and itself together on the land and would not leave until it too had died, thinking it right to share a death for which it imagined that it shared the responsibility. And in memory of this calamity the inhabitants of Iasus have minted their coins with the figure of a boy riding a dolphin.
>
> —Plutarch, High Priest of the Dolphin Temple,
>   Athens

Alexander the Great (356–323 B.C.) appointed a boy to be the High Priest of Poseidon at a Dolphin Temple in Babylon after the boy was befriended by a dolphin. It would come to play with the boy, taking him on his back out into the sea each day "at the hour when the gymnasium was dismissed."

A man named Koreanos bought a dolphin from some fishermen who had caught it in their net and set it free. Later, in a shipwreck, he was the only man who survived, because he was rescued by dolphins. When Koreanos died, a pod of dolphins came to the beach where his body was being cremated, floated quietly, then left at the end of the ceremonies.

The Dolphins both rejoice in the echoing shores and dwell in the deep seas, and there is no sea without dolphins; for Poseidon loves them exceedingly....

—Oppian, *Halieutica*

This other excellent deed of the dolphins have I heard and admire. When fell disease and fatal draw nigh to them, they fail not to know it but are aware of the end of life. Then they flee the sea and the wide waters of the deep and come aground on the shallow shores. And there they give up their breath and mortal man may take pity on the holy messenger of the Shaker of the Earth when he lies low, and cover him with a mound of shingle, remembering his gentle friendship; or haply the seething sea herself may hide his body in the sands; nor any of the brood of the sea behold the corpse of their lord, nor any foe do despite to his body even in death. Excellence and majesty attend them even when they perish, nor do they shame their glory even when they die.

—Oppian, *Halieutica*

The Palladium: Powerful Dolphin Magic

Among the most intriguing tales of dolphin magic in any time, in any land, is the story of the dolphin guardians of Troy:

Greek mythology tells us that a war was fought between Aphrodite, the Trojan Sea Goddess, and Poseidon, the Greek Sea God. The economic history of this era would say that the worshippers of Poseidon wanted free access to the narrow seaway that leads from the Mediterranean to the ports of the East that line the shores of the Black Sea. Jason and his Argonauts had sought and found their gold there. His descendants wanted continued free access. Aphrodite's city, Troy, would not yield. The Trojans continued to extract a tax on Greek shipping.

In the war that developed from this dispute two divinely charged objects, carved from the bones of dolphins, guarded the city of Troy. Both had been worshipped in the Greek communities of Italy, the early "colonies" of Greece. Their citizens made the divine objects available to their relations in Troy for its protection during the war. Although these powerful things were of Greek origin, they were used against the Greeks by the Trojans.

The first power object was the shoulder blade of ancient Pelops, which had been fashioned from dolphin bone. Due partly to their ivory-like texture, dolphin bones were used to make sacred items by the priest/alchemist/artisans of the Dolphin Temple. Dolphin bodies were taboo to all but the priests. This shoulder blade prosthetic had been fashioned to replace the shoulder of a man who was mistakenly eaten by a goddess in a mythical episode. It was brought to Troy from Pisa, where it had been worshipped for centuries.

The other power object was a statue of Pallas Athena, called the *Palladium*. As familiar as this word is today, it is especially remarkable that almost no one remembers its origins.

This mysterious object, of which no images have come down to us, was also made of the bones of dolphins, and may have represented Athena in the form of a woman worshipping a phallus, with her eyes looking upward. Athena herself, with her ever-present helmet, is sometimes representative of an erect phallus. Her name is both male and female, and although she is the most powerful of all warriors, she owned no weapons of her own, being loaned them when she needed them. Pallas Athena embodies an androgynous power, male in effect and female in her strategies. The dolphin also has no obvious male or female form but possesses the qualities of both.

The Palladium held secrets of great importance, understood by Apollo's priests. Its power was real.

One story of its origin says that it was made to be displayed in Olympus, but it had been defiled by Electra as she was enjoying the sexual attentions of Zeus and it was cast out of Heaven. In this tradition it was described as "a legless image, over 3 cubits tall."[4]

Idaes brought the Palladium to Troy from a Dolphin Temple in

Italy. It protected the city until the end of the war, when it played a pivotal role in the defeat of Troy. The war was lost when it fell into the hands of the Greeks in a betrayal by the son of the king of Troy and his wife Theano, a priestess in the temple where it was enshrined.

Theano helped the Greek heroes Odysseus and Diogenes to steal it after the Oracle at Delphi revealed the importance of this sacred and powerful icon and its protection of Troy. With the city weakened by the loss, the war went quickly against the Trojans after the theft, bringing to an end ten years of strife. It was a victory for Poseidon.

The shoulder bone of Pelops was lost at sea on its way to Greece after the war, and then retrieved by a fisherman many years later. The Oracle at Delphi advised him to give it to ambassadors from a small city that were looking for a cure for a plague. They honored the fisherman for his gift by making him the priest of the temple built for the relic. It is not known what became of it.

It is rumored that the Palladium may still exist. It has been traced from Troy to southern Italy, where it was guarded and worshipped by a group of dedicated virgin priestesses, the famous Vestal Virgins. Their worship was primarily in service of Vesta, the Goddess of Fire, whose main icon was the public hearth of sacrifice. In their sanctum, where they guarded their relics and those of other cults, was said to be the Palladium. Although many temples claimed to have the Palladium after the Trojan War ended, it is likely that Aeneas took it to Italy. Virgil's epic poem, *The Aeneid*, tells the story of the wanderings and battles of Aeneas as he "brings his gods to Italy" to found the empire of Rome.

If the Palladium exists today, perhaps it is hidden in the collections of the Vatican. The High Priest of the cult of the Vestal Virgins who guarded the sacred relic was called *pontifex maximus*, or supreme pontiff, a title and position later taken over by the Roman Catholic Pope.[5]

The Palladium lives on in our imaginations. It is used most often to represent something of power or special beauty. Matthew Arnold, a poet in the 1800s, wrote his famous *Palladium*, comparing it to the enduring soul:

> Set where the upper streams of Simois flow
> Was the Palladium, high 'mid rock and wood;
> And Hector was in Ilium, far below,
> And fought, and saw it not, but there it stood.

> It stood; and sun and moonshine rain'd their light
> On the pure columns of its glen-built hall.
> Backward and forward roll'd the waves of fight
> Round Troy; but while this stood, Troy could not fall.

> So, in its lovely moonlight, lives the soul.
> Mountains surround it, and sweet virgin air;
> Cold plashing, past it, crystal waters roll;
> We visit it by moments, ah! too rare.

> Men will renew the battle in the plain
> To-morrow; red with blood will Xanthus be;
> Hector and Ajax will be there again;
> Helen will come upon the wall to see.

> Then we shall rust in shade, or shine in strife,
> And fluctuate ' twixt blind hopes and blind despairs,
> And fancy that we put forth all our life,
> And never know how with the soul it fares.

> Still doth the soul, from its lone fastness high,
> Upon our life a ruling effluence send;
> And when it fails, fight as we will, we die,
> And while it lasts, we cannot wholly end.

Dolphins, Science, and the Arts of Greece

Aristotle studied dolphins very closely. He was the first major Western scientist, a man who applied reason and the experimental method (whereby replicable results are obtained). Aristotle surprises us today with his detailed knowledge of dolphins.

In his book *The History of Animals*, he makes nearly forty statements of fact about dolphins. With recent research, we can now say that only three of these were incorrect, two of which may have been added by translators. He was aware that dolphins are mammals, that they breathe air through their blowholes, make sounds similar to speech underwater, have difficulty making the sounds of consonants, give birth to live infants, suckle their young, and are endlessly friendly toward humans. He even managed to deduce how a dolphin sleeps and mentions that they have been known to snore. An example:

> The voice of the dolphin in air is like that of the human in that they can pronounce vowels and combinations of vowels, but have difficulties with the consonants.
> —Aristotle, *Historia Animalium*

Aristotle is not otherwise known for having used dissection as a means of learning about the insides of animals, but it is clear that he had specific information about the internal organs of dolphins. There can be little doubt that he studied them under ideal conditions, perhaps in a royal seaside pool on the island of Lesbos, where he lived and wrote his animal book in 347 B.C.

This connects us to another thread in the story of Arion of Lesbos, the original "boy on a dolphin." His father was so well pleased by the dolphins having returned his son to him alive that he ordered a channel to be dug from the sea to the inner court of his palace, where the dolphins could come to spend time in a pool with Arion, where they lived "the life of luxury."[6]

This is the second oldest record of a human-constructed facility for dolphins, the circumstance that is now called "captivity." The first was the zoological gardens of a Mesopotamian king in 879 B.C.

The father of science apparently did his dolphin studies in a sort of Dolphinarium. This bears noticing.

Science and mythology were intimately interwoven in those times, as we can see in a passage from Plutarch:

> Wherefore they (the Syrians) reverence the fish as of the same origin and the same family as man, holding a more reasonable philosophy than that of Anaximandros; for he declares, not that fishes and men were generated at the same time, but that at first men were generated in the form of fishes....

This is an especially interesting observation by Anaximandros, who seems to have known that if we examine the fetal growth of both human and dolphin embryos, they are almost indistinguishable from one another for many months. He may have been speaking as a poet, describing a mythical view of their origins, but his view is not entirely without substance. Plutarch, as a high priest of the Dolphin Temple, was more inclined to accept the Syrian idea (which is where Nineveh was, the center of Dagon worship), that we and "fish" are of the same family.

Dolphins were central to the development of the civilizing arts. The Delphic Oracle instituted the Olympic Games. Games, or celebrations of the Divine in each person, laid open the opportunity for anyone, aristocrat or peasant, to demonstrate how much the gods favored them with speed, grace, agility, the command of language, or artistic skill. The plains of Olympia became the most famous place for the games, but their origin was in Delphi. The arena in Delphi still stands.

A winner at the games was not the recipient of grand prizes, officially being rewarded only with a wreath of wild olive branches. The winners were honored socially for the remainder of their lives.

The concept of the Games—the recognition of the human potential to reflect some of the perfection of the Divine realm through beauty, grace, and perfection of form—arose from the self-awareness that Apollo had been awakening during his time at Delphi. His credo, "Know Thy Self," was the unspoken acknowledgement of the essential divinity of man's innermost self. Democracy, that dangerous idea of the value of hearing each intelligent, mature voice in a city, was the same. Democracy is a form of governance derived from the Delphic Wave in Greece. We still aspire to the full implementation of this acknowledgement of our universal divinity.

> What a marvel shalt thou contemplate in thy heart
> and what sweet delight,
> when on a voyage, watching when the wind is fair and the
> sea is calm,
> thou shalt see the beautiful herds of dolphins, the desire of
> the sea;
> the young go before in a troop like youths unwed,
> as if they were going through the changing circle of a mazy
> dance;
> behind and not aloof their children come the parents great
> and splendid,
> a guardian host, even as in spring the shepherds
> attend the tender lambs at pasture ...
> even so the parent dolphins attend their children,
> lest aught untoward encounter them.
> —Oppian, *Halieutica*

CHAPTER FOUR

From Mystery to History: Why God Disappeared

The Chaldeans (descendants of the Sumerians) were known for their study of the stars and other esoteric matters, and from them came many teachers and wise men to the Mediterranean. From the ancient Chaldean city of Ur came Abraham, a nomadic Semite who settled in the hills south of Jerusalem after many years of wandering. He was visited by a god who blessed him as the father of an important lineage—his descendants had been chosen to be the priests of a new religion. Abraham fathered two sons whose descendants played major roles in Judaism, Christianity, and Islam.

Abraham came from a tradition in which there were many gods and goddesses, where the most benign and benevolent god was called EA. According to linguists, the name EA is equivalent to Y-A, pronounced "Yah." In the Old Testament story of Abraham's life there is no reference to the name by which he called his god, except when he is referred to as The God Most High. It was later traditions that ascribed the name Yahweh to the God who blessed Abraham. It is not inconceivable that Yahweh had originally been known as EA.

EA was a biform god, with a body that was both human and fishlike. He was the son of NAMMU and came from the sea. He was the master of the Oceans, the Deep, and the Apsu.

In an ancient tale EA was the god who warned Utnapishtim to

build a boat in order to save the people and animals from an inundation sent by the gods. He swam to Utnapishtim's house, which was on stilts over the marshes of Ur, and spoke through a screen from the water outside. Most scholars consider the Sumerian tale of Utnapishtim to be the forerunner of Noah, Xithusrus, Deukalion, and other heroes directed by one of the gods to build a boat to survive the coming floods.

EA (also known as Enki) is usually depicted with water around him, his robes decorated with water symbols, or surrounded by a wreath of water in which fish are swimming. He is said to be the father of agriculture and civilization itself. In some stories, he is the Creator who made the first humans.

Abraham would have brought with him the worship of EA as he traveled toward his destiny. At a turning point in his story, his substitute wife, Hagar, meets the Lord at a well where He informs her that she will bear Abraham's son. In Genesis 6:13 we read: "She gave this name to the Lord who spoke to her: "You are the God who sees me," for she said, "I have now seen the back of the One who sees me." The well was thereafter named "well of the Living One who sees me (Beer Lahai Roi)."

This brings us to a secret tradition buried deep within the teachings of the Abrahamic religions (Judaism, Christianity, and Islam): Yahweh was originally an "abomination," a repulsive God.

Abominations and the God Most High

In the days of the Old Testament, there were many forms of God, including nature spirits, beings comprised of various animal body parts, and lumpen "gods" who were worshipped because of their miraculous origins: bizarre minerals, crystals, and meteorites. Today we look upon the "demonic figures" of early worship and see devils, bad spirits, and dark designs. Back then, the demons, the "abominations," were amalgamated beings, combining the attributes of animals, humans, and imaginary beasts. Not evil, they were simply beings whose realm was that of the mysterious. Much of the early imagery of the "abominations" depicts nightmare beings, fearsome combinations of the terrible aspects of dangerous creatures, bringers of death. And yet, death is not extraordinary, it is part of the every-day world.

An abomination is something we are deeply conditioned to avoid. In the days we are exploring, what came to be called an abomination was originally a god whose body may have been weird and unsettling to look upon. Their forms were hidden behind the curtains of their shrines. Being hidden became part of their identity.

The two primary concepts of God become evident here. One is the personalized God, the God with a form, a body, a Presence in the worlds of space and time. This God has existence within the reach of the human spirit, even if it is vast and beyond our capacity to fully embrace. The other concept of God is that of the impersonal and non-embodied God, the God that is absolutely beyond contact, not defined by the manifested Universe, without form and diffused everywhere. These two concepts of God may be seen as developmental stages. First would have been the personalized god, the mysterious powers in creatures and the natural world supplying examples of His abilities. As the god concept matured, as explanations for natural processes were formulated, it had to become formless and absolute, beyond our ken.

A personalized God whose attributes were fearsome, whose form was weird and un-natural, might have become a hidden God, hidden from the congregation, unseen behind the curtains of the inner sanctum. Could this be the origin of the Jewish claim for representation of the Highest God, the one more powerful and more inclusive than all other Gods? They had begun with Abraham's worship of the Chaldean Gods, the "abominations" (Belus, Baal, Dagon, Apkallu, etc.), then merged that with a tribal god (Yahweh), who was capricious, jealous, and merciless. His enclosures and trappings were elaborately described in the Torah, and were designed to reveal nothing of His form. (His primary instrument, the object through which he manifested, called the Ark of the Covenant, was covered in dolphin skin.) It was not until long after Abraham that the Jewish priests compiled a God-concept that required Him to be absolutely invisible, unquestionable, and supreme.

The Sumerian god EA was of several natures, and was not easy to look upon. Described as lying lengthwise in the swamp, he could have been modeled on a stranded whale, a misshapen mountain of a creature who breathed, sputtered, clicked, and watched them with intelligent eyes.

We arrive at an odd conclusion: The concept of the Invisible God who could not be known or seen could have been developed by a priesthood serving a repulsive God. The hidden "abomination" that had first been worshipped by Abraham became a secret Almighty Being.

As Robert Temple asks in *The Sirius Mystery*, "How many Jews know that their God was originally amphibious?"[1] Temple points out that a strange creature can be thought to be beautiful by a child and horrid by an adult. A semi-amphibious creature, encountered on a beach in some remote place, of some mysterious or even extra-planetary origin, could be seen as repulsive without it being an "abomination" as we think of it today. If a dolphin or small whale were found on the shore and taken to one of the pools on the terraces of a ziggurat, one can easily imagine the natural reverence that would have arisen. Dolphins readily survive for hours, in some cases for days, without being in water and are always willing to allow humans to help and interact with them. Were dolphins among the original "abominations"?

The "establishment religions" have gone to great lengths to eradicate any knowledge of these early gods, yet glimpses can be found here and there. A tantalizing description is given in the Bible, in Ezekiel 8:1-18, as we shall see in a few pages.

As the odd form of a living being, whose attributes they were emulating, gradually disappeared behind the curtains of the holy shrines, the "Invisible God" gave the Jewish people a basis to claim a relationship with a more refined Godhead, one beyond human conception. Their having been "chosen" by this god eventually gave the Jewish people the sense that they were occupying the moral high-ground, an unassailable position from which to pursue their aims. The Jewish religion depends upon its God being the Highest, the One beyond Whom there is no Other. From their perspective, this must not, cannot be questioned.

Dagon, the Torah, and the Ten Commandments

The Phoenicians were known as the Sea People. They were also known as the Philistines. They worshipped Dagon, described as a legless man, in the body of a fish, his hands and head extending from his fish body. With a fish-like body and human attributes, he would have appeared much like the Matsya incarnation of Vishnu and the Oannes creatures.

Dagon was one of the main gods of the time. Certainly descended from EA, for centuries he was revered by more people than Yahweh and played a major part in the traditions of the coastal people of the eastern Mediterranean. Yet his image, his "body," the objects made to represent him, and the ceremonies conducted to worship him have been so thoroughly erased that we know almost nothing of him today.

Dagon and his worship are referred to in several places in the Old Testament. For instance:

- When King Saul was killed, his head was displayed in the Temple of Dagon.[2]
- Samson was imprisoned by the Philistines. His hair grew back after Delilah's betrayal, so that his strength had returned, but this fact was not recognized by his captors. He was brought out of his cell to be made a mockery of, and chained to two pillars at the entrance to "the Temple of Dagon" in Gaza. He pulled the pillars down on himself, killing the three thousand people who were around or on the roof of the temple. This gives us an indication of the size of the temple.[3]

- After the Ark of the Covenant was stolen by the Philistines, they put it in the Temple of Dagon at Ashdod, a seaside town near Gaza. When the doors were opened the next day, they saw their idol, the statue of Dagon, lying face down in front of the Ark. They stood the statue up. When they returned the next morning, Dagon was not only face down, but his head and hands had broken off, returning him to the form of a fish. Chastened, they returned the Ark to the Israelites in hopes of preserving their God.[4]

Leviticus is part of the Torah, on Old Testament book that consists of a list of actions to do and acts to avoid, attempting to define correct behavior in all circumstances. In Leviticus, verse 11, lines 9-12, there is a rule about not eating cetaceans:

> These shall ye eat of all that are in the waters: whatsoever hath fins and scales in the waters, in the seas, and in the rivers, them shall ye eat. And all that have not fins and scales in the seas, and in the rivers, and all that move in the waters, and of any living thing which is in the waters, they shall be an abomination unto you: they shall be even an abomination unto you; ye shall not eat of their flesh, but ye shall have their carcasses in abomination. Whatsoever hath no fins nor scales in the waters, that shall be an abomination unto you.

This law was probably derived from Philistine practices, the traditional observances of the worshippers of Dagon, written into law by the Israelites as early as the ninth century B.C.[5]

A special place is held by cetaceans in the beliefs of Judaism, Christianity, and Islam for this reason as well: they were the first earthly beings made by God. It was on the fifth day of Creation, according to Genesis 1:21, that the great whales were created. Humans were created on the sixth day.

And most revealing of all is this: among the Ten Commandments is an indirect mention of whales and dolphins as god-like beings. It is the first commandment, in Deuteronomy 5:7-10:

7 You shall have no other gods before me.

8 You shall not make for yourself an idol in the form of anything in heaven above or on the earth beneath *or in the waters below.* [emphasis added]

9 You shall not bow down to them or worship them; for I, the LORD your God, am a jealous God, punishing the children for the sin of the fathers to the third and fourth generation of those who hate me,

10 but showing love to a thousand generations of those who love me and keep my commandments.

This is a very stern warning from the invisible and jealous God of Israel. He is making it clear that no worship of the biform gods or any other natural and *visible* thing is acceptable. And certainly not acceptable is the worship of whales or dolphins. One can only assume that this must have been an option or a recent practice to warrant mention.

When Jonah was called on by the Lord to speak to the people of Nineveh about righteousness, he fled and boarded a ship. When a storm came up the sailors looked for a cause and discovered that Jonah was fleeing a command of the Lord. They tossed him overboard and the storm ended.

Jonah was swallowed by a whale.

After being in the belly of the whale three days, Jonah prayed to God for help, and God insisted that he keep his promise to go to Nineveh. Jonah agreed and the whale spewed him up, onto the land. Jonah survived this horror and went on to chastise the people of Nineveh, and was afterward a good man. ("Nineveh" means "City of the Fish" and was a center of Dagon worship in Syria. This tale leaves one wondering what his sermons would have referred to as he chastised the "fish" worshippers.[6])

This story has been commented on many times and seems mostly to be a cautionary tale about defying God. It also can be seen as the whale taking on the role of teacher, enforcing a lesson upon a defiant man. The man is saved by the whale, then brought to land. The whale serves the Lord, and man learns to do the same.[7]

Cetaceans in Jerusalem

Jerusalem grew into a powerful city, where the descendants of the Semitic Chaldean, Abraham, established themselves. As a walled city, the gates were very important. Each of the gates was named, some with obvious meaning, some not so obvious. The Dung Gate led to the middens of the city, the Damascus Gate was on the road to Damascus. But what about the Fish Gate, in the north wall of Jerusalem? There is no river near the ancient north wall, nor is there ready access to a port from that gate. Excavations have uncovered, outside the Fish Gate, an amphitheater with a pool in the place of the stage.

When Ezekiel was taken to see the iniquities of the Jewish people and priests who had fallen away from proper worship, prior to a purge of Jerusalem by the jealous Yahweh's angels, he was taken to the *north* wall of the city. There he was to look into temples, to observe the worship of idols, images of animals, and other "abominations" in the eyes of Jewish law.

In Ezekiel 8:3–10 we read of his guided tour of a temple of abominations, where he encounters an image he is told is the "image of jealousy," or the thing of which Yahweh is jealous:

> 3 … the Spirit lifted me up between the earth and the heavens, and brought me in the visions of God to Jerusalem, to the entry of *the inner gate that looketh toward the north*, where was the seat of *the image of jealousy, which provoketh to jealousy.*
>
> 4 And behold, the glory of the God of Israel was there, according to the appearance that I saw in the valley.
>
> 5 And he said unto me, Son of man, lift up now thine eyes toward the north. And I lifted up mine eyes toward the north, and behold, *northward of the gate of the altar, this* image of jealousy in the entry.

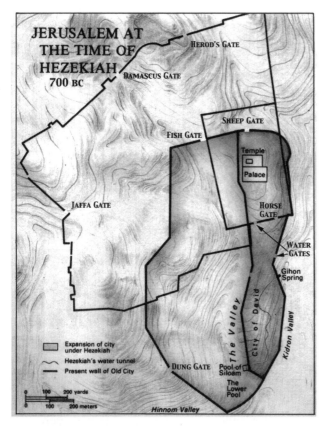

Figure 10 JERUSALEM

Jerusalem in 700 b.c., about one hundred years before Ezekiel was taken to the north wall, near the Fish Gate, to see the hidden and prohibited worship of Dagon by Jews. It was at this place that the Jealous God revealed His jealousy of his main rival. Dagon was an "abomination," half human, half fish, and reverence for his teachings was banned.

6 And he said unto me, Son of man, seest thou what they do? The great abominations that the house of Israel commits here, to cause [me] to go far off from my sanctuary? And yet again thou shalt see great abominations.

7 And he brought me to the entry of the court, and I looked, and behold, a hole in the wall.

8 And he said unto me, Son of man, dig now through the wall; and I digged through the wall, and behold, a door.

9 And he said unto me, Go in, and behold the wicked abominations that they do here.

10 And I went in and looked, and behold, *every form of creeping thing and abominable beast, and all the idols of the house of Israel,* portrayed upon the wall round about. [emphasis added]

We can only speculate what those abominable images, which provoked such jealousy, might have represented. It is likely they included Dagon, the Fish God, since his worship was so popular and ancient.

The legendary king Solomon, the wizard of the Old Testament, recognized the whale as a source of power. In the Talmud is the curious story of his ring. To this day, the ring of Solomon is a popular metaphor, imagined to be an object of extraordinary magical power. Where did his ring come from?

According to the Talmud, his ring had the name of God engraved upon it, surrounded by four jewels. These magical jewels were the source of Solomon's power over the living creatures of the world, and the whole ring made him lord of the spirit world and of the winds and waters. Four animals had given him the four jewels: an eagle, a lion, a serpent, and a whale.

The early Jewish prophets foretold a Messiah, a redeemer who would free the Jewish people to fulfill their destiny as the priests, the arbiters of the hidden God. He would be known as Dag. Dag is a Semitic word for fish. Yeshua Ben Joseph (Jesus) fulfilled the prophecy but was rejected, relegated by the Jews to the role of teacher. (Curiously, "Nun" is a word for fish in Hebrew, the name taken by women who have become the Brides of Christ. Jesus was also predicted to come as the *"Son of Nun."*)

John and the Mystery of Baptism

Another mystery of the Matsya/Oannes/Delphic Wave story as it moved westward concerns the curious figure of John the Baptist. He was described as a wild man, a man who lived far from people, and whose mission was the declaration of the coming of the Messiah, preparing people to be saved by Him through the act of baptism.

Baptism is an old tradition, much older than John the Baptist. It seems to come from either India or Babylon (Chaldea) and is symbolic of immersion in the waters of the original ocean, the waters that existed at the beginning of time, before the creation and "fall" of man. It cleanses and renews the soul.

In the early development of the sacraments of the Christian church, baptism was the covenant that connected non-Jews to the Christian movement, which we must remember was originally a kind of restructured Judaism. To be Jewish required not only bloodlines but circumcision, which was resisted by the Gentiles. Baptism was accepted as a replacement for circumcision, the act that preceded admission into the community of the "dolphin" (Jesus).

Could the baptism ritual be a remnant of the ancient teachings of Oannes about the ocean, the waters of life, and the origins of humans?

In the secret teachings of today's Roman Catholic Church—those reserved for the Bishops—John the Baptist is called Joannes, which is Oannes with an added J. He is a waterside figure who brings redemption through the Spirit that lives in water. (There is some mystery here: the Roman Catholic Church officially uses Latin as its language, yet the current Pope signs his name "Joannes Paulus, PP II". Ioannes is the Greek form of the name John. The Eastern Orthodox Church throughout its history has had hundreds of bishops, archbishops and saints named Ioannes. Both seem to be honoring Oannes.)

. . .

Looking for non-symbolic reasons for baptism's vital role in religious traditions, we discover that the physiological state of apnea creates a powerful mental change. Apnea is the cessation of breathing and the automatic suspension of some body functions that occurs when one is submerged in water. The brain quickly becomes fixed on survival, a deeper issue than one normally focuses on, which manifests as a plunge into a meditative state. Upon sudden submersion, a deep peace comes over one as the heart slows and the brain becomes abstracted, pulled away from the senses and the outer world.

Baptism is a brief re-enactment of the return to the peace and stillness of the amniotic fluids of our origins. It is a visit to the underwater realms that cleanses us and prepares us for salvation. As we rise from the baptismal water, we may find memories of the loving grace of the dolphin, who is the master of the waters, diving and rising effortlessly.

Zoroaster and Baptism

Zoroastrianism is an ancient religion still barely alive in the Middle East. It originated about 700 B.C. and served many millions of people with its clear definitions of evil and good.

The Zoroastrian canon tells us that the divine awareness of the priest and prophet Zoroaster manifested after he was baptized and arose from the waters. It was this event that gave him his original vision, upon which his teachings were based. As he walked away from the river where he had partaken in an ancient Vedic (Indian) ritual of purification, he found himself in the presence of a "shining Being," an angel, who led him into the Presence of *Ahura Mazda*, the singular God whose sons divided manifestation in two. His epiphany came while he was wet from his immersion.

Zoroaster, who lived two thousand seven hundred years ago, is to be the father of the prophesied Savior who has not yet come. This

Saoshyant (one who brings benefit) will be born of a virgin who bathes in a lake in which has been miraculously preserved the semen of Zoroaster. (How his semen comes to be left in the lake is not described.)

Astvat-ereta, the savior, is depicted as having human parents, even though his conception is magical. He is not separate from mankind, but is a paradigm of righteousness.

And, suggestively, not only is he conceived in a lake, he seems to live in the lake: Divine Grace "... will accompany the victorious Saoshyant ... so that he may restore existence.... When he emerges from the lake ... this messenger of God ... will drive the Lie out from the world of Righteousness."[8]

This episode of the arrival of the Savior is predicted to occur near the end of time. We may well add this suggestive tale to the long list of prophecies concerning the arrival of a water-being who will assume the role of savior.

The Edge of History

We have traveled from the depths of mystery, the misty realms of myth, where truths are poems, where symbols float in a fog of meaning, and where our dreaming imagination is our most reliable guide.

With the coming of Jesus, we enter a new era, both as recorded history and as a new chapter in the story of human progress.

Like a dolphin among fish, Jesus moved and lived in unique ways, rising to another plane to gather his life energies then plunging back in again to share his love with the people of his time.

CHAPTER FIVE

Jesus the Dolphin

The occupation of Palestine was not going well. The Romans were troubled by rumors of a Messiah coming to liberate the Jews. John the Baptist was campaigning for cleansing in preparation for His arrival, and secret congregations had been gathering. The Roman and Jewish authorities, with all of their rules, held the people in a net, restraining their desires for growth and change.

It was time for the appearance of Yeshua Ben Joseph (*Yeshua* can be translated as "son of the fish"). His mother was Mary ("of the sea"). His ministry began as He rose from the waters of baptism. His most famous miracles were with bread and fishes, walking on water, calming a storm, and transforming water. As he was being crucified, water poured from his chest wound. He was given the acronym ICHTHYS, which means both Fish and Jesus Christ, Son of God, Savior. His Incarnation had much to do with the mysteries of water.

If we look at His story reflected in water, the story to be read in the stars, we see that Jesus was one of the Avatars of the Piscean Age, whose emblem is two fishes. This was an age of devotion, of passionate belief. He inspired the yearnings of millions of followers, seeking redemption through feeling and pure belief. He promoted a healthy way of living together, with compassion for each other. All these are Piscean traits.

He chose to celebrate his life's work with an intimate dinner. Along with the invitation to the Last Supper came directions to the party. Jesus told his followers to watch for a man with a pitcher of water and to follow him to an upper room. This was where their last meal was to be eaten. This foreshadows the coming Aquarian Age, climbing toward human destiny by following the "water carrier," the zodiacal Being who pours the water of life upon the constellation of the Dolphin. The plot is in the stars....[1]

Self-awareness manifested in community is the Path of the Dolphin. Mastering our human challenges while living in community— what could demonstrate our achievements better? This was what Jesus demonstrated for us all.

He was called the Christ, which means the Anointed One. Anointing was a common practice in Greek and Roman times, a ritual that consists of pouring and spreading oil over a consecrated object or person. Oil was precious, requiring much labor and time to produce, whether the oil of olives, plants, asphaltum from Babylon, or oil from the body of a dolphin. Oil extracted from the jawbone of a dolphin has long been recognized as one of the finest of oils, and was treasured by ancient people. (This oil was later used to lubricate the finest of hand-made timepieces.) The most precious oils were reserved for the most powerful ceremonies. It is not entirely unlikely that one of the oils with which Yeshua Ben Joseph was anointed was the oil of the dolphin.

The Delphic Teachings of Jesus

Jesus came to anchor a new stage of human development, to eliminate the old rigid system of laws governing every aspect of life, and to replace it with a bold new advancement: recognition of the intuitive, original source of wisdom within the heart and mind of every person. He came to replace the Rule of Law with the Rule of Love.

His is the most powerful life ever lived demonstrating the "Delphic Path."

Jesus showed us that humans could have direct knowledge of the Will of God. He taught a personal method for gaining insight into living in accord with the greater life in which we all exist. He counseled that the Kingdom was within, its guidance found in the small voice of the heart, the conscience.

He taught that laws are unnecessary for those who live according to the living, liquid truths of the inner kingdom.

Jesus taught his apostles about the perfection, the godliness of each human soul. His work among the poor and sick was intended to demonstrate that each person, each life is precious in the eyes of God, each is moving toward greater perfection, and that the spirit-guided community is the answer. This parallels the Greek revelation that underlies democracy—that the combined voices of the masses will shape a more perfect way through the difficulties of life. It was an extraordinary break from the path of the kings and priests. Placing one's faith in the inner voice as the guiding principle of a culture was a new concept, challenging and dangerous.

Jesus anchored this radically new paradigm. It was beyond the capacities of the people of his time. Quickly, his teachings were modified, changed to accommodate a system of intermediaries. The lessons became watered-down, less challenging. More recently we have realized that to live as he suggested and to have a valid democracy we must provide education to generate an informed populace, and we must have adequate nutrition to ensure mental development of children so that they can be educated. He set a high goal that we have yet to reach.

This is still one of the great questions we face today: Are we committed to a belief in the inherent divinity of humans, and are we ready to make the necessary adjustments in our values and lifestyle to ensure a standard of universal human rights to food, medical care, and education, thereby enabling us to have an intelligent global democracy?

It is a sad fact that the church that claims to have consolidated Christianity does not acknowledge the divinity of the average person. Catholic and Protestant policy is to insist on the role of the priest, just as the Jews do. Only Islam, among the three major religions that come down to us from Abraham, does not insist on the intercession of a priest on behalf of the individual supplicant. Jesus was not in favor of having a priesthood and encouraged his disciples to teach freedom of personal spirituality, a private process of seeking the kingdom of God within the human soul. He taught that only in a one-on-one relationship with God does each person become an instrument, a vehicle for perfection. Free to be our own divine, diverse selves, we will create a world of wonders, Jesus told us. He affirmed that each soul is divine.

To this end, Jesus taught us that life is continuous. This was not, however, the central and most important teaching he left us. The immortal human soul had been demonstrated many times previously, with death overcome by many mages, seers, and holy people. The resurrected God, in the body of the re-born King, had been celebrated for centuries before Jesus' time. The most unique and powerful parts of his teachings were about *yielding* as a path of power, and about the source of freedom, which is the divinity that lives within us all, which I have called the Rule of Love.

Jesus was the first Jew to teach about personal spiritual insight through the exercise of intuition and conscience, and the life that can be led by the average human in accord with this inner guidance. Buddha, in India, had taught much the same to his followers, but Jesus appeared in the midst of the Jewish world, where religious laws were deeply entrenched and fiercely upheld. These radical changes in spiritual practice that he suggested played a large part in the rejection of Jesus by his own people.

He came to remind us of a path of correct human behavior, to give us techniques for living in a free state, one that mankind had long held to be ideal. Ovid, a Greek poet who lived at the time of Jesus, described a similar Golden Age in his *Metamorphoses:*

> That first age was golden: all was then fresh and new, and so
> arranged that out of spontaneous goodness, men, without the
> compulsion of laws or fear of punishment, kept their faith

with one another, behaving with decency, fairness, justice and generosity.

Called a Fisher of Men, Jesus was the exemplar of the Delphic Path. His teachings about worship, the community of believers, and the ways of male-female relationship were the roots of a timeless and therefore sustainable practice. Jesus encouraged people to gather into groups without formal leaders, without priests, to share goods in common, to raise children in an extended family, to treat men and women as equals, and to worship in personal, private ways, using simple meditative techniques.

If we are to accept the ideal of a dolphin-like life, living in harmonious groups, sharing our major possessions, loving all children as our own, giving and receiving love among our close companions, worshipping in private ways, we must recognize the failings of the age-old institution of the Christian churches.

And the Jewish way, steeped in rules and empty rituals long past meaning, governed by rigid forms of priestly privilege, must also yield to the gentle path of trust that God has spoken to us about, through the Dolphin Messenger, Jesus.

In Islam, we find the teachings of a path of surrender, yet it too has succumbed to rigid forms of worship and extremes of intolerance. Surrender has been re-framed by many Muslims into a path of fierce disregard for diversity and a rabid hatred of those who have not surrendered to Allah.

The mission of Abraham has been fulfilled. Each of the religions descended from his legacy has given us its gifts and has now become a pale shadow of its original self. It is time for a new revelation.

Each age, each major culture, has had its Avatars, its teachings that demonstrate another step in the progressive revelation of the divine life, which we have called the Delphic Path. Each of these teachers has taught lessons that can be learned by a study of the lives of dolphins. Tolerance, equality, compassion, altruism, joyousness, gentle methods of teaching, community sharing, celebration—all of these are attributes of the lives of dolphins.

With the Rule of Love, Yeshua's teachings were not only about the individual and his or her inner life; they are the core lessons for how community must be managed. Rather than a hierarchy of control, the governing of a group of people becomes a process of "consensus of spirit," a coming together of agreement using both intelligence and intuition, tempered by love.

The times we live in today demand a new form of community, and we will find that the successful path toward that long-desired state is guided by principles found among the dolphins and the lessons of the Delphic Path.

> Jesus knew this transcendent immanence of the divine light-consciousness to be the truth of the universe and the truth of each human consciousness; he knew that its realization in human life brought with it a vibrant, boundary-shattering energy of love and wisdom, pure freedom beyond all possible human categories. He knew that this love and wisdom-energy was the building force of the Kingdom, the force that had to be released into the real for the real to be transformed into the kingdom.
> —Andrew Harvey, *Son of Man: The Mystical Path to Christ*[2]

The Gift Is Taken

After Yeshua's disappearance following his crucifixion, his teachings were loosely developed into a new form of worship. There was no institution called Christianity until many years later. Powerful groups of individuals, swept up in the freedom they were discovering through his teachings, began to appear across the Roman Empire, able to resist the fear-based system of control exercised by the army, priests, and governors. The upstart Jewish cult called Christians had a mysterious set of beliefs that made them invincible.

Realizing this, some began scheming on how to use this new

power. Saul of Tarsus, a formerly brutal tax collector and enforcer, became convinced he that had been given a mission to shape the scattered followers of Yeshua into an organization. He had a seizure while walking through the desert and came out of the fit with a glorious vision of a new religion. He saw large revenues being collected from the scattered congregations of gentiles he was convinced were the real "Christians."

Throwing off the Jewish trappings of the teachings, he invited everyone to join the new community, stating that the regulations concerning circumcision as a prerequisite were no longer in effect, that baptism was sufficient.

Unfortunately, many people began to accept Saul's interpretation of the life and teachings of Yeshua. The actual disciples of Jesus whom he met over the years roundly disliked Saul, and his distortions of the original teachings have repercussions that live on, even today. Some of his insights were truly beautiful, but many distortions of Yeshua's message entered into the common Christian system of beliefs.

Paul, as he began to call himself, claimed authority and began a redefinition of the teachings, more in line with the aspirations of the powerful and ambitious. His proselytizing of the non-Jewish population was ingenious, and thousands of new believers came under his sway, which in turn came to be seen as proof of the divinity of his revelation.

And so the simple truths of personal divinity within each of us came under an ever-increasing set of rules and doctrines. By 251 A.D., a split in the church was only narrowly averted when it was decided that rather than a community of saints, the church was a school for sinners.

Yeshua had gathered a community around him that he elevated above their past, relieving them of every kind of sin, helping them to see themselves as "saints" in the making, purified by their inner work of reconciling their own desires with the supremacy of love. In only 250 years, the community was driven from its heritage.

. . .

Judaism, Christianity, and Islam are unique among spiritual traditions in that they all address one God, who is transcendent and impersonal. There is no adequate description of God, no image or manifestation that embodies this universal Presence in the Abrahamic religions as originally formulated.

Curiously, Christianity alone among the three has attempted to find a means for those people who require a personality, a single image of God, to be comfortable with an omnipresent and invisible God. In a convoluted process, the church has declared that Jesus is God, inseparable from Him, and has been in the world as a man. God is not to be thought of as limited to the body we have seen, yet He is fully represented by the Jesus of history.

This logical impossibility, to be greater than, to be the "container" of all that is, and at the same time to be inside, manifested within the world, caused a great deal of intellectual struggle among the growing priesthood, and by 300 A.D. the religion as a whole was in turmoil, about to split.

Was Jesus God? Or was Jesus a Teacher, an embodiment of Divine Truth, an Avatar of the new way? In our terms, he could be known as the Dolphin, the One who showed us the Path of Love. *(See Plate 9.)*

Freedom of the individual soul, free to live out its life with an inner connection to a deep source of wisdom, was the message of the Dolphin. Could freedom be advocated for the masses by the new church? Could one's inner voice be trusted?

The Disappearing Dolphin, the Rising Cross, and the Pope's Hat

It was the question of whether or not Jesus is God that brought the patriarchs of the early Christian movement together, called to a council by the Roman Emperor Constantine. A dispute had raged for years. Seeing that the movement was about to shatter into separate churches, Constantine stepped in. He wanted to consolidate the church, to create a monolithic power structure embracing religious, military, economic, and governmental power in one organization, one elite hierarchy that would dominate the world of humans. In the year 325, he convened the Council of Nicea to address these issues.

The Christian church, which had only recently begun to coalesce into a movement, revealed the new power of people who could withstand torture like no one else. The implications of this as a power base were a strong inducement to the ambitious. If these people could be "rounded up" into an organized force, nothing could stand in their way.

In Nicea, a city in what is now Turkey, 220 priests and representatives of congregations (although only two from the Church of Rome) gathered to settle differences.

By the end of the Council of Nicea, Christianity was redefined.

Far from the original teachings, this new Christianity managed to take on the authority of a message from God. A wonderful history of thinkers delving into questions of freedom, spirit, and human dignity has come from this church, but so much hatred has been supported, so much distance has been allowed between the church and its followers, that its policies have alienated millions. More people have lost their lives from Christian ideals than any other religion in history. Sadly, the unbridgeable distance between worshippers and God has come to be accepted.

Jesus was known as the Dolphin before the Council of Nicea. He was explained to the pre-literate people of his time as a Savior. He was not the militant Messiah yearned for by the political Jews, but a gentle teacher of souls who lifted one above the drowning waves of the world, where suffering and slavery were the norm, to a new level of self-determination, where one becomes free. He was like the dolphin who saves drowning sailors, providing a friendly lift out of the waters of the world.

At Constantine's urging, the various books then in circulation supposed to be the "official" records of Jesus' life were analyzed

Figure 11 DOLPHIN
AND CROSS

Early Christians used the image
of a dolphin to symbolize the
Savior. After Constantine forced
the Christian churches to accept
one way of interpreting the
message of Jesus, his symbol
became that of the cross.

Image after a stone carving near Avignon,
France, 4th century.

for a continuity that would support the new, official policies of the
church. It was at this time that the Torah, the early books of the
Old Testament, was joined to the books we know today as the New
Testament, making up the Bible.

In addition, "official" symbols were chosen for the church. The
symbol of Jesus was changed to the cross, eliminating the dolphin.
The so-called "fish symbol" used to indicate Christian burials and
gathering places in early Rome was the symbol for the dolphin, the
gentle teacher and savior. The cross did not appear in the iconog-
raphy of Christianity at the beginning, whereas the fish symbol had
been there from before the beginning. Slowly, it was phased out.
Part of the reasoning for this change was that the dolphin was too
much like the "abomination," the ancient Sumerian God, Dagon.

Devotion to the lessons of Jesus' life became centered on his
resurrection instead of his life, on the sacrifice he made, showing
us how to leave behind the lower aspects of our nature as opposed
to focusing on the communal life of the self-aware man or woman
and the empowerment of the individual. Both lessons were important, but the choice was made to follow the Path of the Cross. The
pod-oriented dolphin was the example of the living, joyous God,
but the cross and the necessity for sacrifice became the focus. He
was a Savior, but the pagan religions demanded a resurrected god-
man, so, to attract them into the fold, his story was made to con-
form to the ancient tales of Osiris, Tammuz, and Orpheus, who had
all overcome death.

Among the most curious influences of the ancient Apkallu/Oannes traditions to leave their mark on Christianity are symbols surrounding the Pope. As the Roman church expanded into new territories, it found it useful to adopt certain old traditions. As the vestments of the Pope were being developed, the headgear of the high priests of old was assumed. The mitre that the Pope wears today, his ceremonial hat, is a direct link to the Sumerian era, when the priests wore the fish-skin cape. The mitre represents the head of the Oannes, the Fish-God who brought wisdom from the mysterious depths. Only bishops and above, in the hierarchy, are permitted to wear the mitre, those who have been initiated into the secret teachings of the Catholic faith. *(See Plates 5 and 6.)* The Pope's round cape, the pallium, may also be related to the Palladium, as is easily seen by the similarity of the words, as well as the connection to Pallas Athena, Goddess of Wisdom. The pallium is bestowed on the Pope at his investiture as a symbol of his divinely inspired wisdom. Even the familiar Gothic arch can be seen as tracing the shape of the mitre, the head of the dolphin.

Persistence of the Delphic Ideas

Cetacean tales surface periodically in Christian history and myth. St. Brendan searched the North Atlantic seeking the fabled Promised Land of the Saints. For each of the seven years of their search, he and his fellow wanderers were led back to an island to celebrate Easter mass. The island was actually the back of a whale named Jasconius. In this case the whale was the refuge, the haven of peace to be found in the world while one seeks the realms of paradise.[3]

Dolphins associated with saints include St. Martian, St. Basil the Younger, and Callistratus, who were all saved from drowning. St. Lucian of Antioch was killed and thrown into the sea. His body was carried by dolphins to the town of Drepanum, where he was recognized and given a proper burial.

By the Middle Ages, stories of dolphins were fading into the mist. Fewer and fewer tales were being told of contact with them. Apparently, it was time for mankind to slow down and let all that had happened sink in. For hundreds of years, beginning with the time of Constantine, the dolphins and whales virtually disappeared from the records of civilization. We might surmise that in the ocean depths a new dream was being developed, a new path being devised for man. The night of the fish had come.

> "So many fishes bred in the water, and saved by one great fish," says Tertullian of the Christians and Christ and the Church.
> —H. P. Blavatsky, *The Secret Doctrine*[4]

CHAPTER SIX

Faith and
the Gnostic Star

The Council of Nicea settled some weighty questions. Or did it? The new church was based on only one iota of difference, literally (iota is the ninth letter of the Greek alphabet). The orthodox church position was that Jesus was *identical (homoousios)* with God the Father, while the Arian "heretics" held that he was *similar (homoiousios)* to God the Father. Similar does not equal sameness. No longer could Jesus be a model for human aspiration, an evolved human. He was now superior in origin and possibility. He was from elsewhere, and humans could only worship, without the need for understanding. Out of the insistence upon this scintilla of difference came a flood of change, redirecting the flow of human history, taking centuries to harden, to extrude the impenetrable shell of the Christian reality tunnel.

Constantine had created an organization, the Roman Catholic Church, with consolidated principles. Now it was time to create policies and practices.

A split occurred with the Nicean decisions. Disliked by the majority of the new priesthood, these issues were to be fought over for the next 250 years. The mental contortions required to dethrone the rational, self-discovering mind were painful and lengthy.

To such latter-day followers of Plato as Proclus, whose leadership of the Platonic Academy in its final days was the terminal dance

of a long and beautiful celebration of the rational human, the new
Christian belief system was shallow and devoid of the knowledge
needed by intelligent leaders. Proclus worked long and hard to re-
instate the Platonic concepts of the Knowable God Within and was
unrepentant in his paganism. But his efforts were in vain. The newly
remodeled Christianity forced the closure of the Academy (A.D. 485)
that had begun under Plato more than six hundred years earlier.
The Oracle at Delphi was forced to stop speaking.

This signaled the end of the era of direct Delphic influence that
we have been following. This is not to say, of course, that dolphins
did not continue to save sailors, play along the shorelines, or weave
their playful dance in the bow-waves of ships. But there was a time
of retreat, of more hidden influence. Jesus the Dolphin slipped back
into the waters, diving deep into the mysterious ocean of time.

From Reason to Faith

We are, by necessity, taking the long view. Not detail, but movement itself, gradual growth, is our subject. This phase of human
awakening was like the shift from breathing in to breathing out.
Natural, inevitable, and completely contrary, the story of the Roman
Catholic Church is the story of the change from reason to faith. The
transition was gradual—from the insights of brilliant Greece, itself
a synthesis of all that came before, to an age of passions that bypassed
the need to understand—and it took many hundreds of years.

The Age of Faith sounds like a name for a wonderful time of
heartfelt inner progress, which to some degree is correct, yet it must
also describe a time of denial of the role of understanding.

Some examples:

- By A.D. 386, the Church had decided that all priests must be celi-
  bate, removing them from the community as fathers and family
  members. In North Africa, a movement that demanded that
  priests be sinless, living exemplary lives that modeled the principles of Jesus, was crushed. The church decided that its priests

were not to be held to such high standards. This is a unique policy among the religions of the world, where most priests are accomplished metaphysicians, students of wisdom, and experienced in the ways of the mystic realms. Instead, the Roman Catholic priest was not expected to be a man of exceptional spiritual insights or accomplishment.

- When Nestorius stated that Mary was not the mother of God, but the mother of Jesus, he was excommunicated. Nestorian Christians fled to the east, escaping the reach of the Roman church; their descendants make up small portions of the Christian population of Africa, India, and China today.
- In A.D. 385, St. Jerome was asked to retranslate the Bible into a more accessible form of Latin. He was a rabid ascetic, whose influence on the church was profound. He made saints out of anorexics and led a wave of austere religious fanaticism, setting the stage for extreme practices that both stimulated and frightened the average Christian. Few could match the religious fervor of these mad monks and nuns, thus further setting them apart from the majority of Christians.
- In A.D. 450, Pope Leo I demanded that all authority in matters of belief and church policy be centered in Rome, taking away the power of Jerusalem, Antioch, Alexandria, and Constantinople. A gulf opened between the Roman church and the Eastern church that remains to this day.

In the midst of the excesses, there were some few who absorbed the Delphic Message and deserve the status of sainthood given them by the church. St. Paulinus and St. Martin gave their personal fortunes to the poor, served them tirelessly, worked in the fields to provide for their own needs, lived simply, and were a part of their communities. They were the exception.

St. Francis was also an extreme example of the Christian saint, and his formula for simple, ecstatic holy living was not suited to the many who tried to follow in his footsteps. Within one hundred years, Franciscans were burned at the stake for trying to emulate him, judged by the Church to be heretics. His teachings about holy poverty were softened and in time became much less ascetic, aligned with the comforts enjoyed by other orders.

Then came St. Augustine. By A.D. 400, he wrote the fundamental books that ended a millennium of rationalism, instituting the Age of Faith, which was an emotion-based lifestyle. His book *The City of God* created the rationale for theocracy, a form of government that places spiritual authority over secular. The Roman Catholic Church was set to rule, its power based on a hierarchical structure of passionate priests, ignorant of the world, their authority coming not from personal depth of spiritual understanding and experience but from following the dictates of a distant authority.

It is difficult from the distance of the centuries to understand the need to turn away from reason and understanding in favor of blind faith. So much suffering, so many millions killed or forced to live in abject conditions, without understanding, denied the knowledge of the Delphic teachings of Jesus and the advances of the mind that the Greek philosophers had made popular—the teachings were all slipping into obscurity. This is hard to reconcile with our sense of a steady ramp-like progress toward our destiny. And yet, there was some sense in it when looked at from a deeper perspective.

In some metaphysical traditions, where the Earth is thought of as passing through seven rays of light or planes of existence in an ascending spiral, this period of history is described as the beginning of the influence of the Ray of Devotion.[1] The world passed out of the Ray of Knowledge and slipped into the new energy of one-pointed aspiration, focused from the heart on a transcendental goal. A necessary aspect of human character, devotion enables us to move toward soul awareness, soul manifestation, by creating a form of selflessness. It is a move in the direction of a more inclusive mindset, leaving behind the narcissism of pure self-awareness. Simply put, this is the change from self-consciousness into selflessness, a step on the path toward true Self-awareness.[2] The mind becomes secondary, left to follow the heart, the romantic ideal, which is an early stage in the development of intuition.

In this model of spiritual evolution, the personality of a human is constantly being perfected to enable the soul to make itself manifest through the outer shell. In lifetime after lifetime, the body, the emotions, and the mind are being refined, balanced, and clarified to make an ever-more perfect vehicle for the soul. The destiny of each of us is, therefore, to become a fully embodied soul, a state of being that is spiritually sustainable, within a designed world of ecological sustainability—in short, the Path of the Dolphin.

The Legend of the Golden Dolphin reveals that a decision was made by the Cetacean High Council a thousand years ago to stop inspiring the human mind, which was starting to show signs of awakening, and to begin the process of awakening the human heart.

The message of Jesus was a key to human destiny. Mankind had to find and fit the key to the lock, to open a new way of living. But first, it had to go through ten centuries of adjustment. The Delphic Wave had come from the east to the Mediterranean like the earlier flood from the bursting Black Sea, and like a wave arriving at a beach, it had subsided and withdrawn. The ocean's tides were rising, inexorably.

Islam and the Delphic Heart

Mohammed, the prophet of Islam, arrived on the world stage in the seventh century, near the beginning of this era of Faith, bringing another message, one of passionate surrender to God. The peoples of Arabia adopted his teachings, and the holy message quickly exploded across northern Africa, giving the desert people a rationale for abandoning their former worship of nature spirits and rough tribal gods.

The fire of Islam burned in the hearts of these people. With the unifying name of Allah on their lips, they found themselves living in a vast land of common belief. When the invading Goths sacked Rome and moved south into Spain, some Moors (Moslems) were asked to help when strife developed among them. Finding little resistance to their military prowess or ideas, the Moors quickly moved north, bringing the cultures of the deserts of Africa and the Middle East into the southern heart of Europe.

Mixed with Latin and Gothic cultures, Islam took on a new character, full of passion, heat, and grace. The Delphic Wave had a new face, with dark eyes, black hair, and a glittering smile. Out of the Mediterranean Moors came the troubadours, the idealist bards singing of perfectly devoted non-physical love, where souls find and join their soul mates. They carried the Tarot cards, a systematic form of teaching aids used to get past the church's guardians. The mystic Heart of the Delphic Wave was making a subtle appearance.

In Islam, the secret power of water and the sacred wisdom from the sea was woven into the fabric of belief:

- The requirement for all worshippers to first bathe, to ritually wash, is central to Islamic prayer. A fountain of some sort is always part of a mosque, a place to be touched by water.
- In the Koran, 7:163 (The Heights), it says:

> And ask them about the city that overlooked the sea and what befell its people when they broke the Sabbath. Each Sabbath the fish used to appear before them floating on the surface of the water, but on the day on which they did not keep the Sabbath they never did come near them. Thus we punished them because they had done wrong.

The city referred to is Eilat, on the Red Sea. This is where a modern dolphin-interaction facility exists today. There, a natural cove is separated from the Red Sea by a net to protect a pod of dolphins who have befriended humans. As fish do not float on the surface of the water, visiting people, it seems that the punishment meted out for not keeping their holy commitments in this example was to withhold interaction with dolphins.

In an odd passage in the Koran, 18:60–63 (The Cave), Moses is traveling with a servant and says:

"I will journey on until I reach the land where the two seas meet, though I may march for ages."

But when at last they came to the land where two seas met, they forgot their fish, which made its way into the water, swimming at will.

And when they had journeyed farther on, Moses said to his servant: "Bring us some food; we are worn out with traveling."

"Know," replied the other, "that I forgot the fish when we were resting on the rock. Thanks to Satan, I forgot to mention this: the fish made its way into the sea in a miraculous fashion."

There is no further explanation of this. Did Moses intend to eat the "fish"? What kind of fish can survive being carried any distance? What kind of fish can make its way back into the water "in a miraculous fashion" and swim away after being out of the water?

Knowledge of the ancient influence of the dolphins still remains in Islam. To the Bedouin people, Muslim nomads who live in the deserts of the Sinai and along the coast of the Red Sea, the dolphin is known today as Abu Salam, which means "Father of Peace."

The Gnostic Star

In Sumerian times, long before the Christian era, a simple idea took root. The idea was that by inner processes of mind and passion one could gain personal knowledge of God. Many techniques were used, from ascetic lifestyles to ritual trances. Meditation practices were developed, often focused on the image of a wheel turning, or wheels turning in opposite directions simultaneously.

Different from the religions of the masses, in which an ignorant populace was led by priests through a ceremonial procedure to ease their worries, this process of inner discovery was very personal, and was practiced by the more intelligent minority.

Over the centuries, a body of images, messages, and techniques accumulated that came to be called Gnosticism, meaning "knowledge from direct experience."

Gnosticism was a handy term for this emerging form of personal spirituality, applied by outsiders to the practice. One did not belong to a Gnostic church, or go to a Gnostic priest. This practice was both personal and universal in that it was not limited to any culture. Anyone, in any age, who denies that he or she is awaiting salvation by another and thus claims responsibility for his or her own initiation into spiritual awareness is a gnostic. Since there is no institution surrounding it, the history of gnosticism is a mystery. We see it in the Jewish community before the time of Jesus; it appears as a powerful antidote to the "churchification" of Christianity; and such practices were, and still are, a vital part of Sufism (the mystical side of Islam).

Beginning in the second century A.D. gnosticism was brought into Europe by the Jewish and Arabic communities. And later, in a spectacular delusion lasting several centuries, the Crusaders' goal of liberating the Holy Lands from the hands of the "infidels" was to achieve nothing except this: the returning aristocrats had been exposed to the gnostic wisdom of the east. The roots of an important movement began growing amidst the chaos of this dark age. The Rosicrucians, the Masons, the secret societies that will appear later, at a crucial moment in history, all began during this time, influenced by the ancient Delphic knowledge of the Greeks, Egyptians, and Sumerians.

The Jewish form of gnosticism was mostly a set of practices called the Merkabah, which means Throne or Chariot. In synagogues built in the fifth and sixth centuries, the mosaic floors often depicted the merkabah as a chariot driven by a sun-god, Helios or Apollo. (Apollo was here again invoked as an icon of self-awareness; He who drives the chariot of destiny, with its rotating wheels.) One Merkabah technique involved sitting in a chair, placing one's head between one's knees, breathing rhythmically, clenching the fists, and imagining a wheel of light with six spokes overlaying another wheel of light with six spokes; or alternatively, two triangles forming the "Star of David."

Plate 1 WHALE TAIL ROCK

Along the south-facing coast of Australia is this huge whale's tail,
where the Mirning say that Jiderra pressed his body against the land.
The cliff leads to a natural blowhole, where the Mirning for centuries
have honoured the Stellar Whale.

Image by: Kim Kindersley/Heart Magic

Plate 2 A MIRNING CALLS THE WHALES

The Mirning are recreating their ancient traditions, sitting on the cliffs,
tapping their click-sticks and singing to call the whales. The Southern
Right Whales rise up and roar beneath them.

Image by: Kim Kindersley/Heart Magic

Plate 3 NICKY

Dolphins are usually depicted as graceful, beautiful creatures. Sometimes, up close, they can appear alien and frightful, perhaps leading to the names of several of the Apkallu which translate as *repulsive* or *abomination*.

Plate 4 APSU TANK

This stone tank once stood in a temple in the ancient city of Assur (Iraq). Almost four feet deep and over ten feet square, this tank was large enough for fish, or for a river dolphin to live in for a short time.
Photo from the Vorderasiatisches Museum, Berlin Germany.

Plate 5 MARDUK PRIEST AND MITRE

This scene depicts Marduk in his fish-skin cape attended by a flying god and a priest as a ritual is conducted. Note the similarity of the fish-head hat to the mitre of the Pope.

Image after a cylinder seal from Assyria.

Plate 6 THE POPE'S MITRE

The Pope, also known as the Pontifex Maximus (Supreme Ocean Bridger), wears the mitre, ancient head-dress of Marduk, the dolphin-like head of Oannes. Around his neck is the Pallium, the symbol of wisdom derived from the sea.

Plate 7 ZULU DOLPHIN

The green stone dolphin suspended from the ceremonial necklace of Credo Mutwa. Here *Hlengeto*, the Zulu Saviour, holds the golden tablet of the Law as his gift to mankind.

Image by Kim Kindersley/Heart Magic

Plate 8 COINS

Greek coins display a wide range of styles, from primitive to extraordinary beauty. In this assortment covering hundreds of years and many city-states, we see the prevalence of the dolphin in Greek culture. Dozens of other examples exist.

Plate 9 CHRISTUS DELPHIS

Jesus as we might see him, emanating the ageless love of the Delphic Spirit, blessing us all with his radiant message of Freedom from Law, establishing the Rule of Love, embodied in the Golden Dolphin.

Plate 10 BEAU AND CRYSTAL

Beau Ives and the large double-terminated quartz crystal that he blessed and dropped in the sea off Point Barrow, Alaska on September 29th, 1988. It was this act that called three whales who became trapped in the ice, bringing about the largest animal rescue in history and the beginning of Glasnost, the cooperation that ended Communism.
Image: Beau Ives

Plate 11 SHADIA

Dolphins who live in human-managed environments are now living long lives that are safe, well-cared for and in increasingly excellent surroundings. Shadia, at a Dolphin Discovery facility in Mexico, brings up her new baby among humans.

Plate 12 MK 7 DOLPHIN

Some US Navy dolphins have been trained to find and help retrieve bombs and missiles from the sea floor. Others have been used to locate and place underwater explosives. This dolphin is designated a "Mark 7 Mine Searching System."

Image from a US Navy web site.

Plate 13 NAVY DOLPHIN PENS

The US Navy has been experimenting with dolphins and Beluga whales for many years. Here we see sixty-four pens and training areas in San Diego harbour.

Image from US Navy web site.

Plate 14 SQUIRT, MASTER THERAPIST

Squirt, the author's best friend. She taught me how a dolphin swims, how to engage a dolphin's attention and most importantly, that dolphins love to work and live among humans. She is a master therapist, working at her clinic, Island Dolphin Care, in Key Largo, Florida.

Plate 15 DEANE-PAUL

Dean-Paul Anderson has had only Dolphin-Assisted Therapy. His future was predicted to be bleak, with little hope of overcoming his Down's Syndrome. Dolphins helped him become an out-going, charming and quick-learning person.

Image by Cathy Anderson/Dolphin-Assisted Therapy Association

Plate 16 DAT FOR K

Dolphin-Assisted Therapy holds promise for disabled humans. Here an autistic girl is carried by Squirt, attended by Deena Hoagland of Island Dolphin Care. The child is being drawn out of her inner world.

Plate 17 K LOOKS
         AT US

K, an autistic child, has just completed three weeks of Dolphin-Assisted Therapy, working with two human therapists, on the left, and her mother, on the right. For the first time, she is curious about the world around her, and looks directly at the camera.

Plate 18 CARLI AND NICKY

The joyous interaction between children and dolphins has inspired
humankind for as long as we have been human. At Monkey Mia,
in Western Australia, dolphins have established an embassy
and playground. People of all ages are visited by generations of wild
dolphins.
Image by Claire Leimbach.

Plate 19 CALAMITY AND DIANE

Hundreds of
centuries of kindness
by dolphins toward
humans has finally
paid off. The future
will bring us even
closer, as we accept
the responsibility to
care for our best
friends in a manner
that equals the gifts
they have given us.

Figure 12 GNOSTIC STAR

The Gnostic Star, as
depicted by Leonardo
Da Vinci. He reveals in
this drawing the three-
dimensional nature of the
star-tetrahedron, used in
the ancient Merkaba
tradition. Only in
meditation can the many
additional dimensions of
this transcendental object
be experienced.

The wheels or triangles turn slowly, then more rapidly, in opposite directions. The visualization of these spinning forms was known to take the practitioner into a mystic trance, wherein he might encounter a vision of seven heavens, revealing the nature of God.

Islamic gnostic techniques were similar, coming from contact between Muhammad, the Jewish mystics of his hometown, and the much older Sufi traditions. Among Islamic practices were meditations, sacred sounds, spinning dances, an alphabet of postures and breathing techniques, and zen-like questions, posed by the Sheikh to the student, which were used to dislodge the mind from its foundations, freeing it for direct perception of transcendent knowledge.

Eventually the Catholic Church set out to crush gnostic practices. Perceived as a threat to the power of the church, Gnostics were pursued angrily and their practices rooted out. Sadly, this was literally done by ritually torturing and burning people to death. They had been found to be practicing the very thing that Jesus had advised, which was to know within oneself the Kingdom of Heaven.

In their simplest forms, gnostic practices were, and still are, a system for producing self-induced hypnogogic states. This is also called the Theta state, the temporary condition that the mind enters just as one passes from waking consciousness to sleep, and that peculiarly lucid condition that we experience as we wake up. When one is measuring this brain state, it is characterized by slow cycles of activity just above the speed at which our brains sleep. This threshold state passes quickly and constitutes those few moments when the conscious mind is allowed access to the superconscious mind, which sees beyond the limits of time and space and is the mental aspect of the soul.

Here is another link to our main theme: theta-wave prevalence in the brain is what we commonly find in people who have just swum with dolphins. There is no current explanation of how this occurs.

The description I have given is an almost dangerous oversimplification of several thousand years of traditional mystery teachings and practices. I must caution the reader to recognize that deeply mystical states are uncommon, and produce an experience of *union with the Divine*. Union with the divine is very different than visions and *a sense of divinity*. These are far more common, and are accessible through psychedelic substances, meditations, and systems of breath control. But even these lesser techniques ought to be explored with great caution and under the guidance of very experienced teachers.

For people who are ill-prepared for mystical experience, the visions accessed by the Merkabah techniques are overwhelming. In *Hekhalot Rabbat*, a Jewish mystical text from the second century A.D., instructions are given for dealing with the terrors that might overcome someone not fully prepared for the vision of the Merkabah:

> As soon as that man entreats to descend to the Merkabah, Anaphiel the prince opens the door of the seventh palace and that man enters and stands on the threshold of the gate of the seventh palace ... Five hundred and twelve eyes ... appear like lightning, and they dart to and fro. In addition, there are the eyes of the Cherubim of Might and the Wheels of the Shekina, which are similar to torches of light and flames of burning coals.

This man now trembles, shakes, moves to and fro, panics, is terrified, faints, and collapses backwards. Anaphiel, the prince, and sixty-three watchmen of the seven gates support him, and they all help him and say: "Do not fear, son of the beloved seed. Enter and see the King in His magnificence. You will not be slaughtered and you will not be burnt."[3]

For centuries people have made the mistake of seeing themselves as prophets, saints, and even messiahs after exploring these realms. From visions, they mistake themselves as having made a *union with God.* Even today we find a common delusion among practitioners of Merkabah techniques[4] and other mind-altering paths of self-discovery. All too often we see people assuming the persona of an imagined perfection after a temporary visit to the realms of spirit.

In this light, when the medieval Catholic Church's watchdogs noticed people avoiding church services there was deep concern. When forms of madness appeared among the people, the Church took it for a certain sign that Satan was afoot. The Inquisition was instituted to uproot the Gnostic heresy. The Church had an answer: Save their soul even if it means taking their body from them. For six hundred years, across Europe people who practiced a personal religion, seeking their own experience of God, as Apollo and Jesus had suggested, were hunted down, tortured, and killed.

As the European era progressed, the Church Fathers succeeded in demonizing the "abominations," all of the former Gods. As one of the primary gods with which Yahweh had had to contend, the Oannes/Dagon/Osiris amphibian god was linked to the Leviathan, the Dragon of the Deep who had terrified John as he wrote his Revelations. As proof of one's faith one was required to renounce the abominations, the pagan, animal-derived gods. St. George was required to slay the dragon. Here we return, full circle, to the connection between the Dragon and the Whale, the Rainbow Serpent and the Great Sea Beast from the stars. Just as Fu Hsi, Osiris, Zeus, and Matsya all had tails, not legs, they were the serpent's children, the dragon gods. It was the end of their time.

Across many cultures we find this new imperative, the slaying of the dragon. Persian miniatures, Indian paintings, early Muslim depictions, and the hundreds of images from Europe of St. George all depict the wiping out of the old worship of a visible God, in favor of a God who is absolute, invisible, and not to be found in this world. Only faith, the conscience being born in the human heart, could take one to God. And faith is hard to hold onto when reason is denied.

Corruption set in and Europe descended into a riot of decadence. Monks sold blessings, ignoring their vows of poverty and chastity, nuns ran brothels out of their convents and murdered their babies, courts became filled with vicious schemers, children were put on thrones to enable illegitimate men to rule nations as their regents, Popes bought their elections, and all reason and understanding of the true and the beautiful was on the run.

All cosmological explorations and technological inventiveness came under the watchful eye of the Church, and "natural philosophers" (later called scientists) were burned at the stake as heretics.

The Christian Church had become catholic, universal. It had control of the hearts and minds of Europe, and needed new sources of income and power. It decided to encourage one area of technological development: the building of ships. Blessings of the church were upon explorers who desired to seek new commercial opportunities. The three aims of exploration that were condoned in that terrible time of repression and control were, in order of importance: God, Gold, and Glory.

So Columbus, Magellan, Vasco de Gama, Cabeza de Vaca, Henry the Navigator, Cortez, and all the rest were encouraged to sail the seas, looking for potential new citizens of God's kingdom — and their gold. The explorers themselves were allowed the glory, as long as it was done in service to the Church and the King or Queen.

By the mid–1400s, ocean-going ships were being built that could take long voyages. So, onto the bounding main they went, where they quickly encountered the whale.

The value of whale oil as a source of clean-burning, bright white light was beginning to be appreciated. Also, the ropes so vital to ships depended on both hemp and whale oil, which was used to soften the coarse fibers of the cannabis plants so they could be wrapped and twisted into rope. When the magnitude of the resource of the millions of whales swimming freely in the oceans was realized, an eager new industry was born.

With minds quieted by reasonless faith, living in a culture of fear and repression and with only a few sparks of enlightened self-interest among the elite, European adventurers fell into the depths of forgetfulness. Now the majestic whales, Nommo of old, were to be hunted aggressively, slaughtered mercilessly, and sacrificed on the altar of human need.

. . .

A chronology of whaling before 1700:

Ca. 1100 Basque whalers hunt whales from shore in the Bay of Biscay. The Basques are considered the first large-scale commercial whalers.

Ca. 1400 Basque whalers begin extending their range out of the Bay of Biscay into the North Atlantic.

Ca. 1550 Basque whalers have reached the New World and are spending summers at stations along the north shore of the Strait of Belle Isle in Labrador.

1607 Henry Hudson returns from a voyage in search of a Northeast Passage with a report that waters near Spitsbergen are teeming with whales. Within a few years, British and Dutch whaling ships are competing to control the Spitsbergen grounds.

1613 Dutch merchants combine to form the Noordsche Compagnie and win a monopoly over the northern whaling grounds. It enjoys a monopoly until 1642.

1617 Dutch whalers on Amsterdam Island erect the first buildings of their main shore station at Spitsbergen. This place, called Smeerenburg (Blubber Town), grows into a thriving summer settlement until it is abandoned in the 1640s as the whaling begins to move offshore.

Ca. 1650 Shore whaling begins on Long Island, New York. This represents the beginning of the American whaling industry.

Ca. 1670 The Dutch whaling fleet is the largest and most productive in the world and dominates the industry.

—Adapted from *A History of World Whaling,*
by Daniel Francis

CHAPTER SEVEN

The Four Elements:
Whale Oil,
Coffee, Chocolate,
and Tobacco

The Whales lay so thicke about the ship that some ran against our cables, some against the ship, and one against the rudder. One lay under our beake-head and slept there for a long while.
—Jonas Poole, 1612

By the late 1500s, from the far corners of the world a flood of new products began pouring into Europe. With a smile, let me suggest that there were four primary substances that came to Europe and changed everything.

Whale oil was the first because it could be found nearby, and it was already known as a precious commodity. With the exploration of the world, and especially the Americas, came the other three—Coffee, Chocolate, and Tobacco.

These materials remain primary elements in our cultures and lives today, with only whale oil having been replaced by petroleum.

In an age when the church stifled all research into the natural world, crushed the age-old path of self-initiation through mystical practices, and created an atmosphere of fear, dominance, and control, the arrival of these four elements was like a sun coming up. Into a world newly emptied by the millions who fell victim to plagues, with a gradually collapsing feudal system, a corrupt church, and the revolutionary new invention of the moveable-type press, came these four elements.

If we place any credence in the existence of nature spirits, that is, the over-arching spirit that accompanies a flower, tree, or animal, we might see the new products' arrival as the advent of the Spirits of Energy (coffee), Pleasure (chocolate), and Imagination (tobacco), lit by a clear, white flame of Joyous Mind (whale oil).

The first major change brought on by the four elements is the institution of the coffee house. There, people of all kinds could gather to discuss the news, gossip about the King and his mistress, chat about the latest printed books, and generally carry on a spirited dialog. Coffee gives energy and stamina to everyone, regardless of class. Although most coffee houses were frequented by the educated elite, they were remarkably egalitarian. Having a jolt of java was everyone's favorite thing to do once it caught on.[1]

Imagine the scene:

The local coffee house, the Whaler's Inn (which is different from a pub, because everyone stays coherent), has a bustling business in the evening. The almost-burnt, rich smell of the coffee beans warms the air outside, leading customers in. A new shipment of chocolate has just arrived in port, and blocks of the hard sugary stuff are being broken up and melted down to make a crude kind of "hot chocolate" as an alternative to coffee. Some customers are mixing the two together. People are feeling the uplift of the caffeine and the theobromine/caffeine "love feeling" of the chocolate, when someone enters with a pouch of tobacco. The early form of tobacco, a strain called *"rustica,"* is nearly psychedelic. It's potent stuff, sending the smoker on a mental ride. The clientele is buzzing....

Once the new printers had filled the demand for Bibles, which only the small number of literate people could read, they began exploring the manuscripts at hand to see what else was free to be published. The ancient Greek texts, collected by the Medici brothers of Italy, were dusted off and printed.

All the radical ideas about Freedom of the Individual Soul, the Nature of the Good, the Republic of Enlightened Kings, Democracy, the ideals of Beauty, and all the excellent thoughts of 1,500 years before that had survived the Inquisition suddenly were on the "best seller" lists.

With whale oil lamps to see by, far superior to olive oil, coffee to help one stay up late, chocolate to make one feel loving and open, tobacco to stimulate the imagination, and of course the coffee houses in which to debate new ideas, we had a fertile environment from which to expect changes to arise. And did they ever!

"The Enlightenment" was a term that could have been used in reference to the effective brilliance of the whale oil lamps that lit the coffee shops of Europe, where the dreams of a New World were born and the free human spirit reawakened.

The great documents of the age were all written under the light of whale-oil lamps and candles: Martin Luther's proclamation founding the Protestant churches, the Declaration of Independence, the books of Voltaire, Rousseau, Descartes, and Isaac Newton. The Constitution of the United States and the sailing orders of Captain James Cook would all have been written under whale light.

No longer was the long reach of the church's authority acceptable. No longer were the edicts of the inbred nobility, with their rampant excesses, able to contain the growing dissatisfaction of the educated. No longer were the limits of Europe and its small landscape and even smaller elite class able to command allegiance. Unwittingly, the church had created an underground trade in ideas. With new animal and plant specimens coming from around the world, a new culture of knowledge was being born. Martin Luther wrote: "We are now in the rosy dawn of the life of the future, for we are beginning once more to acquire knowledge of the creatures."

New prosperity was flowing in, with incredible new wealth being built by a merchant class. Even the craftsmen and women of Europe were beginning to see some wealth from the outfitting of so many ships.

To people with insight who were seeking advantage in a new

world of markets and opportunity, it was evident that Europe was no longer big enough. For many reasons—including the desire to create a new moral environment where effort and good works could bring one favor in the eyes of God, instead of appealing to the corrupt priesthood for indulgences (which was one of the roots of the Protestant reformation)—people began to dream of a new world, a new beginning.

Designing a New World: The Americas

The New World was literally thought of as the New Jerusalem, the place where man's destiny led him, where he would complete the process of ascending to his freedom as a soul.

The Masonic movement was well established by the 1600s when the first settlers began to create a new world in the Americas. The Masons were, and still are, a fraternity devoted to the development of men who are free from the petty prejudices of church. Their system of belief urges its members to honor every religion, to accept every form of worship in an atmosphere of equality and fairness. The Masons established a hierarchy that is accessible, and a secret commitment to mutual benefit that has remained strong for centuries. Whereas the Rosicrucians were concerned with the legacy of ancient sciences, the mysteries of alchemy, and occult insight, the Masons' arcane philosophies led them to be involved in politics, commerce, and the public world.

As the Americas were being settled by Europeans, the Masons of Europe were deeply interested and involved. The typical Mason was educated, financially well off, and free-thinking. Into their clubs had come the Four Elements, stimulating their study of ancient ideas.

It could be said that the Delphic Spirit, a self-aware spirit embodying compassion, mutual benefit, joy, and freedom, was brought to America in the vessel of Masonic tradition.

The fantasy of escape from the degenerate Kings of Europe had been brought to life by the Masonic Brotherhood, with their Egyptian regalia, unitarian religious tolerance, and expanding business interests. A new country was now the dream, where the ancient Greek (Delphic) experiment could be tried out by creating a democratic nation where anyone could be a citizen, have the opportunity to rise to whatever station in life their aspiration could manifest, and find a kind of freedom never allowed before for the human spirit.

The Masons did their job well. They designed a new country, an original concept in itself. They gave it symbols from ancient times, such as the Phoenix, born anew out of the ashes (which was the original bird on the seal, before being changed to the American Eagle); the mottos *E Pluribus Unum* (Out of Many, One); *Novus Ordo Seclorum* (A New Order for the Ages); and *Annuit Coeptis* (He has Favored Our Undertaking) inscribed on the money; the gnostic star-tetrahedron of thirteen stars, floating above the eagle; and of course the Pyramid, with the all-seeing eye, the Christ Eye, floating above it as a capstone (see Figure 13).

To further anchor the Masonic design and the Delphic Wave, the first designated capital of the United States of America was

Figure 13 US GREAT SEAL

The Masonic and Rosicrucian influence in the design of America is evident in the Great Seal of the United States. Look carefully and you will find many elements of esoteric wisdom. Note the Gnostic Star over the head of the eagle.

called "Philadelphia." You may recognize that, contrary to the standard definition given in public schools all over America, the meaning of "Philadelphia" is not "City of Brotherly Love" but is actually *Lovers of the Dolphin.*[2]

A wave was beginning to wash over the world with the American experiment. It was the first consciously designed country, with a belief in the essential goodness of the human spirit at its core, trusting that its correct governance would be found by empowering every citizen with the right to vote, to share his inner voice with the world. It gave the Delphic Spirit a new birth, after many years of darkness and submission to the necessary changes wrought by the ferment, the composting of the old, in Europe.

Once again, the Delphic Spirit brought ancient teachings across the sea to initiate a culture into the arts of civilization, just as it had in Australia, India, Sumeria, Egypt, Africa, and Greece. Into America poured the many cultures of the world. Inventiveness soared, the age of mechanisms and industry came clanking into view, and the world began to systematically hunt the whale.

CHAPTER EIGHT

Blood on the Waters

Can he who has discovered some of the values of whalebone and whale oil be said to have discovered the true use of the whale? Can he who slays the elephant for his ivory be said to have 'seen the elephant'? These are petty and accidental uses; just as if a stronger race were to kill us in order to make buttons and [whistles] of our bones....
—Henry David Thoreau, 1864[1]

There is a period in human history that marks us for all time as the ones who murdered nearly all of our most constant and dedicated friends. We will live with the infamy of our deeds forever.

Perhaps this will serve to keep us humble as future humans. We will remember our barbarity, our dumb harsh ways, and be ashamed. Not a crippling shame, but one that keeps us always tender, gentle, and careful to be kind.

Perhaps this will keep us from behaving badly toward other races, other beings who do not appear to be equals in the hierarchies of life. Perhaps we will use the dynamic contamination of our history, the story of how we acted toward the cetacean families, as a key factor in becoming Masters of Compassion.

The price for our awakening has been their suffering. May our awakening be in time to prevent their disappearance, and ours.

For tens of thousands of years, the dream of human awakening had been underway. Slowly growing around the great sphere of the Earth, from its Australian origins, a wave of gentle kindness had been soaking its way into human awareness.

A pause, a caesura, a moment between waves....

It gave us time to absorb the lessons of the past and to add faith to our strengths. We gained but we also forgot. We began to see the cetacean families as resources, no longer divine but treasures to be wrested from the seas, to be boiled down into oil and bone, meat and tooth.

When we stopped worshipping them, we went to the other extreme, hunting them relentlessly until, with ever-increasing efficiency, we were killing them at the rate of one every twenty minutes, year round—thirty thousand in a year. Millions of tons of meat were dumped into the sea when only "oil and buggy whips" were sought, millions of gallons of blood poured overboard.

- The U. S. Constitution and its Bill of Rights were written under the light of whale oil.
- The lighthouses that guarded the coastlines, showing the way to weary whalers, immigrant millions, colonial armies, and the dark and densely packed slave ships, were lit by the oil of the whale.
- The first typewriter had springs of whalebone.
- The first oil that could dissipate the high heat of machining, enabling the evolution of precision tools, was whale oil.
- City streets, to keep "villains and robbers" at bay, were lit by the oil of the whale.
- Until the early 1800s, washing one's body with soap was done only under the advice of a doctor. Then, with the surplus of low-grade whale oil, cheap soap could be made by the ton and sold to

the masses. Modern advertising was invented for the purpose of selling soap to those who did not know they needed it.

- Alfred Nobel, whose Peace Prize is one of the highest accolades to be given to anyone living, made his fortune with the invention of dynamite, which depended on glycerine from whales for its manufacture.

- Corset stays, lipstick, linoleum, soap, margarine, paint, photographic chemicals, glycerine for explosives, Rolls Royce transmission fluid, watch lubricating oil, the first hormone-based medicines, buggy whips, flogging whips, golf bag leather, pie crust crimpers, niddy noddies, flageolets, buttons, toys, steaks, bacon, fertilizer, cattle food, cat food, dog food, pig food, chicken food, fuel, candles, umbrellas, shampoo, eyeshadow, upholstery, detergents, brushes and brooms, tennis racket strings, support trusses, sausage skins, stitches, drum heads, ink, insecticides, crayons, leather finishes, carbon paper, parchment, varnish, bouillon cubes, iodine, insulin, skin cream, mink and arctic fox food, anti-freeze, shortening, piano keys and cufflinks, car wax and shoe polish, fishing rods, lubricants for space craft ... all were products from the bodies of the whales.

- Between 1909 and 1935, almost 12,000 blue whales were reported killed in the Antarctic each year for their oil, wasting 380,000 tons of edible meat per year, enough for a six-ounce steak every day for a year for 6,180,000 human beings. From the same whales 210,000 tons of oil were produced, enough to supply 2.5 ounces of margarine or edible oil every day for a year to 8,276,000 humans.

By the 1970s huge factory ships managed to process an entire whale in forty-five minutes. Men in barbed boots climbed the bodies with hockey stick-like knives to slice the blubber away. Saws twenty feet long separated the bodies into sections, cranes lifted body parts to specialists in dismembering various portions of the skeletons, and huge mincing machines below deck ground away at the flood of meat and bone, shredding it, flushing it into huge cauldrons for boiling under pressure. An entire whale would disappear into the bowels of the ship, sliding down holes in the deck in small pieces. In the belly of the ship mammoth tanks filled slowly with golden oil. Driers and grinders turned meat and bone into dust, blown into bags that were stacked in mountains in the dark holds below.

In the Antarctic, hundreds of carcasses floated in the harbors of South Georgia Island, the oil taken from the head of the sperm whale, the rest left to rot and eventually slide to the bottom of the sea.

Under sail, the wooden ships of the earlier era of hand-thrown harpoons were scenes not unlike Hell itself. The whale, tied to the side of the ship, was torn apart by sharks while men stood on the carcass. By poking great hooks into the thick blanket of blubber, the whale was spun slowly as the strips of fat and skin were peeled off. Long pieces of dripping flesh were swung onboard, then dropped on the deck, where it was cut into shorter sections, then minced by men wearing whale penis-leather vests. The chunks were tossed into huge black iron cauldrons that sat over open fires, fueled by the "cracklins," the boiled-hard flesh of the whale's body. Dense black smoke rose into the sails, much of the boiling being done at night, the ship looking like a reddened den of demons dancing around a hissing and spitting fire, long ladles skimming off the hot oil into cooling vats.

If a sperm whale was taken, the head was severed from the body and hoisted onboard. A hole was chopped into its forehead, into the "case." The hole was made big enough for a small man or a boy to climb inside, to carefully scoop out buckets full of spermaceti, the glowing pearl-like essence of the whale's liquid acoustic lens. Quickly, the "sparm" would cool and begin to harden into a soft wax, an exquisite substance that wafted its delicate and volatile scent through the dank and foul smoke of the onboard holocaust.

The men would wear the same oil-soaked clothes for months, finally boiling them to extract the last bit of oil before tossing them overboard on the voyage home.

Photographs show them to be sullen, uncouth, hardened men living desperate lives far from civilization. Men who had been at sea, sometimes for two years or more, slaughtering, sailing, butchering, stabbing, slicing, sailing, were hardly fit company for their wives and families. Many shipped out again within a month or two of their return.

A barbarous underclass of men, they infested the ports of the world, especially dirtying the South Sea islands. They were raping, drunken murderers, foul and feral, bringing the many diseases of the European world to paradise. Children born to island women, abandoned by their whaler "husbands," were outcasts, often becoming whalers themselves. Propagating their own kind, they left a legacy of brute stupidity, of harsh and uncivilized behavior.

The churches followed, bringing "the salvation of Jesus" on the heels of the whalers, and the idyll of island life was destined to end. Rules and regulations, diseases and a cash economy were brought in exchange for the oil and bone of the whale.

How Could This Happen?

How are we to understand this? How, if the cetacean families are so intelligent, did they let this happen? Could they not avoid the ships by diving and disappearing into the blue deeps?

Could it be that they *did* know what was happening? Could their Nommo nature be so sure of the course of life that relinquishing a body was seen as a fair price to pay? All for the opportunity to return as a human, one who lives on the edges of creation, a new and unproven species, stumbling toward the end of history?

Could their love of us be so great that they could allow the Holocaust, the endless burning of their own flesh for fuel for the fires that melted them, to go on month after relentless month, year after year, waiting for us to catch on, to "get it," and finally stop? Could the accumulated wisdom of thirty million years have given them acceptance in the face of death?

According to the Legend, a thousand years ago the Dolphins decided to stop touching the Human mind—it was sufficiently stimulated. The decision was made to awaken the human heart, even if sacrifice were the price. *Could anyone have that much love?*

With a heart the size of a chest of drawers, and 15,000 liters of blood, with heart vessels large enough for a child to crawl through, a tongue ten men could stand on, and a brain weighing twenty-two pounds, a great whale probably knows what it is doing....

If we ask this question of the cetacean ethologist, he must answer that he does not know. What culture could resist the relentless pursuit of its members by a technology completely alien? To many of these whales, no boundary had ever been encountered before, save that between water and air. No hard thing, other than ice, had ever been seen. No creature hunted them, no strategic games had been played attempting to take their lives before their confrontation with man.[2] Their only resistance came once they had been pursued, when they either swam away, or circled to protect their families. Millions of years of peace had left them majestically, serenely peaceful, beyond any thought of murder.

It is appropriate to note here the impact of whale killing on both global warming and the growing hole in the ozone layer over the southern hemisphere. These processes have followed the wholesale removal of up to 95 percent of some species of whales in that region. Is there a connection?

Perhaps there is. The biomass of that part of the globe is responsible for production of a larger percentage of our oxygen than anywhere else, far more than the Amazon Basin or the jungles of Africa. The rainforests, while being rapidly depleted, damaging our oxygen supply further, are second in production of oxygen compared to the "plankton forests" of the southern oceans. Hundreds of billions of tons of phytoplankton, converting sunlight into life and oxygen, capturing carbon molecules, have pumped breathable air into the gaseous envelope surrounding our planet from the beginning of Earth time.

The whales were the farmers of these vast areas of living, breathing ocean. Keeping the blooms of plankton in a state of balance, harvesting thousands of tons of krill per day, the whales were the caretakers of the oxygen farms.

With whales removed from the system by the tens of thousands, the balance has been upset. Vast phytoplankton blooms now occur without sufficient harvesting of them. The plankton consume the nutrients of the sea in orgies of explosive growth, then die off catastrophically. When the ocean blanket of phytoplankton rots, it gives off immense amounts of methane, a destroyer of ozone.[3]

In the indigenous traditions of Africa, Australia, and North America, the whales are thought of as the record keepers and the caretakers of the planet's breath. The Mirning of South Australia think of Jiderra, the Great White Whale from the stars, as the originator of the air we breathe. Perhaps they are correct....

We removed most of the whales from the southern hemisphere, leaving only the lonely minke whale, too small to be worth harvesting. Now we are turning on them because their populations have expanded in a futile attempt to fill the empty ecological niches of their cousins. Several nations are champing at the bit, pawing the ground, eager to race out onto the seas to begin the final slaughter of the minke, seeking to take us all down with them, into the boiler rooms of doom.

More than one thousand minke whales will be killed this year (2002). The Japanese call it "scientific whaling," by which they are proving that dead whales are dead and that they taste good. In June of 2001, a Japanese Fisheries Department official called the minke whale "the cockroaches of the sea." Their "science" has concluded that there are too many whales, that they need harvesting to prevent them from competing with humans for fish.

The Norwegians don't bother calling it anything other than harvesting dark red meat. They don't have a taste for the blubber, deciding recently to sell the 800 tons they had in frozen storage to the Japanese, despite an international agreement (the CITES treaty).

to ban all trade in cetacean products. At the last minute, the sellers discovered that the blubber was laced with heavy metals and toxic chemicals and had to call off the sale.

And now the Japanese have added the bryde's whale, sei whales, and even sperm whales to the menu once again.

The collective guilt of humanity in this heedless slaughter is immense. We live in homes, drive cars, eat food, and send our children to schools financed by the killing of whales. Every one of us is an inheritor of a world economy built on whales. The hundreds of cities of the coastlines of the world are all connected through their history to the taking or using of the products of the whale. They are harbors of death.

Aristotle Onassis: Gluttony on the High Seas

Aristotle Onassis must be named as the worst example of rapacious abuse of the oceans, the worst whaler ever known.

Before the Second World War Onassis watched the Nazis begin a strategic stockpiling of oils with which to feed their population. To prepare people for the change to whale products, in 1933 Adolf Hitler issued a decree in which he compelled all bakeries and restaurants to display placards informing the public of the use of whale oil in their margarine. Financed almost entirely by Dutch and British financiers (Lever Bros. in England), the Nazis built a fleet of whaling ships, which they had in full operation by 1937.

Herman Goering said that having their own whaling fleet "offered the possibility of supporting the supply of fats to our people, and thereby contributing to the attainment of the great goal of freedom in raw materials and food."

This was a key element in German preparation for war. It gave them complete independence from other suppliers, not only for fats, but also the all-important glycerine needed for explosives.

After the war, Onassis bought what remained of the Nazi fleet, hired the sailors and officers, and began whaling. He converted a tanker into a floating factory ship and christened it *lenger*. Onassis had earned a reputation as a fierce (business of shipping and now brought that spirit

He hired a Norwegian who had been convicte with the Nazis to be his expedition manager and hired an... as captain, Wilhelm Reichert. To complete his mini-fleet, he added at least fifteen catcher boats, with a total crew for the fleet of more than 500 German ex-Nazis.

Onassis ordered his fleet to kill whatever they could find. Mothers with calves, recently born baby whales, humpbacks (notorious for lack of oil)—no matter what size, age or species, it was slaughtered mercilessly.

Called pirate whaling, Onassis' style of whaling disregards all international agreements to protect the stocks of whales. His attitude was that money made more sense than morals.

In 1954, off the coast of Peru, the *Olympic Challenger* chose to hunt whales inside the official boundaries of that country's waters. When the ship and its catcher fleet were taken into custody, Onassis was not worried. He had insurance against seizure, and made more money ($30,000 per day) having been seized than he was making from the whales.

He was "turned on" by killing ("aroused" is the word used by one of his biographers), and even invited friends to accompany him to the *Olympic Challenger* for cocktail parties, where guests were able to fire the harpoon cannons. His private yacht included a saloon where the bar rail was inlaid with whale-tooth ivory, decorated with scenes from Greek myths. In this saloon he had barstools that he delighted in inviting Hollywood starlets to sit upon. He would inform them that they were sitting on the largest penis in the world ... the stools had been upholstered in leather from the penises of sperm whales and had their teeth as footrests.

Eventually Onassis was forced out of the whaling business. Even the Norwegians were infuriated by his flagrant and devastating practices. Just before he was to come under serious legal charges in 1957, he managed to make a deal with a Japanese company, selling the *lympic Challenger* and its fleet of catcher boats for $8.5 million, another tidy profit.

The *Olympic Challenger* was renamed the *Kyokuyo Maru II* and continued to be used by the Japanese until 1970.

The symbolism of the transfer of the Nazis' whaling fleet, via the most bloody whaler of all, to the Japanese, who insist on blindly continuing the horrible hunt, is hard to escape.

Cry for Forgiveness

> "In the world of mammals," writes Teizo Ozawa, "there are two mountain peaks. One is Mount Homo Sapiens, and the other is Mount Cetacea." How odd that the one pinnacle has chosen to lay the other waste....
> —Robert McNally, *So Remorseless a Havoc*[4]

In the grand procession of life across the face of our world, two great brains have evolved. Two ways of maintaining a balance with the systems of life have been attempted. One has been successful, finding homeostasis in the Oceans; the other, humankind, has yet to find the spiritual state of sustainable joy.

Let us, each day, celebrate the gifts we have received and let us remember those who gave them to us. By remembering, we may one day deserve to live among them as friends, humbled and gentle, expending our vaunted abilities on providing pleasure for them and us, building beautiful things out of their large dreams.

Until then, perhaps it would be right for us to go to a Whaling Wall, to cry for forgiveness.

> If our present mad quest for domination and power leads to the obliteration of our species in some terrible conflagration of nuclear war, it is likely that most of the animals of the land and air will be consumed as well. When such dark thoughts come to me, I have a small prayer: that we do not leave this an empty

planet, that the seas will survive. And if one grand life form in those seas might survive us, let it be the whales.

Allow, if others are silenced, the songs of whales to rise up through the darkness to the distant stars. Let these be the guardians of the planet, great archangels of life in the wide seas below. Then, perhaps, it will be them and not us who will lament, sadly aware, in that great brain, that something is gone out of the tumultuous terrestrial world, knowing, no doubt, in ways we cannot know, wise in ways we are not wise.

Then, in a planet empty of life save in those "waters of the beginning and the end," there will be a long, long time of waiting. Eventually, once again, it will be safe for life to creep out upon the land. And perhaps, as life emerges on the shore, in the sea foam the whales will sing again. Huge lullabying midwives to a new world.

—David Day[5]

CHAPTER NINE

A Sublime Brain:
The Sperm Whale

Perhaps the sperm whale is really a genius in disguise; the possibility cannot be totally discounted.
—Edward O. Wilson[1]

Genius in the Sperm Whale? Has the Sperm Whale ever written a book, spoken a speech? No, his genius is declared in doing nothing in particular to prove it.
—Herman Melville[2]

The sperm whale is a unique creature among the cetaceans. It is the largest whale with teeth, and it has the largest brain ever to have been on this world. They live in wandering tribes of females, the eldest sometimes being five or even six generations older than the youngest. It is thought that females never leave their mothers, staying with them and all their female relations for life. The female groups stay in warm waters, away from the freezing northern and southern seas, while the males migrate to the cold zones each year and back again, to mate and socialize. The males do not seem to have particular tribe loyalties, but instead seek out whatever female aggregation will host them.

The head of a sperm whale is the largest head of any known

creature, roughly one-third of its body length, or up to twenty feet. Inside is a huge reservoir of strange iridescent oil. No satisfactory explanation has yet been put forth for this enormous "case." The energy required to develop and maintain this part of their anatomy is huge. It must have great importance to their survival to have become what it is, from an evolutionary perspective.

Sperm whales have a limited repertoire of sounds. Trains of repetitive clicks, rising and falling in frequency from nearly twice as high as humans can hear to low rumbles, organized sometimes into "codas," comprise their entire known language.

Not the largest whales, the males may reach fifty-two feet and forty-five tons, the females thirty-three feet and fifteen tons. At least, this is the size recorded in scientific records. Older records mention sperm whales as long as eighty-five feet, such as the one that sank the *Essex*, a whaling ship whose fate inspired Herman Melville to write *Moby Dick*.

Sperm whale brains are huge. Larger than two basketballs, they are the most elegant physical organ ever to grace our world, capable of providing a massively interwoven, wholistic interface between the mysterious living world and the realms of the unseen. If we are capable of awe in the face of natural phenomena, this is one altar before which we ought to bow our heads and bend our knees.

Certainly the brain of the sperm whale ought to be able to instill enough reverence in us to keep us from killing them. Yet the Japanese have placed the sperm whale in their sights once again, killing them in the North Pacific under the rubric of "scientific whaling."

Moby Dick, We Hardly Know Ye

Moby Dick surfaced in 1851. The tale of the Great White Whale lives large in human culture, a true icon. Often referred to as the ultimate novel, its subject is whales and whaling. Although there are many human characters in the book, they are secondary to the whales. The power of the book lies partly in its evocation of the sperm whale, the creature that embodies one of the greatest mysteries in the living world.

Herman Melville spent years at sea and observed whaling first hand. His accounts of the techniques of whaling and the processing of the parts of the whale are authentic. He uses the story of a madman's obsession with killing the whale who took his leg years before as a framework within which he portrays the mighty sperm whale in his historical, biblical, scientific, and even spiritual dimensions.

To many modern readers, *Moby Dick* is surprising for its humor. Melville is both an excellent caricaturist and a dry wit. His descriptions of the human characters are masterpieces of understatement and subtle allusion. Once the whaling journey that is the central quest of the book is underway, he makes a funny scene out of the creation of a protective apron—a cassock is made from the skin of the penis of a whale. With painfully polite discretion and without ever naming exactly what he is describing, he manages to outline the exact process of its creation.

Melville's spiritual insight can be profound. His chapter on the whiteness of the whale and the subtle portrayal of evil in shades of white is a masterpiece. He turns on its head our normal sense of purity and spiritual perfection in the colorlessness of white. A brief excerpt will illustrate:

> ... Or is it, that as in essence whiteness is not so much a color as the visible absence of color, and at the same time the concrete of all colors; is it for these reasons that there is such a dumb blankness, full of meaning, in a wide landscape of snows—a colorless, all-color of atheism from which we shrink?
>
> ... and like willful travelers in Lapland, who refuse to wear colored and coloring glasses upon their eyes, so the wretched infidel gazes himself blind at the monumental white shroud that wraps all the prospect around him. And of all these things the Albino Whale was the symbol....[3]

Perhaps the most powerful passages are about whale oil, particularly the mysterious spermaceti. Melville speaks so eloquently of the experience of handling spermaceti, one wonders whether there actually is a magical element in it:

> That whale ... was duly brought to the [ship]'s side, where all those cutting and hoisting operations previously detailed were regularly gone through, even to the baling of the ... case. *[Baling the case involved lowering buckets into the whale's head to bail out the spermaceti oil.]*
>
> While some were occupied with this latter duty, others were employed in dragging away the larger tubs, so soon as filled with the sperm; and when the proper time arrived, this same sperm was carefully manipulated ere going to the try-works, of which anon.
>
> It had cooled and crystallized to such a degree, that when, with several others, I sat down before a large Constantine's bath of it, I found it strangely concreted into lumps, here and there rolling about in the liquid part. It was our business to squeeze these lumps back into fluid. A sweet and unctuous duty! No wonder that in old times this sperm was such a favorite cosmetic. Such a clearer! such a sweetener! such a softener! such a delicious mollifier! After having my hands in it for only a few minutes, my fingers felt like eels, and began, as it were, to serpentine and spiralize.
>
> As I sat there at my ease, cross-legged on the deck; after the bitter exertion at the windlass; under a blue tranquil sky; the ship under indolent sail, and gliding so serenely along; as I bathed my hands among those soft, gentle globules of infiltrated tissues, woven almost within the hour; as they richly broke to my fingers, and discharged all their opulence, like fully ripe grapes their wine; as I snuffed up that uncontaminated aroma,—literally and truly, like the smell of spring violets; I declare to you, that for the time I lived as in a musky meadow; I forgot all about our horrible oath; in that inex-

pressible sperm, I washed my hands and my heart of it; I almost began to credit the old Paracelsian superstition that sperm is of rare virtue in allaying the heat of anger: while bathing in that bath, I felt divinely free from all ill-will, or petulance, or malice, of any sort whatsoever.

Squeeze! squeeze! squeeze! All the morning long; I squeezed that sperm till I myself almost melted into it; I squeezed that sperm till a strange sort of insanity came over me; and I found myself unwittingly squeezing my co-laborers' hands in it, mistaking their hands for the gentle globules. Such an abounding, affectionate, friendly, loving feeling did this avocation beget; that at last I was continually squeezing their hands, and looking up into their eyes sentimentally; as much as to say,—Oh! my dear fellow beings, why should we longer cherish any social acerbities, or know the slightest ill-humor or envy! Come; let us squeeze hands all round; nay, let us all squeeze ourselves into each other; let us squeeze ourselves universally into the very milk and sperm of kindness.

Would that I could keep squeezing that sperm forever! For now, since by many prolonged, repeated experiences, I have perceived that in all cases man must eventually lower, or at least shift, his conceit of attainable felicity; not placing it anywhere in the intellect or the fancy; but in the wife, the heart, the bed, the table, the saddle, the fire-side, the country; now that I have perceived all this, I am ready to squeeze case eternally. In thoughts of the visions of the night, I saw long rows of angels in paradise, each with his hands in a jar of spermaceti.[4]

This supposed "rare virtue" of spermaceti might suggest its use in anointing royalty and other special people, possibly even explaining the motive behind this odd ancient custom.

... It is well known that at the coronation of kings and queens, even modern ones, a certain curious process of seasoning them for their functions is gone through. There is a saltcellar of state, so called, and there may be a caster of state. How they use the salt, precisely—who knows? Certain I am, however, that a king's head is solemnly oiled at his coronation, even as a head of salad. Can it be, though, that they anoint it with a view of making its interior run well, as they anoint machinery? Much might be ruminated here, concerning the essential dignity of this regal process, because in common life we esteem but meanly and contemptibly a fellow who anoints his hair, and palpably smells of that anointing. In truth, a mature man who uses hair-oil, unless medicinally, that man has probably got a quoggy spot in him somewhere. As a general rule, he can't amount to much in his totality.

But the only thing to be considered here, is this—what kind of oil is used at coronations? Certainly it cannot be olive oil, nor macassar oil, nor castor oil, nor bear's oil, nor train oil *[train oil is low-grade whale oil]*, nor cod-liver oil. What then can it possibly be, but sperm oil in its unmanufactured, unpolluted state, the sweetest of all oils?

Think of that, ye loyal Britons! We whalemen supply your kings and queens with coronation stuff![5]

John Allegro, in his controversial book *The Sacred Mushroom and the Cross*,[6] says that the practice of anointing is a re-enactment of insemination, by pouring a representation of sperm on an upright image of a phallus. The "sperm of God" is the essence of the spirit that fertilizes the world, and the re-enactment calls upon God to increase abundance and prosperity.

A King is anointed at his coronation to call attention to his representation of the phallus of God, whose words and deeds will result in a better society. He is to be the fertilizer of the fields, the orchards, the seas, bringing life to all.

It makes sense that the sperm of God might be found in the head of the creature with the largest brain. Melville's seeming joke that spermaceti was the mystical ingredient in anointing oil is not far-fetched, and he probably knew of what he spoke. The ingredients of anointing oil are a secret, closely guarded.

The Gift of the Whales: Will We Accept It?

The story of the whales is old and has been very public, yet it hasn't yet been widely accepted as a central element in the gradual uplift of humanity's state and possibly even our souls. We have been too close to it, seeing each episode as an isolated incident. Now, at the time of another turning point, we are being called to take a glimpse backward, along the way we have come. Climbing the twisting road, from a switchback we call the millennial moment, we can see the curves of our progress from the first cetacean-human encounters to admiration and worship; to the shame of forgetfulness; from forgetting to slaughter; from holocaust to remembrance. And now we look around ourselves seeking the redemption brought through remembering. In remembering, we face the living truth of our own divine nature, accepting the responsibility to live within the circle of balance, which is the many-billions-of-years-old perfect system of the natural world.

At the end of *Moby Dick*, as Ahab disappears, tangled in the ropes dangling from the harpoons of the many whalers who tried before him to take the White Whale, the ship sinks, the sailors drown, and only Ishmael survives, having climbed into the floating coffin of the crew's indigenous wisdom keeper. His salvation is found by placing himself within the safe container of ancient wisdom.

The White Whale is the whale known as Jiderra and Nommo. He is a god of the Zulu, Aboriginal Australians, the Tongans and the Chinese, the Dogon and the Greek, the Nabatean and the Hindu, the Chumash and the Oneida. He lives in the hearts of people everywhere. Every continent has its whale and dolphin magic, its stories of the Divine presence in the sea. When we threaten it, it can drown us, taking us down into the smothering waters from where we began and from where we perhaps must begin again.[7]

We are all on the edge of that dark plunge. The whales have been decimated, only small fractions of their former millions now swim and breathe. The northern right whale has reached so low a population it cannot recover. These are its last days. The orca of Puget Sound are so polluted by the accumulated heavy metals and toxins poured into the oceans that they might not survive the next fifty years. The beluga whales of the Saint Lawrence Seaway are nearly all sterile now, poisoned by pollution, and will be gone within the next thirty to one hundred years.

All of them, gone.

Have we passed the limits? Can the system still recover?
Do we know those limits?
Will we discover the limits before we pass them?

> "And I'll tell you a quare thing. So long as they was on the fishing grounds along of we, I never was afeared of anything; no, nor never felt lonely neither. But after times, when the whales was all done to death, I'd be on the Penguin Grounds with nothing livin' to be seen and I'd get a feeling in me belly, like the world was empty. Yiss, me son, I missed them whales when they was gone."
>
> "'Tis strange. Some folks says as whales is only fish. No, bye! They's too smart for fish. I don't say as what they's not the smartest creatures in God's ocean."
>
> He paused for a long moment, picked up the telescope and gazed through it.
>
> "Aye.... And maybe out of it as well."
>
> —Uncle Art, fisherman, in *A Whale for the Killing*,
> by Farley Mowat (1972)

The Building of a New Relationship: Dolphins and Whales in the Modern World

CHAPTER TEN

Waves of Spirit: European Exploration and the Return of Remembrance

The Captain Cook Memorial, on the big island of Hawaii....

I have just kayaked across the bay and landed, alone on this isolated point of land. As I wander into the jungle behind the memorial obelisk, I see piles of stones under the greenery.

There is not much to see now—only loose stone walls mark the ruins of a former royal enclosure. This is where the royal family of Hawaii used to gather for part of the year, coming from all the islands to this hospitable bay. Its natural features, sheltered from the ocean, also attracted Captain James Cook, who had come to visit in 1778. He stayed a year, then left.

He chose an inauspicious moment to leave, running into a storm immediately. One of his ships was severely damaged. When the small fleet sailed back into the bay from which they had so recently departed, some of the younger Hawaiians became suspicious.

When Cook arrived the first time, the Hawaiians assumed he was a legendary figure they had been expecting named Lono, and Cook had never corrected them.

There was envy of the special things the English had on their ships, but this had been tempered by considering that the visitors were gods....

The Hawaiians were caught up in many emotions when Cook returned. How could he be Lono if he could not command the storms? Why did he

return to Kealakekua Bay, instead of simply going to his heavenly home?
Had they been misled and lied to?

A fight broke out when a sailor refused to give some nails to a Hawai-
ian. He was under strict orders from the Captain. The soldier was injured
in the fight and Cook went to his aid. The captain intended to defend the
sailor, but now that it was revealed that he was not an invulnerable god, he
was himself attacked, beaten and killed.

The other sailors escaped. The Hawaiians cut open Cook's chest and
removed his heart, which they ate.

Ducking under a branch, I came out of the dark green shade into bright sun.
Looking down into a shallow pool at my feet, I saw just below the surface
of the water a bronze plaque on which it said: "On this spot, February 14th,
1779, Captain James Cook was killed."

—From notes in my journal, S. T., 1996

We have been following a tale of mystery, selectively arrang-
ing ancient myths, moving forward through time to the more
reliable facts of written history, showing how contact with the
cetacean families— whether benign encounters with sleek dolphins
or deadly attacks upon the majestic whales—has influenced the
path of humankind. This whole enterprise of transfiguring history has
thus far depended on the reporting of others. Have they preserved
a true record of what happened?

From this point on, I will share another aspect of this strange
saga, the mystery as it appears in our own times. It will consist of
personal experiences and more current reporting of world events.
And some of it is necessarily speculation, the product of an inner
search for answers.

When I first heard the panoramic tale of the Dolphin Legend, I
wondered whether its suggestions could be borne out in the world
I live in. Do dolphins and whales have anything to do with recent
history? Is there a faint trail to be found in our own times? What
would this trail look like? Could I find their watery "footprints"?

Delphic Waves: Path of the Mind, Path of the Heart

I went to Hawaii in November 1996 for a week-long meeting with a group of dolphin experts and members of the international "Dolphin Tribe."

The bay where Cook lived among the Hawaiians and eventually was killed is famous today for the local dolphin pods that come to rest within its sheltering arms. I had chosen this auspicious spot to hold our meetings and to formally announce the founding of the Cetacean Studies Institute, in close proximity to the spinner dolphins.

The first day we arrived, I swam among the dolphins in the bay. A large dolphin, whom I took to be a male, played with me in a startling way. He would dive deep and then arrow directly up toward me. As I lay on the surface, staring down, I saw him coming up at me the first time and I could hardly believe my eyes. He came up fast, swerving at the last moment, to suddenly disappear right in front of me as he leapt into the air!

I pulled my head out of the water, looked up, and saw him spinning around, bending and coming back down toward me. He somehow managed to miss me and I stuck my head down again, only to see a universe of bubbles swirling around. As they cleared, there he was again, coming straight up at me!

I watched him intently. He was coming up fast and didn't seem to change course—but he missed me anyway. He left the water no more than twelve inches from my head. I held my breath, wondering again if he would land on me....

No, in an explosion of bubbles again, he landed less than three feet away. I couldn't see him at all, until ... yes, there he was again, coming straight up. He repeated this several more times and then he disappeared from the last cloud of bubbles. I never saw him leave....

. . .

Later that evening I lay on a soft cushion on the veranda, looking out over the bay. I drifted into a reverie, and found a panorama of history unfolding before my inner eyes.

> I drift into my dolphin consciousness. Deep quiet watery oneness. Quiet companionable joyfulness. All-encompassing dolphin deepness. Surging flowing powerful muscularness. Flowing curving plunging gracefulness. Forever everywhere oneness in dolphinness.[1]
> —Chia Gawain

I saw the Delphic Wave—the slow, enlightening wave of deepening awareness, of acceptance of the gentle arts, the reverence for Love, Beauty, and Joy—as it moved around the world, softening the harshness of the human brute. Civilizations flowered, rising to great heights. Finally, as Rome faded and the Catholic Church expanded, the Wave went below the surface and split into two.

One wave went north and one west, taking on two distinctive qualities. In the north, in France and England, began a new awakening of the human Mind. To the south and west, in Spain and Portugal, where Latin blood was being merged with the dark blood of Arabia and North Africa, the Wave awakened the Heart of humankind.

Two Waves, the Mind and the Heart. In time, as sailing ships became capable of long voyages, the two waves were to come into conflict. The Mind Wave wanted to know, to explore, and to encompass the whole world. The firewood of fact was feeding the fire of wisdom. From all corners of the world came exotic spices and foods, fascinating traveler's tales of diverse cultures and customs, and an endless variety of new animals and plants.

Isaac Newton had climbed upon the shoulders of past scientific giants and put the ideas of Aristotle to rest. He demonstrated that the world was knowable, not the inscrutable handiwork of a closely involved God, but a measurable system of laws, a set of fundamental rules which, once grasped, could take mankind to the stars.

God had opened His mind to man, and the modern age of science began.

The other Wave, that of the Heart, had matured in the warmer southern reaches of Europe and grew full, passionate for release. The heat of the heart, seeking fulfillment in chivalry, the ideal of love without physical contact, the love of pure souls, was dynamically opposed to the cold and calculating minds of northern Europe and England.

Profoundly influenced by the passions of Islam, the Christianity of Rome was eager to bring souls to God, to open distant lands to the love of Jesus, and to increase the power of the Church.

The Original Delphic Wave: The Holy Body

In my reverie, I recalled a tradition that the Polynesians are the remnant of a former type of people. According to esoteric history, there existed a huge continent in the region of today's Pacific Ocean called Lemuria. Despite claims that Lemuria was a literary invention from the 1800s, esoteric records state emphatically that there was an earlier civilization that disappeared many tens of thousands of years before Atlantis sank. (Some recent researchers have made the interesting suggestion that Antarctica was Lemuria. Before continental drifting and a sudden tilt of the planet caused the pole positions to shift, this hidden land mass could have been the site of a civilization that preceded all those we know today. It could be the source of visitors to all those civilizations we know to have received language, writing, and sea-borne knowledge from somewhere else. Buried under as much as three miles of ice, Antarctica is the most mysterious of all continents. Could it have been the home of Oannes?)

In those far distant days, according to esoteric history, the spirit of mankind was being born into the new realm of physical bodies. We had been almost entirely spiritual beings before, and we were developing control of our new biological vehicles as we descended into the density of this plane.

Mastery, the ultimate stage of development in any era, was at that time all about mastery of the body. To be in control of one's muscles, to be especially strong, fast, or beautiful, was the height of accomplishment. Some people today seem to have stored in their cellular memory the desire to perfect the body by "body sculpting," weightlifting, and huge amounts of time spent on exercise and image. This is thought to be the ancient remnant of Lemurian tendencies.

With that in mind, let's consider the Polynesians. They are physical in many ways, with classic beauty, great athleticism, and an easy outdoor paradise lifestyle. Their gods are Tikis, grimacing figures standing with arms akimbo, fists tight, and angry faces glaring with bulging eyes. They are very physical gods of anger, war, and power rather than animal-like or ethereal beings. Many, if not all, Polynesian people made the ritual killing of humans a part of their lives. Many ate human flesh.

It was into these cultural traditions that Captain Cook sailed. After many months of friendship with the Hawaiians, he departed only to return immediately. Clearly not the long-expected white brother/god, he was challenged, killed, and his heart was eaten. He had refused to allow nails to be given to the Hawaiians, hoping to lessen the impact of their visit. The men who killed him were attempting to reclaim the ascendancy of the physical body over the mind.

The Mythos has its way....

The Human Mind was reaching out, seeking to embrace the entire world, the globe. It was seeking knowledge to add to the dominion of man. It was Heartless, and the guiding Soul of Mankind knew that all knowledge must be balanced by love. When the nails were withheld, symbolic of the fruits of knowledge that would improve life immeasurably, holding it together, the Body knew that the Mind was living in isolation, which was not acceptable. It had to be stopped.

Cook and Christ

In this historical metaphor, the Mind of Mankind is stopped from its complete dominance of the world by the sacrifice of Captain Cook. His death was sacred, a true sacrifice. By his death, complete dominance of the world by the heartless mind was stopped. The people of the body, the Pacific ancestors, had made clear that mind was not enough, that the body must be honored as well, a body empowered by the heart and led by the light of the mind.

By all accounts, James Cook was a good man, kind, capable, and temperate. His death, for withholding nails, curiously parallels the other good man who was nailed to a cross. His life was also taken in an act of symbolic sacrifice, a moment in time when the family of man was turning in a new direction.

As I lay in the dark warmth, history seemed visible to me. Here by this beautiful bay below a cloud-ringed mountain, with clear blue water at my feet where the dolphins today bring people by the hundreds to swim among them, mankind had lived in idyllic surroundings, without sin, without "knowledge of good and evil." There was perfect climate, abundant food, little need for shelter or clothing, and the easiest lifestyle to be found anywhere. Perfection for the physical body was the gift of the Hawaiian Islands, the most remote islands on the planet.

I was stunned by this insight. What was this? Did this agree with history as we have been taught it? Is this story true? Perhaps the legend, which is always being told and is always alive, had just told another part of its amazing tale.

Until approximately 150 years ago, the world had forgotten its former love and respect for dolphins and whales. At that time wholesale slaughter of whales was in full swing, and dolphins were no longer thought of as divine.

One can imagine something urging the dolphins to engage with us, to accept us again, to initiate interactions that would change our perceptions. And so we began to remember, to be their friends, to move away from the assumption of dominion over all creatures.

The First Signs of Remembrance

In 1862 three dolphins were caught and brought to the London Zoological Gardens. They were placed in a pool and crowds gathered. Two died within a few days. One managed to survive in the shallow fresh water for several weeks. His fame grew and thousands of onlookers came to see him. His health began to fail and a veterinarian, Dr. Buckland, was called in to see about reviving his spirits.

An engraving from a newspaper of the time shows a man in shirtsleeves standing in a pool, with the dolphin's head under his arm, pouring a brisk shot of brandy down the dolphin's throat. The dolphin did not revive, and died within a few days.

At first glance, this seems a horrible way to treat a dying animal. And yet, from another perspective, this was a wonderful advance, a first feeble gesture to attempt care for a dolphin. Until that moment, they were only strange fish that breathe.

Flashing forward, there is a well-known photograph of Dr. John Lilly, taken in 1962, showing him successfully feeding a young dolphin in a glass tank, giving it a nipple from which a rich man-made formula is being suckled.

One hundred years later, how far we had come.

The tale that is unfolding is one of hope. Mankind is changing, rapidly. There is progress to be seen in our growing recognition of our mysterious friends in the sea. There is a growing love of the dolphins and whales. People do care now. We are in a slow-motion turnaround, at this point over 150 years in the turning....

CHAPTER ELEVEN

"How Might We Seem to Them?"

Perhaps "Native Americans" arrived on the American continent by crossing the land bridge where the Bering Strait now exists. Some say this may have happened as long as 12,000 years ago. Other theories propose that humans arrived by boat from across the Pacific, colonizing the South American continent at an earlier point in time. After all, man-made stone objects much more than 12,000 years old have been found at the southern tip of South America. Mormons claim that the Indians of South America are descended from ancient explorers and colonists from Africa, who were the lost tribes of Israel. There is evidence that there were white people as well as dark people at one time in ancient Peru.

However the "Indians" arrived, they have lived in the Americas for a long time but are less "indigenous" than the Australian, African, or Asian peoples.

It is remarkable that at least one traditional American tribe still retains memories of their wanderings, describing the entire nomadic trail from their beginnings near the Caspian Sea. The Oneida tribe today has its home in northern New York State. In her book entitled *The Walking People*,[1] Oneida author Paula Underwood reveals the story she was raised with. Her grandfather identified her as a Keeper of the tribal story when she was a child, and she committed to memory an enormous tale, the story of their ancient trek.

In the story we experience a lesson learned along the way that has profound philosophical and psychological overtones.

At the ocean's edge for the first time, the tribe encountered an entirely new kind of being, a sort of friendly fish.

Here is the tale:

The Great Swimmers
Now
> *It was also a continuous learning,*
> *This living at the ocean's edge ...*
... From time to time
> *Great Swimmers came—*
> *And these were nearly as great as we*
> *And sometimes larger.*
At first
> *The People were wary of these new swimmers*
> *As they were unknown.*
And yet
> *Greater familiarity caused us to learn*
> *That little concern was merited.*
Rather,
> *These ones seemed to take great pleasure*
> *In swimming among us,*
> *So that we began to swim willingly with them*
> *And to learn from them*
> *Some of the nature of the Ocean.*
For
> *It was these ones*
> *From whom we learned*
> *The deeper nature of Ocean*
> *And how to help the young ones swim.*
They and We
> *Being of different configurations*
> *It was not possible for us*
> *To move nor swim exactly as they,*

And yet much that they did
Was possible for us.
From Them
We learned to forget to breathe
For longer times of swimming
And to survive this circumstance
With increasing ease.
There was something
About the patterns of their communications
Which stirred in us some wonder.
One understood from another
And yet
The manner of it was not clear to us,
So that we began to wonder
About how we might seem to them.
The manner of our communications
was mainly shaped in the open air—
As theirs was mainly in the open water.
Yet
Each might transpose this
To the opposite circumstance
With less, yet meaningful, efficacy.
So that through all this
We began to understand ourselves
In ways
Never thought of before.
And we saw how it was
That these great swimmers and we
Did not seek each other
For sustenance
But for companionship
And for learning.
And
We saw this as a great value.

And

> *Asked ourselves*
> *To remember the value of such learning.*
> *Remembering always*
> *To ask the question:*
> *"How might we seem to them?"*

This is a question worth asking, even now.

The other question we have been asking is: Who are the dolphins? Inevitably, we realize that we must ask this question of ourselves as well. By asking how others see us, we are better able to see ourselves.

Much is revealed in the Oneida story.

First, there is the realization that the dolphins are friendly. To people living on the move through dangerous new territory, this alone must have been an exciting discovery. (We will assume these were dolphins or the beluga, the small white whale, based on size.)

Large fish-like beings who "... take great pleasure in swimming among us ..." was an important new concept. By helping the humans overcome their fear of swimming, they proved themselves to be friendly beings in the ocean.

One must wonder what is meant by the phrase "learning about the deeper nature of Ocean." Perhaps they were referring to some of what we experience today when we go to the home of the wild dolphins and put fear aside to leap into the dark blue, apparently bottomless sea. Or was it more?

Learning to "... forget to breathe ..." is a charming way of describing the first efforts to hold one's breath, which may well have been the first time they had any need to do so.

The observation that they were different but that some actions were similar shows a growing awareness, not only of the dolphins, but also of themselves.

Then comes a remarkable commentary on the communications among the dolphins themselves, which begins an important train of thought.

First, the idea of their communication being something of a secret, which enables the dolphins to observe and comment on the humans, gives the Oneida the suggestion that they are being observed.

Second, a tidy bit of logic about how differences in environment constrain language appears in the suggestion that the dolphins and humans might be able to "… transpose this to the opposite circumstance with less, yet meaningful, efficacy." Amazingly, the ancient Oneida were contemplating exchanging speech with dolphins, by somehow speaking underwater or having dolphins speak above water, improving communication, even though it would still be limited.

Just as Aristotle must have been a keen observer of dolphins to make his comments on their pronunciation, and must have been in a situation where the dolphins had become quite adjusted to human presence to be making sounds above water (which is unusual as we know from current research), so the Oneida must have spent a considerable time with some very friendly dolphins to arrive at these conclusions. Remember, for a dolphin to "speak" above water, it must make sounds through its nose, at a very low pitch and at a slow rate of speed.

Can you say "Hello!" through your nose, in a bass voice, very slowly?

Then, in a striking parallel to the Greek statement about dolphins seeking "friendship for no advantage," the Oneida recognize that there is no predation going on between the two species. For people living in the natural world, without established systems of food supply other than hunting, gathering, and opportunistic feeding, an encounter with a being whose interest in them is so demonstrably friendly, "… for companionship and learning …," must have been an entirely new experience. This is reflected in the final stanza, where the lesson that will be carried with them on their journey is comparable to the universal experience of an encounter with the Other: "How might we seem to them?"

This question demonstrates a fundamental shift in self-awareness.

To observe another who has been observing you and then to consider what is going through its mind requires self-awareness that has left behind total self-absorption. It speaks of a mature mind, whose concerns have begun to extend beyond simple self-interest. To care how another thinks or feels about you is the hallmark of someone who has begun to awaken to compassion.

In this remarkable fragment of ancient memory, we see one of the timeless lessons that lie in the interspecies encounter. When one recognizes another mind's presence and attitudes, one becomes larger, more integrated into the all-encompassing field of life.

"How might we seem to them?"

Where Are We Now?

On our circular journey, moving from the ancient land of Australia westward to India, Sumeria, the Mediterranean, Africa, and Europe, we have followed a subtle spirit, a wave of awakening to the Divine component of the human being. We have discovered many stories of a gentle influence, a wise voice from the deeps counseling humankind, giving hints and even gifts of knowledge and inspiration.

At this point in the tale, we have arrived at the shores of North America, where a New World is being born. We have seen how the dream of a new country embodied the ideals that had been developing within the womb of Europe, carrying the hopes of humanity to a new starting place. We have also found an indigenous tradition, moving eastward, of self-awareness similar to the central message that comes to us from ancient Greece, again given by the dolphins.

And what of America? What has become of that dream and all the human hopes? For several hundred years, the American dream has thrived, bringing inventiveness, exuberant economics, and unlimited curiosity. The whole world contributed people, ideas, cultural treasures, and most importantly, the minds of its people to this enterprise.

America became the vessel of promise for the whole human race, a ship in which we all might sail into a future of equality of opportunity, actualized democracy, and freedom for the spirit.

Recent events show us that the experiment has not produced all the effects hoped for. A new ideology is needed; new icons must be emblazoned on flags. Our current world dilemma calls us to find yet another vessel, yet another set of insights. The pattern of the past shows us that it is from the cetacean families that we are most likely to receive the wisdom, love, and guidance we require.

Next we will explore more recent times, the world of today, to see where this wisdom lies, hidden in plain view.

CHAPTER TWELVE

Dr. John Lilly and the Cetacean Nation

It is time to recognize that the human species has maintained a human-centered, isolated existence on the planet Earth because of its failure to communicate with those of comparable brain size existing in the sea. The cetaceans have a reality separate from the human reality. Their realities, defined in their own terms, their social competence, their surviving for the last fifteen million years, are to be respected, to be researched and the consequences to be legislated into human law.

—Dr. John Lilly, *Communication between Man and Dolphin*[1]

As we have seen, after centuries of reverence and respect, humankind fell into a long period of estrangement from the cetaceans. Once human curiosity took people onto the wide oceans we discovered them again. Forgetting our ancient friendship, we slaughtered them by the tens of thousands each year. Then one man launched a scientific quest to understand their minds, to explore their languages. His story is the story of our modern awakening to the gifts of the cetaceans.

Beginning a New Era: Lilly Meets the Dolphins

A scientist working for the National Institutes of Health (NIH) in the 1950s often found himself participating in debates about the relationship between the brain and the mind. The question was: Does the mind have a separate existence from the brain, or is the mind the byproduct of the chemical and electrical activity of the organ in our head?

One such scientist, who was an MD and a psychoanalyst, decided to investigate. He framed the question this way:

"If I isolate a living, healthy human brain from input, removing all sensory stimulation, will it go to sleep, or will it continue to manifest mental activity?"

He designed an isolation chamber, knowing that he could remove most sensory stimulation by floating a person in warm water in the dark. His ethics about experimentation required that he be the first subject. He climbed into the tank and closed the lid.

The first few hours of the experiment proved easily that the mind existed independently, free to go wherever it wanted.

When he questioned whether any other creature experienced this floating state of mind, someone told him about dolphins, living in warm water with brains that might be equal to our own in size. In 1954 he made a trip to Florida to see for himself what dolphins were all about.

Thus begins the story of John Cunningham Lilly, MD. To the majority of people, no one has been more closely associated with dolphins in modern times. His work has changed our world.

Lilly played a large part in the cresting of the Delphic Wave in America. He brought to everyone's attention the exceptional qualities of the dolphins. His discoveries; his self-rescue from the clutches of people with dark designs; his radical change of heart; his courage, his unique style, and publicly reported spiritual quest; the arrival of the love of his life—all are part of a Human saga, a modern-day hero tale. Two movies based on parts of his life have been made, *Day of the Dolphin* and *Altered States.*

His first visit to the dolphins fascinated John, and he quickly raised money for a series of experiments to explore their brains. John had, several years before, received a patent for something that sounds like a torture device, but which had real value in the world of neurosurgery. He had discovered that he could drive specially designed hollow stainless steel tubes through the skulls of monkeys, into their brains. Since the brain itself has no nerves, there was very little discomfort to the monkey, a huge improvement on techniques used by other researchers. These hollow tubes would then allow him to insert thin wires into their brains to exact depths. With the inserted wires given tiny electrical impulses, John could map the entire brain, seeing for the first time a living, undamaged brain reacting to controlled stimulus. He found the pleasure centers, the pain centers, sleep, orgasm, sight, hearing ... in short, he helped mankind advance his knowledge of the physical brain. John eventually found a way to stimulate the brain with no damage whatsoever and was instrumental in changing the way that neurosurgeons treat the human brain.

He returned to Florida. Much to his horror, the first dolphin placed on an operating table and given anesthesia died immediately. John was shocked but requested another dolphin to work with. It also died as soon as it was anesthetized.

Stepping back, John thought deeply. He suddenly understood what had happened. Dolphins must be "conscious breathers," completely aware of every breath they take. If they lose consciousness, they stop breathing. Humans are "unconscious breathers." If we go to sleep, or are knocked unconscious, we breathe automatically.

John worked with a group of physiologists, anesthetists, and cardiologists to design a method for supplying dolphins with air. His basic design for a dolphin respirator is still in use today. Despite claims to the contrary by a Navy veterinarian, it was Dr. John Lilly who first made it practical to care for dolphins under sedation.

As a byproduct of the unfortunate deaths of the first dolphins, John had the opportunity to observe firsthand the extraordinary size and complexity of the brain of a bottlenose dolphin. After years studying the human brain, he was stunned to see the similarity. Under microscopic examination he saw that their brains are as dense with neurons as ours, and even more convoluted. (The surface of a brain is folded more and more intricately as we go up the ladder of intelligence and sophistication. More convolutions allow for more surface area, which is a measurable sign of complex activity.)

John asked himself a new set of questions: What if he were to dedicate himself to studying the brain of the dolphins, and not only their brain's physiology, but their use of that brain? Quickly he drew up the criteria for an ideal laboratory (on a shore with warm water; close to the US; access to scientific colleagues; not in a city or town) and set his sights on St. Thomas in the US Virgin Islands.

He designed and built one of the most futuristic laboratories ever created. The lab overlooked Nazareth Bay from Dolphin Point. It had a pool underneath it that was recharged by wave action, constantly refreshing the natural seawater. Upstairs were laboratories for sound, photography, computers and electronics, and a unique apartment.

The apartment was built to be flooded to the depth of eighteen inches. It was designed for a project wherein a human would live side-by-side with a dolphin. The apartment was connected to the pool below by a special elevator that enabled John to lift a dolphin up to the labs. (The elevator was designed to allow the dolphins to operate the controls themselves as well.[2])

John's early research into electronic stimulation of brains had put him in a spotlight, trained on him by the military. The US Navy was interested in using remote-controlled animals as deliverers of weapons of mass destruction. Could a horse be remote-controlled, directed to walk up to a command post where its load of explosives could be set off? To the military mind, unwitting animal "suicide bombers" was a reasonable proposition. Lilly's research seemed to say it could work.

He was approached by the Pentagon and asked to give a briefing. John had to learn quickly how to be diplomatic in extricating himself. That he managed to avoid being ensnared in military schemes is a testament to his insight that only public awareness of his work could protect him, that by going public he would be too visible to be coerced.

John set up his Communications Research Institute (CRI) with headquarters in Miami and its main labs in St. Thomas. In Miami John had two dolphins in a swimming pool, and he invited numerous scientists to visit. Carl Sagan came and afterwards wrote a long narrative about his visit. He and John shared an interest in extra-terrestrial intelligence, and the dolphin research was John's method for exploring it directly.[3] It was at this time that John began envisioning the cetaceans as actual "ETs," non-terrestrial beings, and the need to protect them with human laws.

Aldous Huxley also visited the "Miami Dolphins," enjoying immensely his time swimming with them. Another visitor was Gregory Bateson, a well-known anthropologist, who was to become one of John's lifelong friends. Bateson moved to St. Thomas, where he took over management of the research programs while John sought funding and developed a strong advisory board and support system for CRI.

It was Bateson who discovered Margaret Howe. She was a college graduate with a degree in biology who was skilled in observation. She was working at a local hotel on St. Thomas. Bateson hired her immediately to work at CRI.

John conceived of a project in which Margaret was to live with Peter, a large male dolphin, for ten weeks in the flooded apartment. Six days a week, Margaret would interact with Peter as his only companion. Margaret was to attempt to teach Peter English words. John observed that a dolphin was more likely to learn to speak as we do than we would be able to speak as they do. Compared to humans, a dolphin's sonic range overlaps the frequencies used in radio technologies, and dolphins are familiar with an extremely complex sonic world. We are almost deaf to the world they live in.[4]

The experiment was a success, showing that a dolphin will learn easily from a human, adapting his behavior to suit the conditions. Communication between the two of them improved rapidly, with Peter mimicking Margaret's voice remarkably well.

One of the more unusual discoveries from this experiment in interspecies co-habitation was the way in which Peter transferred his sexual attentions to Margaret. Dolphins are very sensual beings, endlessly playing games of caressing, stroking, and tickling each other. They have sexual encounters very frequently and with whoever happens to be near, with no reservations as to sex or age. Theirs is an extraordinarily exhilarating sex life, free of all restraint.

Peter was horny. He had been separated from his two female companions, who were just downstairs, and with whom he carried on continual conversations even though they were out of sight. Peter made his needs evident to Margaret, who was uneasy with the situation. She wondered whether Peter was telling his girlfriends about her "frigid" behavior. Peter was gentle, eventually keeping his penis inside his body, instead of erecting it and sliding it around on Margaret's legs. He liked to mouth her legs, as a form of dolphin foreplay, but she didn't like that, so he would jam a rubber ball in his mouth, to keep it from closing too far, and then slide his teeth up and down her calves. Margaret was frustrated by all the time taken up by Peter's advances, so she decided to stimulate him manually, to gain a moment's release from his desires. This worked well, and research was able to continue.

Photographs of Margaret and Peter show a warm companionship that developed during those amazing ten weeks in the Caribbean in the summer of 1964.

John solved a mystery during those years in the Virgin Islands that had puzzled many researchers. Have you ever wondered how a dolphin sleeps? Floating in water continuously, breathing through a hole in the top of their head, they cannot afford to doze off. Nor can they go unconscious as we do. A process of careful and continuous observation, which his laboratory design enabled, answered the question. John had built one of the world's first "participatory" labs, where it was possible to live with dolphins, and he discovered that the dolphins sleep in one of the most amazing ways imaginable.

In higher animals brains are divided into two hemispheres. Each is a mirror of the other, although different functions take place in each side. We are familiar with the idea that each side has different characteristics. Yet, for most of us, this is an abstract idea that we use to talk about the different types of thinking, or the differences between men and women, or different people, one more "rational" and one more "intuitive," one more "linear" and one more "artistic."

For the dolphin, an awareness of the two sides of the brain is not abstract at all. To sleep, they put one side of their brain to rest, which causes the eye on the opposite side of their head to close. They keep the other half of their brain awake, alert to dangers, breathing and navigating. After about twenty minutes of rest they awaken the rested side and put the other half to bed. Dolphins don't sleep much, but when they do, they really know how to "turn it off."

John had two locations for CRI, and they were very different. The Miami offices and labs were traditionally scientific, focused on hard research and administration of measurable results. In St. Thomas, a softer, more interactive approach was taken. In context, this was a huge breakthrough.

Science at that time was "specimen-based." All creatures were seen as organisms whose internal and external processes were the provinces of cold analysis. Little to no care was taken for their comfort or emotional needs. Even the suggestion that an animal might have feelings was debated for many years, and the idea that they might have higher functions was unthinkable.

In a report delivered to the American Medical Association in 1963, Dr. Lilly said:

> The feelings of weirdness came on us as the sounds of this small whale seemed more and more to be forming words in our own language. We felt we were in the presence of Some-

thing, or Someone who was on the other side of a transparent barrier, which up to this point we hadn't even seen. The dim outlines of a Someone began to appear. We began to look at this whale's body with newly opened eyes and began to think in terms of its possible 'mental processes,' rather than in terms of the classical view of a conditionable, instinctually functioning 'animal.'⁵

A New Tool for Exploring the Mind

John was rapidly approaching a dividing line, drawn on the water.

Ivan Tors had made the movie *Flipper* with John as a scientific advisor. Tors was inspired by John's work, and when the film was completed he gave John three of the dolphins who had been in the film. Tors was to go on to produce the *Flipper* TV series, which had an enormous impact on the world, stimulating a wave of love for dolphins.

Tors' wife was a well-known psychological researcher, whose work with LSD was very influential. John had been encouraged to try using LSD during his years at NIH, but had always refused. He didn't want his isolation tank investigations to be confused by the addition of another element. But now, with Constance Tors as a guide, he decided to give it a try.

He flew to California for the session, and had a magnificent experience. He had hoped to discover the source for his migraine headaches, and not only discovered their source, but was able to correct the problem internally, and never had another migraine. He tried another session a short time later with Constance, but was not in a good emotional state, and was somewhat disappointed.

It was 1963, and LSD was still legal, and considered very promising in the field of psychological research. John obtained a supply of it from NIH and took it to St. Thomas. He wanted to know whether the combination of isolation and LSD might lead him to more important understandings of the mind, but was not certain whether his body might forget to breathe, or might drown while on the drug in his float tank.

He decided to give LSD to several dolphins.

When he ingested the drug in California, he found himself among the stars, without any of the familiar surroundings from his Earth life, just floating in limitless space. When he watched the dolphins' reaction to the LSD he observed that they would look at the walls and floor of their pool and appeared to not trust what they were seeing, so they used their sonar to scan the floor and walls. He theorized that perhaps their experiences might have some parallels to his own.

The six dolphins given LSD had no noticeable problems with the experience and afterward became even more friendly and sweet-tempered.[6]

John then decided to try floating in the isolation tank while on LSD. He injected himself with the magical elixir and climbed into the tank. The warm salt water supported him well. Closing his eyes, he left his body consciousness behind. He became a point of Self, a focus of awareness and knowledge. He could feel the dolphins in the pool below, and found himself in deep communion with them.

In that experience, John Lilly made conscious contact with the dolphin's true nature, a moment that they had awaited for many centuries. John recognized that dolphins are sentient beings, self-aware, with a consciousness not totally unlike our own, yet certainly alien. He had encountered the Other. He saw, as if in a flash of light, that dolphins and whales are the most successful species the planet has yet hosted. He realized that the oceans of the world are their vast "homelands," a nation, and that they are the citizens of that nation, the largest and greatest nation on the planet. He was saddened to recognize the uses that he and others had put them to, while they persisted in their loving kindness toward us.

It was after this encounter that he made a famous decision. He said:

> It's time I went away and studied my own mind, for the wonder of the dolphins poses the question of where we humans

are heading. Apparently into darkness, with the wiping out of an underwater civilization that has managed the oceans with superb poise and conservation for millions of years before upstart Man appeared and began to ravage Earth and Sea.[7]

John was exposed to the telepathic awareness of the dolphins when he decided to close his labs. Of the eight dolphins he had at that time, five chose to commit suicide within days of his decision, before he had told anyone of his choice.

As part of the scientific establishment, John realized the limits of traditional Western thought about the mind. He knew of only one direction to turn for guidance. He began a deep study of religious texts about the nature of the mind, particularly the Yoga Sutras of Patanjali. These texts focus on mental control through concentration, meditation, and contemplation leading to stillness. The state of stillness becomes a vessel for the Soul to manifest itself through. John had been fascinated by the LSD experience and he joined his science, his spiritual studies, and his passion for exploring the vast possibilities of the mind into a personal "yoga" that led to years of experimentation with psychedelic drugs.[8]

He wrote about his insights and his system for codifying the levels of operation of the mind, his experiences with ECCO,[9] and his adventures among non-human intelligences. His insights have led hundreds of thousands of people into clear understandings of their own inner landscapes. His books are considered classics and remain very valuable resources for the cybernaut.

Years later, Dr. Lilly returned to dolphin research. He set up a project in California to explore a computer-aided interspecies language called JANUS after the Roman god with two faces. He made an agreement with two dolphins to bring them into the program, take excellent care of them for five years, and then release them back into the sea. The project was successful on many levels, but was hampered by the slowness of computers in the early '80s. Given the speed of the average desktop computer today, his experiments would now go much further, much faster.

His dolphin friends, Joe and Rosie, were eventually released, seven years later, by a group of dedicated individuals who willingly took over responsibility for their preparation and release. Documented by *National Geographic* Magazine and receiving much publicity, this project was not without controversy. At the end, Rosie became pregnant. Many friends of Joe and Rosie—people who took an interest in their well-being after befriending them at John's research site—took this to be a sign that they wanted to have a baby among human families.

John had thought of this years before, and his wife Toni eagerly pursued the idea of having dolphins and their babies living side-by-side with young human couples who were themselves having babies, so the children could grow up together. John's dream of many years had been to live in an "interspecies village," but Joe and Rosie were on the road to release, and it was not to be. The momentum was too great, and the man who took on the role of "untraining" them saw an opportunity for himself to redeem his former occupation, as a dolphin trainer for oceanariums and the *Flipper* TV series.

On the day chosen for their "release," Joe and Rosie swam away from their canal-side pen slowly, returning to swim among their human friends a few last times, trying to get their attention. But the humans had decided to ignore them, believing this was best for them. They were last seen heading down the canal, toward the open sea.[10]

The Cetacean Nation

In 1996 I became a friend of Dr. Lilly's. He was in his late 70s when we met and he was still as brilliant and irascible as ever. When I asked him what legacy he would be most proud to leave behind, he unhesitatingly said, "The Cetacean Nation."[11]

Proposed long ago in his writings and repeated often, the idea is simple and elegant: John has pointed out that cetaceans deserve protection under law just as much as humans do. He asserts that they have inalienable rights, just as we do. His suggestion is that they be given representation among the community of nations, to protect their interests.

Yes, that means a seat in the General Assembly of the United Nations. Or rather, a tank. Like so many things about dolphins, it is not without a sense of humor that this image comes to mind, but it is also deadly serious.

Along with recognition of their status as special creatures, with highly ordered minds, sophisticated social skills, and complex language and forms of communication that may place them far above us on a scale of self-awareness and conscious interdependence, John saw the need to understand them much better. It is not a well-known story of how John Lilly came to seek interspecies communication. Why was he interested in learning to speak Delphinese, or to have a dolphin speak English?

The answer is simple: so they can represent their interests in the United Nations. Short of having a dolphin in a tank in the General Assembly with headphones on, listening to debates over the Law of the Sea, it might be feasible to have some form of communication that could be used to inform human representatives of their thoughts and desires.

John and I both spoke at an international conference on this topic, sharing the podium for our common passion.[12] He graciously invited me to use some of his presentation time to articulate our common goal, with a vision of how it could work. We later did a live internet broadcast together, discussing this idea.[13] In each instance John asked me to articulate how I see the founding of the Cetacean Nation.

In my mind's eye, I see a wave of children walking across the plaza in front of the United Nations Headquarters in New York, nearly eight hundred of them, led by a girl and a boy. The children are from every nation on Earth, four from each country. They walk up to the door and knock. An adult comes to the door and invites them all inside. They flood into the great hall, and the two who led stand before the podium of the General Secretary to address the General Assembly.

They read from a scroll. The scroll states the desires of the children of the world for the people of land and sea to have peace between them, forever. They ask that the oceans be recognized as a single, world-surrounding nation, and that the cetaceans be represented as one people among the community of nations.[14] This extraordinary document is signed by all species of the cetacean family, by proxy.

A petition is also presented with hundreds of millions of signatures, accompanied by endorsements from scientific, religious, and political groups and the sponsorship of several nations. Televised to the world, this will serve as a unifying moment, a time when people everywhere accept a more humble human role in nature.

A globally important ceremony like this, marking the moment when humans accept the presence of other minds, other self-aware beings, would be like a doorway into a new life for us all. By this one symbolic act, we can begin the balancing process that must take place for the human family to become sustainable, integrated into the system of life.

Among the ideas around this initiative, I see a special school established where carefully selected young people are educated in interspecies diplomacy, prepared to mediate between the human family and the cetaceans. They will have to be exceptionally healthy: physically, emotionally, and mentally.[15] They will be given every advantage to learn the subtle nuances of communication with the ancient races of the seas, and they must be trained to link their human identities into a larger whole, a group mind, just as the dolphins and whales do. This cadre of people will act as guardians of the Cetacean Nation's interests, and as representatives to them of human needs.

Aspiring to be a dolphin advocate, an interspecies diplomat trained in every way to be an optimized and balanced human, would give an exciting new goal to millions of young people.

Until this dream becomes actualized, we can begin by placing the need for healthy oceans at the top of our priorities. We can speak for the necessity of stopping pollution, ceasing the destruction of critical habitat, stopping all unsustainable fishing practices, and of course, the end to all whaling and the killing of dolphins.

Toward Recognition of the Cetacean Nation

A small group of interested people has formed around the Cetacean Nation initiative. We have been developing certain basic understandings and starting points. We are each aware that we ought not to claim communication with dolphins or whales until we can demonstrate it, so we use our critical faculties to define certain unequivocal, basic, life-sustaining principles, shared by all self-aware beings. From principles come policies, from policies can be developed practices.

As a first principle, we recognize that their nation is the water of our world. The policy of the Cetacean Nation is to willingly cede each coastal nation certain rights to use and help protect the waters. They ask that all water everywhere be protected, respected, and returned to the use of the citizens of the waters. By accepting responsibility to regard water as the home element of the Cetacean Nation, mankind will begin to clean up the world. We owe it to them, and we will all benefit by doing so. (See dolphintale.com.)

All we have to do is get past smiling about the idea, and do it. This is one of those Dolphin things, funny at first, but deeper than it looks.[16]

The Momentum of our Belief

In terms of the Tale that we have been following, it was John Lilly who was the modern herald of the new era, with its kinder, more correct relationship with the dolphins. When he announced to the world in 1961 that dolphins have minds and language, many things changed in that instant. No longer were we alone in Universe. Suddenly there was publicly spoken awareness that we are part of an intelligent, inter-communicating matrix of life, mysterious and vast. What histories might the whales and dolphins have witnessed? Could they hold memories of former epochs, such as Lemurian tales or Atlantean sagas from continents long since washed away, submerged, or buried under miles of ice? Here on Earth for 150 times as long as humans, they may know far more about us than we do.

Perhaps they don't speak in the way we do because they already did that, and have discovered better ways to share their inner selves.

To the average person, the importance of John Lilly's news in 1961 about dolphins was not immediately apparent. Take a look at the popular culture in those days, though. You will see a proliferation in the magazines and Sunday comics of cartoon scenes with people talking to dolphins. You will see Flipper at the movies and on TV, the book and movie *Day of the Dolphin*, the SETI project, *Time* magazine and many others reporting on Lilly's research, and a flood of other interspecies themes. Like a health-enhancing virus, this positive realization quickly spread.

We are all creators of a set of beliefs that we encourage each other to maintain. We share some basic agreements, no matter what our other biases might be. For example, nothing keeps us from smashing into each other as we drive down the road except the commonly accepted symbol of the strip of paint that separates us. We also tend to believe that animals can be treated with less respect than humans.

One could characterize the massive scale and momentum of our beliefs as a supertanker, a vast ship sailing on the open sea. So much conviction, so much effort to build and maintain a stable belief system has gone into our way of thinking that it is not easy to change course. What rudder can be turned to change direction? Where is the steering wheel, the helm of our destiny?

Like the real supertanker sailing our oceans this very moment, taking many miles to change course, fifteen miles to come to a stop, the system of human belief is resilient and resistant to change.

When a new, fundamentally different idea comes to us, we are not usually different the next day. So it was with Lilly's announcement to the world that dolphins have minds and language. A bright flash for an instant, but the steady course of history seemed unchanged. Was it?

> We are often asked, "If the dolphins are so intelligent, why aren't they ruling the world?"
>
> My considered answer to this is—they may be too wise to try to rule the world. The question can easily be turned around. Why does man or individual men want to rule the world?
>
> I feel that it is a very insecure position to want to rule all of the other species and the vast resources of our planet. This means a deep insecurity with the "universes" inside one's self....
>
> It is my deep feeling that unless we work with respect, with discipline, and with gentleness with the dolphins that they will once more turn away from us. Apparently at the time of Aristotle or just preceding his time, the dolphins approached man. By A.D. 50 in the time of the Romans, they had turned away from man not to come back until this century.
>
> —Dr. John Lilly, *The Mind of the Dolphin* [17]

CHAPTER THIRTEEN

Songs from the Sea: Humpback Whales and the Birth of Environmental Activism

F loating there, I was in a trance, hypnotized not by any jewel, but by the singing of a massive humpback whale. It sounded close, so very close. But where was it? It seemed I could see forever down, and all around. At forty-five to fifty feet in length and up to 90,000 pounds, this titanic mammal should have been easy to see.

Holding my breath, I slipped silently beneath the surface and allowed myself to glide downward. The further I descended, the louder became the haunting, sepulchral melody. Through my fins, up my legs, until my entire body actually vibrated, I could feel the resonance of this leviathan. I was so damned near! Yet there was not a thing to see in any direction except blue. Endless, brilliant, featureless blue. The sea around me was saturated with song, as if I were in a cathedral with a 45-ton pipe organ filling the air. I was enveloped in the spirit of this phantom whale, spellbound, with time suspended. I felt as if I were drawing energy directly from the sound waves, alive with this life force pulsing through the water, coursing through my body, then dispersing through an infinite sea.

I could have kept going down. That was the easy part. Getting back up would have been another story. I never did see the Whale, but it hardly matters, for his song is within me still.[1]

. . .

Less than ten years after Dr. Lilly's announcement to the world of the presence of other minds on our planet, two researchers studying sound and the weird noises of whales were sitting in a boat in the warm waters off Bermuda. It was late at night, and they were listening through headphones to the sounds of the underwater world.

On that fateful night, one of the two men was a concert cellist. As he listened, he realized that he had just heard the same phrase repeated. The sounds were accurately recreated, structured into phrases, and it suddenly became evident that he was listening to a *song*.

Drs. Roger Payne and Scott McVay published a paper describing their discovery that whales sing songs within the ocean depths. This was in 1967, when the world was just beginning to get used to the idea that dolphins talk. Eventually it was determined that humpback whales from the same ocean all sing the same song, and that the song changes each year.[2]

With this new idea appearing in the minds of millions, yet another "course correction" was made to the rudder of our "belief ship." People began to dream of hearing the songs of whales, and Dr. Payne satisfied this desire by issuing an album that has sold more copies than any other album of natural sounds, called *Songs of the Humpback Whale*. I venture to say that everyone reading this book has heard this recording, many times over. If not the entire album, you have certainly heard excerpts from it in commercials, pop songs, symphonies, and soundtracks.[3] When the *Voyager I* and *II* spacecraft were sent on their long missions to escape the bounds of our solar system, a plaque was placed on the outside showing two humans, with directions for any intelligent alien finding the craft to be able to figure out where we are. Also onboard was a recording of sounds from Earth. Among them was a selection from *Songs of the Humpback Whale*.[4]

Payne and McVay gave us another piece of the picture forming in the minds of millions of people, of an intelligent and loving presence in the sea. In this case, it was science that supplied this delightful image.

Dr. Payne went on to become a pre-eminent whale researcher and spokesman for their protection. His book *Among Whales* is a powerful and beautifully written prose song, a 400-page gem of science, observation, passion, and prose that lifts the spirit and changes forever the way we see the whales. Or at least, one must hope his message does this.

> ... I believe that the principal gift that whales offer humanity is that they are the only animals that can impress us enough to persuade us to change our minds about the importance of the wild world ... whales escape much turmoil. With increasing size comes increasing serenity. Large creatures find less and less extremes, less upheaval.... With size comes tranquility. For a whale a passing thunderstorm is but the footfall of an ant, and a full gale an annoying jiggling of its pleasant bed. If you were a whale, all but the grandest things would pass beneath your notice. As the largest animal, including the biggest dinosaur, that has ever lived on the earth, you could afford to be gentle, to view life without fear, to play in the dark, to sleep soundly anywhere, whenever and however long you liked, and to greet the world in peace—even to view with bemused curiosity something as weird as a human scuba diver as it bubbles away, encased in all that bizarre gear. It is the sense of tranquility—of life without urgency, power without aggression—that has won my heart to whales.
>
> —Roger Payne, *Among Whales*[5]

Payne has made the painful observation that the health of the oceans is in great peril, out of balance, unable to correct its chemical mixtures, temperatures, currents, and contents as the oceans have done since the beginning of time. As he puts it, the oceans have AIDS. Their defenses against environmental ill-health have been so compromised that we must now think of the oceans as being in dire straits, struggling for life.

Greenpeace

Once the public heard that whales sing, a new value was found in them. But, although a sense of the majesty of whales was widespread, there was no substantial popular sentiment about protecting them. By the time a group of radical adventurers decided to interfere with nuclear testing in the Aleutian Islands and was unable to successfully sail there, the protection of whales was conceived as a worthy alternative.

Thwarted in their anti-nuclear campaign, the adventurers created this new task for themselves: they would save the whales. They set out in the rusty *Phyllis Cormack* looking for the Russian whaling fleet, the largest in the Pacific Ocean. Using coordinates given them by an insider at the Pentagon, they hoped to film themselves in the act of harassing the whalers, preventing them from harpooning a whale.

This is the beginning of Greenpeace, a ragtag mix of scientists, hippies, and eco-freaks who wanted to do something, anything, to make a difference. They had sailed out to sea and found nothing. They were alone, almost out of fuel, at the turning point when their supplies were only adequate to return to port, when a fog enveloped them. No sign of the whalers had been seen. The captain pulled out his *I Ching* (a Chinese oracle book) and consulted it. It told him that stillness was a virtue. He decided they would remain where they were. The next day he consulted the oracle again, and this time it said, "The Southwest furthers." He set course for the southwest, knowing he would have to stop soon. They broke out of the fog bank to find themselves in the midst of the Russian fleet.

The rest is well-known history. Images flashed around the world of men in small inflatable boats, racing in front of giant ships. Harpoons were aimed at whales just in front of the little boats. A few whales were protected; several were killed despite these heroic efforts. Harpoons flew over the heads of the protectors and buried themselves in the backs of the whales in scarlet explosions, blood bathing the protectors in torrents.[6]

The world was stunned. The very idea of a human putting their own life on the line to protect animals was unthinkable before this. What could have made them do this? Then the haunting sounds of the whale would come from the radio or the TV, and the two images merged.... "Oh, yes, whales sing, don't they? I think that is just beautiful. I'm glad someone is out there trying to protect them."

One can make a strong argument that the environmental movement itself, the massive popularization of concerns for the living system of the planet, came from the early work of Greenpeace and their dedicated efforts to protect the whales.

Minds, language, songs, lives on the line ... this all fits the Tale, the story of their esoteric influence, their deep effect on our mutual history. We awoke to oceans full of song. The cetaceans, persevering through time to provide images and ideas, without speaking, without artifacts, were changing the course of history.

> We come to speak Truth
> and to wage ImageWar
> on Ogo, animal man.
> —Peter Shenstone, *Legend of the Golden Dolphin* [7]

A Carousel of Whales

Tales of highly-charged encounters with the wisdom of whales could be a book in itself. An example: When a group of whale enthusiasts was taken out to the Farralon Islands off California's northern coast a few years ago, a young man came along with a didgeridoo, the Australian drone instrument. When whales were sighted on the horizon, he went below and placed his instrument against the steel hull. On deck someone was watching the whales with binoculars. At the same moment that the musician began playing, the whales changed course, making straight for the boat. Someone tugged on the sleeve of the man with the binoculars, saying, "Hey, you better check this out!"

He dropped his spyglasses and looked around. Whales were converging on them from all directions. The musician was told to keep playing by his excited shipmates. The whales arrived, circling the boat. Several species were noted—blue whales, fin whales, and humpbacks. Then several of the blue whales moved into a tighter concentric ring, closer to the boat. They were vigorously swimming in a circle, rising and diving like a living carousel. Astonished, the people on the boat fell silent, realizing that the whales were stirring a huge vortex in the ocean with them in the middle. Their eighty-five-foot sailboat began to spin....[8]

One can hardly credit this to chance. Some great wordless intention was evident to those present, and the effect was life-changing for many on board. An interaction had occurred between two self-aware species, a dance to music that brought everyone present into the circle of celebration.

This lively spirit, dancing in circles around our confusions, singing to us of ancient and future memories, of a world that is worth celebrating, has inspired people everywhere. Around the world today, people by the millions are recycling cans and bottles, making compost of their kitchen scraps, asking for cars that don't pollute, building more energy-efficient homes, and doing what they can to clean their local environment. Millions of volunteer hours are poured into campaigns to make the world healthy again while building a joyous spirit of community. Everyone who does these practical things to reduce their "ecological footprint" is, in a small way, acknowledging that the system has limits, yet this is not limiting to our joyous spirits. All this was somehow set in motion by our love of the dolphins and whales, another appearance of the Delphic Wave in our time.

CHAPTER FOURTEEN

Dolphins in the Net

The dolphins of the eastern tropical Pacific Ocean have a mysterious relationship with yellowfin tuna. For reasons no one knows, the tuna like to swim in large schools underneath dolphins. Recognizing this, fishermen learned to set nets around the dolphins to catch the tuna, hauling them all out of the water. When this practice first began, the dolphins were disregarded, allowed to drown in the nets as the tuna were brought in. Tens of thousands of them were killed each year. Known to scientists, this problem had been written about, films were made about it, and endless debates occurred, attempting to find solutions to what was perceived as an economic issue. Could the tuna be caught, without huge expense, in any other way?

Tuna is a widely loved fish, well liked in most culinary traditions, but especially loved by the Americans and Japanese. Less prosperous countries in Central and South America, with limited exports, consider the tuna fishery a vital part of their economy.

By 1974 as many as 194,000 dolphins were being killed each year in the Eastern Tropical Pacific tuna fishery. To grasp the enormity of this slaughter, let me re-state this: twenty-two dolphins per hour, every day, around the clock. One dolphin dying as "bycatch" and tossed overboard every three minutes of every hour. The death toll was beyond belief.

In an effort to lower this number, when the Marine Mammal Protection Act was being developed in the United States, provisions were included to discourage American and foreign involvement in this type of tuna fishing. Once the law was passed in 1972, the effect was dramatic. Observers were posted on boats to record the deaths of dolphins, new gear was developed to allow the dolphins to escape, and both captains and crews were given classes in how to avoid endangering the dolphins. Dropping from the hundreds of thousands to around 20,000 per year, the death toll was greatly reduced.

Then reports began coming in from onboard observers whose lives had been threatened. They had had explosives thrown at them to drive them inside their cabins, they had been offered bribes, and they had been told they would be dropped overboard in the night if they reported the actual numbers of dolphins being killed.

Earth Island Institute mounted an extraordinarily well-organized campaign to bring public pressure on this dolphin-killing industry, calling for a consumer boycott of all tuna and particularly brands that were not "dolphin-safe." They had begun campaigning for change in 1984. There was some response, but little changed.

Then two unlikely factors entered into the picture that did the trick.

The first was a young biologist who daringly went undercover to see for himself what was actually happening. He signed onto a Panamanian tuna fishing boat and became a cook's assistant, brought along a small video camera, and acted like he was not mentally healthy. He told the fishermen that he was videotaping the voyage to prove to his father that he could hold a job.

The famous videotapes by Sam LaBudde shocked the world: horrible images of dolphins trapped in netting, being dragged up and over pulleys, thrashing and squealing; dolphins flopping on the deck of the boat, being kicked into the water or ignored as they died, gasping amidst the machinery. Over and over the images were played on TV, at conferences, and around the world. I attended a presentation given by LaBudde and Paul Watson in January of 1990 at a private college in Colorado, where we all sat aghast at the images we were shown. Sam had placed his life on the line. Many of us were outraged by the callousness of the industry and pledged not to eat tuna again until this practice stopped.

That same year a group of young female high school students took a trip to Florida to spend a week at The Dolphin Research Center. They returned to their school near Denver, Colorado, with a determination to do something about what they had learned regarding the tuna-dolphin problem.

At their school they saw that tuna was on the menu in the cafeteria. They decided to ask the school board to ban tuna from lunchrooms. One of the girls' parents was a friend of a newspaper reporter. He managed to get an article and a photograph into the next day's local paper, and bigger papers noticed the story.[1] Soon the successful school lunch protest by the girls was making news around the country. Other schools followed quickly, and the issue was placed before the public in a new way.

Public pressure, led by Earth Island and other activist groups, now amounted to a real threat to the economics of tuna fishing: people stopped buying it. The combined images of the dying dolphins and the smiling faces of the young women somehow added up to a convincing argument, swaying the minds of millions of consumers.

On April 12, 1990, the three largest tuna-selling companies in the US agreed to cease buying any tuna "caught by methods that harm dolphins or other marine mammals." A voluntary program labeling tuna as "dolphin-safe" was instituted, and the death toll dropped by another 95 percent.

Cocaine and Dolphins

The issue remains, however. Dolphins are still killed by the thousands in the Eastern Tropical Pacific in the pursuit of tuna. In 1996 the *Los Angeles Times* reported that fishing boats sold after the boycott were bought by the cocaine cartels of South America, who operate them without restraint. Estimated to be one of the major pipelines for cocaine imports into the US, two dolphin-killing tuna boats were apprehended in 1996 with millions of dollars' worth of cocaine onboard. The drug is sometimes called "atun blanco," or "white tuna" by the cartel. In addition, demand for tuna around the world has allowed them to maintain a lucrative business in these fish, affording them a means to launder their ill-gotten gains from cocaine.

The Global Agreement on Trades and Tariffs (GATT) and the North American Free Trade Agreement (NAFTA) have now threatened the laws instituted by the US to protect dolphins, and the labeling of dolphin-safe tuna has been compromised. Stringent laws protecting marine mammals and other species have been called "barriers to free trade." Under global agreements protecting corporate commerce, the laws of individual nations are falling by the wayside. There is still much to be done to protect marine mammals.[2]

> Dolphins are not an accidental catch in the tuna purse seine industry. They are chased for approximately an hour until they are exhausted. Then the mile-long net is set around them. During closure underwater bombs are detonated near the areas where the net is still open to keep the dolphins in the net, that is, to prevent the dolphins from escaping from the net (because tuna will escape with them). Thousands of dolphins can be encircled in this way, and all of them can end up dead, especially during equipment breakdowns at night. I have seen hundreds of dolphins die in single sets of the net, and more often than not, the net only had dead dolphins and no tuna.
>
> The best way to enforce the existing law prohibiting the import of tuna which kills dolphins is to require that all tuna boats who provide the tuna be inspected and not be allowed to have speedboats. The speedboats can be replaced with boats of more appropriate velocity—fast enough to carry out efficient net work, but too slow to chase dolphins.

In addition, the common practice of ... shooting all of the rough-toothed dolphins, pilot whales, and false killer whales in the area before setting the nets ... should be banned and enforced.

—Congressional testimony of Dr. Ken Marten, former National Marine Fisheries Service porpoise observer and dolphin research biologist[3]

That We Care At All

For our purposes let me point out another, deeper aspect of this situation, namely, that the story of Greenpeace and the dolphin-tuna issue would have been unthinkable as recently as forty years ago.

We can see it this way: around the world came the Delphic Wave at a critical moment when humans required a new way of seeing themselves as part of the world. The whales sang out, they called us to protect them and to clean up the world, to save it from ourselves. The dolphins showed their suffering to a young man and swam gracefully into the dreams of young women, asking us to act with compassion. A redirection of humanity has been occurring around us and through us for the last forty years. The whales braved the harpoons; the dolphins died in the nets; all to startle the human world into wakefulness.

The idea that dolphins ought to be cared for, that they are different than tuna, that the plight of being captured and killed as a "bycatch" is anything to care about, is extraordinary in itself. When millions of other fish and wildlife are killed indiscriminately in virtually all other fisheries to bring to our tables the foods of the sea, why do we single out the dolphins for such protection? What is it about the dolphins that tugs at our heartstrings, causing us to "take up arms" against those who abuse them? What hidden cord ties their fate to our hearts?

I believe that the presence of dolphins among us—close enough to touch, to laugh and clap with, to swim among, and to witness the mysteries and magic of their smiling souls—has taught us that they are special beings, full of the many traits we wish for ourselves. Many millions of people have seen the exuberance, willingness, and creativity of the dolphins who live in the embassies we call oceanariums and aquariums. They come away knowing that a dolphin is a very special companion, a planetary partner whose intelligence and good will match or exceed our own. This has been a powerful lesson for us all. The sacrifices of these few, if in fact it has been a sacrifice, have been the salvation of millions of lives.

We have personalized the cetacean families, and we no longer can tolerate their suffering. They are now being recognized as our friends and allies.

CHAPTER FIFTEEN

The Crystal Whales

Nerrivik lives at the bottom of the sea, and the dirt in her hair is the animals that my people hunt. Because Nerrivik has only one arm, she needs help combing her hair. The shaman helps Nerrivik to comb her hair, so the People can hunt and eat. In his spirit body he goes to her. The assistance of the shaman in altered states of consciousness brings the whales and dolphins to the People.

—Interview by the author with an Inupiat Elder, 1992

The Flower of Life

In 1991 I converted a school bus into a home, with solar panels on the roof and a complete living space inside, including kitchen, bedroom, dining space, and bathroom. I moved my little "home" onto a piece of land in northern New Mexico, a magnificent location far from anywhere. I was on an open plain, without trees, but with one of the best vistas in the world. I could see 150 miles in the brilliantly clear, clean air. It was isolated and perfect for me at that time in my life.

I was in retreat. I had spent almost three years with a group of people developing a body of teachings called the "Flower of Life." We had set up the Naakal Mystery School where we offered three-day residential workshops on the esoteric subject of "sacred geometry." These included the teaching of a special meditation called the Merkaba. The classes were exciting, mysterious, and elegant. There was an air of something powerful happening, something very important. One of my roles was to help adapt the teachings for a wider audience.

I had not joined this group of people as a "surfer," simply riding a wave of speculative spirituality. My initial interest in the Flower of Life and the Merkaba meditation arose from an unrequited desire to find a way to communicate with dolphins. I had reasoned that a language based on breathing and images of perfectly pure forms might be universal, understandable by all self-aware creatures everywhere. Perhaps by teaching ourselves how to breathe consciously and to deeply identify with ideal forms we could find a way to talk with dolphins.

At the time I was unaware of the history of the Merkaba tradition. Only years later, while tracing the Delphic Wave back into Sumerian history, did I discover for myself its ancient origins. As a Gnostic mystery teaching, it had survived hundreds of centuries of oral transmission. It had first been taught by the Apkallu, the amphibian dolphin-men of old, eventually passing into the traditions of Jewish Kabalism, Sufi mysticism, and even para-Christian secret societies such as the Rosicrucians and Masons.

Part of my fascination with the Flower of Life teachings was the connection between special breathing and expanded consciousness. In the practice of the Flower of Life version of the Merkaba traditions, one visualizes a tube of light passing through the vertical axis of a pair of tetrahedrons of light surrounding one's body. As the tetrahedrons are spun in the imagination, the breath is transformed. It seems to enter the top of the head, and to expand into the mind and heart.

It takes no great leap to imagine this as being similar to the experience of a dolphin, who is actually breathing through the top of its head. Since the latter stages of the meditation open vistas of transdimensional insight, I was drawn to wonder how dolphins experience themselves. Do they have an inner worldview akin to this, of interconnectedness and light? At this early stage in my research I saw the Merkaba work as a gift that was leading me toward the dolphins.

I was unaware of its dangers.

In 1985 I had been the first person to be taught the meditation of the Merkaba by a man who claimed to have learned it from a discarnate being. That means it could have come from another plane in the universe or a faraway world of highly intelligent dolphin-like beings. He was introduced to me as Akbar, a sewing-machine repairman and ex-student from a Sufi community. However, when we founded the school in 1987, he peremptorily announced that his name was actually Drunvalo Melchizedek and that he was a "walk-in" from the thirteenth dimension. He had traveled across millions of years of galactic time and arranged to "borrow" the Sufi's body.

Eventually I was asked to be the school's first director, a job I was happy to take.

But human issues got in the way. My directorship of the Naakal Mystery School lasted only a few months. In effect, I presided over the collapse of an experiment in "multi-dimensional ethics." Confusion was a byproduct of the work we were doing, which was not our intention. We had entered a world of bright light and deep darkness that we had little real skill in navigating. The thirteenth dimension does not fit easily into the realities of our 3-D world, but that is another story for a different book. We closed the school and I bought some land nearby. I moved my converted school bus onto it to see where the Dolphin Story might lead me next.

The Wave Comes to My Door

My neighbor began coming to visit me because I had electricity for nighttime light and a stove to make tea on. We would eat together, and became acquainted. One night he asked me about my connection with the Dolphin Story.

When I finished telling the tale, he was smiling a big smile. He said he had a Whale Story. By the time he was finished telling me his tale, I realized that the Delphic Wave had found its way to my hideaway high in the mountains, almost as far as one could get from the ocean in North America. His story follows.

A Journey of Faith

Beau was from the Midwest, a misfit like myself, drawn to the Southwest years before. He had moved to Aspen, Colorado, where he found himself living among a group of friends who were interested in spiritual pursuits. One member of the circle began to "channel," allowing a spirit named Enoch to speak through him. The group had decided to work with the Kabala and the Tree of Life. They undertook a sequential study of the ten positions on the Tree and were consulting with Enoch as they went. At one point on the path, they asked for the task that lay immediately ahead for them. When Beau asked, he was told that he could "contribute to the return of the Spirit of Peace to our planet" if he were to undertake a special mission.

He was told to place a consecrated quartz crystal in bodies of water, no more than fifty miles apart, all along the mountain "spine" of the Americas, from the north end to the south end, from Barrow, Alaska, to Tierra Del Fuego, Argentina. Beau owned a small plane and had only recently gotten his pilot's license. Somehow, it all fit with his sense of adventure and destiny, and Beau agreed.

A box of crystals was acquired and he began his odd task. Flying over lakes, rivers, or ponds, he would drop crystals into the water. Mapping his progress, he quickly covered the contiguous United States. Winter was coming, so he decided to fly to Barrow to place the northernmost crystal in the ocean there.

It was late September 1988. He flew his little plane north and left it in Anchorage. He took a commercial flight to Barrow, arriving on the 28th. He brought a video camera along to document the adventure. He was in the most northerly town in the world, in blowing snow, just before the onset of full winter. Unable to talk any of the local fishermen into taking him out in a boat so late in the season—with a hard freeze expected any hour, thus making travel on the ocean very dangerous—he was stopped in his tracks.

Finally Beau talked a young taxi driver into being his accomplice. They borrowed a small aluminum boat and an outboard motor and drove out of town, to the Point, the northernmost tip of America. There, they probed with a paddle and found a way to the edge of a sea of slush. They put the boat in, attached the tiny outboard motor, turned on the camera, and launched themselves out on the nearly frozen sea. Going several miles out, they aimed to be beyond the edge of the continental shelf, where the pack ice wouldn't push the crystal onto land in years to come.

The scene is tense, as the frail boat slices through the slush, looking for open water, any moment potentially being caught in the ice. They make it to open water, near a floating iceberg, and Beau hands Eric (the taxi driver, a local Inupiat man) the camera.

Beau takes off his gloves and holds the crystal up. It is a magnificent double-terminated crystal, about fourteen inches long, thick and heavy. He says a powerful prayer over the crystal, asking that it serve to end the illusion of separation in the world. He reaches out and pauses, then drops the crystal through the slush, into the dark blue sea. *(See Plate 10.)*

They make it back to shore.

Beau flies out the next day, and a storm blows in, dropping the temperature to sixty degrees below zero, the ocean freezing for the winter. Beau retrieves his plane and heads south. He flies to Texas, where his brother lives, for a visit. Arriving feeling ill, he is taken in to recuperate. His sister-in-law, who had no idea where he had been, tells him of a weird dream she had about him. She saw him far out at sea in a tiny boat, surrounded by ice. He said a prayer and dropped a shiny crystal in the water, and she followed it down, where it fell to the bottom, rolled down a slope, and finally came to rest. In her dream the crystal began emitting a signal of some kind, and whales came to investigate.

Sitting in front of the TV, wrapped in a blanket feeling flu-ish, Beau watched a story appear on the news of three baby gray whales, trapped in the ice off Pt. Barrow, Alaska. An effort was going to be made to save them.

Beau was amazed. He called his taxi-driver friend, Eric, to see what was going on.

"Beau, you won't believe this! Those whales are trapped about 200 feet from where you dropped that crystal!" said Eric.

I would be skeptical about this tale if it were not for the videotape. Beau had been a secret part of setting the scene, playing a mythical role. He had been following a magical path as a choice, making the effort to believe he could work magic. He succeeded beyond all expectations.

The latter portion of this tale was widely and thoroughly reported. This incident has had books written about it. Beau's entire story is just as true, with only the dream of his sister-in-law not a verifiable fact.

As Beau was telling this story to me, I got chills up and down my spine. It was not the cold of Alaska I was feeling. I sensed many layers of destiny, waves of incredible meaning suddenly washing over me as I sat in my odd little home on the windswept plains of northern New Mexico, so far from the sea. What had been an intellectual pursuit, a fascinating esoteric mystery tale that inspired me to follow it, had now become an exoteric fact. The Golden Dolphin and its Wave had become visible.

The Greatest Animal Rescue in History:
Who Was Saving Whom?

As it happened, an Inupiat, the captain of the local whaling group (which has permission to hunt a few whales each year) had gone out onto the newly frozen sea just after Beau left, to see if there were any easy pickings that year. The Inupiat eat only the bowhead whale, and they consider the gray whale inedible. The tribal people of that part of the world have a name for the gray whale: "The whale whose meat makes you shit." He was disappointed to find only three baby grays trapped in a small breathing hole, not worth the effort to kill.

Barrow, Alaska, is isolated but the town has benefited financially by the oil exploration and drilling in the region. The Inupiat have received millions of dollars in depletion royalties and invested much of that windfall in their community, including a modern telecommunications system, primarily for long-distance schooling. Sophisticated, with satellite uplinks, a production studio, and its own modern building, the TV station in Barrow is an oddity in the icy north.

The gossip at the local bar that night included the story of the three baby whales. The TV station manager thought this was a nice little story of nature and its challenges, so he reported it on the evening news.

The satellite broadcast from Barrow was picked up in New York that day, and Ted Koppel decided to put the story at the end of his evening report as a teaser—the kind of heartstring-pulling tale so much loved by Americans—and the public immediately asked for more.

The story captured the imagination of nearly everyone. Over the next week 150 reporters were sent from countries around the world, making this the biggest story to ever come out of Alaska (until five months later when the *Exxon Valdez* poured its oily contents into Prince William Sound).

As the situation became more desperate for the three small whales, the humans were propelled into an amazing whirlwind of energy. Cindy Lowry of Greenpeace made a concentrated effort to find a way to free them. She began putting together a coalition of players unheard of before. VECO, the largest construction company in Alaska, contractors to oil giant ARCO, were asked for the loan of a hover-barge to crush the ice, to make a path for the whales to escape. The US military was asked to use two of the most powerful helicopters in the world to tow the hover-barge 270 miles from Prudhoe to Barrow.

Then-President Ronald Reagan asked the National Marine Fisheries Service to cooperate with the Inupiat whalers to assess the situation. Everyone offered to help.

Parts for machinery were flown in by military jet, huge machines were moved from storage where they had been frozen to the ground for years, and tens of thousands of dollars in fuel was used flying reporters and visitors and scientists back and forth to where the whales were bobbing up and down, trying to stay alive.

Billie Bob Allen of VECO decided to fly to Alaska to supervise the hover-barge operation, and when he arrived in Barrow, was taken out to see the whales. He walked over to the hole in the ice and looked down. A whale rose up in front of him, paused, then slowly sank down again. Billie Bob turned to the watching scientists, Greenpeace activists, and native people and said, "I don't know how much you will need, but the checkbook's open." VECO eventually spent hundreds of thousands of dollars on its part of the rescue operation.

It has been estimated that at least $5,750,000 was spent freeing the whales. It took twenty-two days, from beginning to end.

One whale, the youngest, died before the channel was opened.

The Inupiat had cut, with chainsaws, rectangular holes in the ice for the whales to follow, places for them to breathe, for more than five miles across the frozen sea.

It was as cold as sixty degrees below zero during this operation. In the end, it was the Inupiat hunters who did the most to save the whales, but many people played crucial roles. One of the unsung heroes of the story was Jim Nollman. Jim had gained notoriety over the previous years by playing music to animals in an attempt to communicate with them. He authored several books and created a non-profit organization to further his research.[1] Cindy Lowry of Greenpeace remembered that Nollman had helped rescue a misguided whale near San Francisco by playing sounds to it, and she called upon Jim to come to Alaska immediately. Jim observed the situation closely for a few days, then had a small hut dragged out onto the ice for his equipment, hoping to keep it from freezing. The challenge was to entice the whales to leave the familiarity of their original breathing hole to take advantage of the new holes made for them by the Inupiat whalers, which would eventually lead them to their escape. His efforts worked dramatically, and almost immediately.

Mikhail Gorbachev called Ronald Reagan to offer help. He was under pressure within his own government, and the public in Russia was also clamoring for something to be done after seeing the American efforts to rescue the little whales. The Russian Merchant Marine was directed to bring its biggest ice breaker, a nuclear-powered monster, the *Admiral Makarov*, and a smaller icebreaker, the *Admiral Alexenyov*, from a site three hundred miles away, where they were just finishing a six-month job building a floating research station. Ironically, the request to the Russians came from David McTaggart, the head of Greenpeace. The Russians were motivated to become involved by the opportunity to gain positive publicity to counter the fact that they had harpooned 169 gray whales that year and were under attack by Greenpeace for their pirate whaling. A US Coast Guard officer was flown by helicopter out to the *Admiral Makarov* as it arrived, and the first official government-sanctioned military cooperation between the US and the USSR since the end of World War Two occurred in the ensuing hours.

The Russian icebreakers, using ice data gathered by a brand new American satellite rushed into service before its scheduled startup to aid this operation, broke a path through a pressure ridge of mounded icebergs for the whales to escape. After three weeks of bobbing up and down, and the loss of the weakest of the three babies, two Pacific gray whales swam free.

The cost had been enormous. Was it worth it?

Yes.

Far away, the government of Iceland was swept up into a bizarre situation: in the middle of a recession, Iceland was dependent on fish exports to Europe. Activists working against Iceland's whaling industry, which was not stopped by the global moratorium on commercial whaling, took advantage of the international media coverage of the whale rescue and talked the largest importer of Icelandic fish in Europe into canceling a $3 million contract. The news shocked the newly elected Prime Minister of Iceland, and he was forced to offer a deal: re-instate the contract for fish, and Iceland would stop whaling forever.

The deal was done and Iceland no longer kills whales.[2]

The Russian people saw that the propaganda machinery of their government had lied to them about the American people, and they began to clamor for more openness in their news and their society. It contributed to the changes occurring within Russia, and the walls surrounding the communist failure came crumbling down shortly thereafter. *Glasnost* was on everyone's lips, and within a year the Berlin Wall came down. A new spirit of peace had come.

To those who follow political history, there are defining moments, sometimes small moments, that herald a new beginning. The so-called "ping-pong diplomacy" that enabled the United States and China to open a dialog after years of official non-communication was one of those moments. Two ping-pong teams wanted to compete against one another but they couldn't due to their respective countries not recognizing one another. Richard Nixon decided to use this situation to open up a dialog, and the rest is history.

The story of the collapse of the communist system, which was stimulated by Glasnost, and the opening of real dialog between America and the USSR, can all be traced to the cooperative effort to save the whales off Pt. Barrow in the fall of 1988.

Somehow, the small efforts of one man to choose to follow a message from the world of spirit, to allow magic and mystery to guide his life for a while, had precipitated a worldwide cascade of events that changed human history forever.

And in the center of it all were three baby whales.

A whale of a story, indeed …

Trust the Magic

For me, this brought home the premise of all the legends, ancient myths, and fishy tales I had been collecting. It illuminated the Mystery.

Today's world is just as much affected by the esoteric influence of whales and dolphins as ever. We can hear the circular and rhythmic song of life, the deep wisdom about how to live sustainably and gently. All we have to do is listen, treat our fellow world citizens with all due respect, and commit to acting on what we learn.

And to trust in the magic.

In a converted school bus at 7,300-plus feet of altitude on a sparkling, star-lit night, as I listened to a friend tell me his story, the Souls in the Sea came to me, through him, asking me to tell their story.

. . .

PRAYER OF THE CRYSTAL WHALES

Kodoish-Kodoish-Kodoish—Adonai Sabayoth
Kadoish-Kadoish-Kadoish—Adonai Sabayoth
Kadoish-Kadoish-Kadoish—Adonai Sabayoth

Dear Father, I thank you for this opportunity to be of
    service to this World
and all the Peoples upon this World.
May this small gesture in this humble way bring the light
    nearer to us all on this planet.

The prayers and ceremonies of all the Peoples of this Earth
are within this crystal....
May the connection be re-established for all the Peoples
and for the Universe.
For all the four-legged and the two-legged,
and those that fly and those that live within the Earth.

May the connection be re-established for the purification
and for the realization
of the non-separation ... knowing that separation is only an
illusion.
May we find this as a true understanding soon upon this
Earth.

I ask you this Father in the name of your most Holy Son
Jesus, the Christos.
And I thank you Father.
IN THE NAME OF
YOD HEY VOD HEY
YOD HEY VOD HEY
YOD HEY VOD HEY
And of all the energies which give us the creation of this
ceremony.
May the purification begin for all the peoples, and I thank
you Father.
For the People of the far North, may you live in Peace and
Love. May we all reconnect.
SO BE IT, IT IS DONE.
Into the cold Arctic Ocean I put this beautiful crystal
with the blessings of the people of this Earth.
SO BE IT ... GOOD-BYE MY BEAUTIFUL FRIEND
—The prayer spoken over the crystal, by Beau Ives,
Point Barrow, Alaska, September 29, 1988

(To obtain a copy of the video of this event, see: www.graywhale.com)

CHAPTER SIXTEEN

The Challenge of Self-Awareness in Dolphins

Ever since Dr. Lilly announced that dolphins have minds and language, the questions have been asked: "How smart is a dolphin?" and "What are they thinking?" Instead of lengthy and technical descriptions of the debate that still rages over these issues, I propose that the more pertinent single question is "How are they smart?"

There is no longer a debate as to whether dolphins are intelligent. It is the type and use of their intelligence that are still being defined. This is not my observation, but one that has been voiced by many researchers, frustrated by other scientists who seem to have a religious need to retain the highest pinnacle of creation for humankind.

How Is a Dolphin Smart?

There are several issues involved in answering the question of how intelligent a dolphin is. The first is the definition of intelligence itself. Always hard to pin down, intelligence is not simple awareness, nor is it to be defined in terms of living skills. Awareness is evident in inanimate objects such as light-sensors, and snails are quite successful at living snail lives. Perhaps the best definition would be "a mental process that leads to flexible response to change." In this definition, we refer to intelligence as adaptability as a result of thought. Therefore, higher intelligence would give a creature some better survival skills in a wider range of environments. Snails cannot avoid capture easily. Frogs can, but they cannot escape the change of seasonal moisture variations, except by going into hibernation. Dogs adapt well to many conditions, but are not innovators, nor do they deliberate mentally to determine the relative value of options. Humans and apes rate quite high on this scale, but the apes fall behind in both their languaging skills and the range of innovations they are capable of. Dolphins have been known to adjust very well to captivity, some thriving and healthy after being in the same pool for over thirty years.

Karen Pryor, at Sea Life Park in Hawaii, decided to see how creative a dolphin can be. Pryor is a passionate believer in operant conditioning, the mechanical view of animal behavior that does not attribute self-awareness to any animal. This model of intelligence and mental ability uses reinforcement as its method for getting animals to repeat actions. Primarily for food and attention rewards, dolphins respond to requests by their "trainers." Pryor let a dolphin know it would only be rewarded for novel behaviors. No repeats of known tricks or actions would elicit a fish reward. Only unique actions would be rewarded. She found that once a dolphin understood this challenge, it was able to vary its actions *ad infinitum*. There seemed to be no limit to its antics, movements, sounds, or games. A dolphin must have superior mental control to do this. It would have to remember each previous action so it would not be repeated and be creative enough to improvise every time it was set this task.[1] No creatures other than human and cetacean can do this, and this ability is one of the strongest facts to be woven into any analysis of the mental state of cetaceans.

· · ·

For many years, intelligence in humans was judged by a set of standardized tests, giving a final result in terms of a fraction called the intelligence quotient, or IQ. When it was proven that white, upper-middle-class young males had an advantage in these tests, since the questions were not sensitive to cultural, racial, or economic differences, a new way of measuring intelligence was sought. One group of researchers decided to question whether there was actually only one form of intelligence, and they eventually developed a circular diagram consisting of seven different kinds of intelligence.

These areas of intelligence include: Verbal, Visual, Kinesthetic, Logical, Intrapersonal, Interpersonal, and Musical. When a person is measured with this scale, everyone turns out to be intelligent, with different combinations of levels of competence. While making the question of intelligence less easy to answer simply, it is much more sensitive to the variety we find among ourselves.

By understanding that intelligence has many forms, we can begin to see that the intelligence of a dolphin must be measured in ways that relate to his or her special life experiences, such as living underwater most of the time, having a sleek body with an onboard ultrasound imaging system, and being from a lineage that is so old that some rocks are younger than they are. It is not their intelligence we ought to be seeking to understand, but their wisdom.

The Mirror Test

As I write this (May 2001) I am hearing the television from downstairs, where the evening news is reporting a breakthrough, a piece of solid evidence that dolphins are self-aware. Two scientists, Dr. Lori Marino and Dr. Diana Reiss, have just released a report in the *Proceedings of the National Academy of Sciences* that tells of their research with dolphins, using what is called "The Mirror Test."[2] The TV reporter says this will require a re-evaluation of current theories about intelligence and self-awareness. What the reporter is not saying, and may not know, is that both scientists have been publishing much the same results for at least nine years, and other researchers have done virtually the same experiments as long as twenty years ago. Why the long delay in accepting this idea?

Science can be either a fine, delicate instrument or a blunt club. It can evoke the minutest details from a set of observations, and it can refuse to see the nose on its own face.

In the case of dolphin intelligence, with all due respect, science has made a laughingstock out of itself to those who know dolphins. What has been required of Drs. Marino and Reiss has been an exacting and almost silly experimental procedure that can withstand the most acidic and skeptical investigation. In this way they have reached a position that is unassailable, but it has cost us a long delay in the process. Simple observation by children and the scientifically innocent sees the extraordinary intelligence and obvious self-awareness of dolphins, but there are positions to be defended, beliefs to be shored up, and entire careers dependent on keeping the debate open.

What careers could possibly depend on whether a dolphin is self-aware? Quite a few, actually. Many you wouldn't expect....

Who's Afraid of the Big Bad Dolphin?

Throughout the time I have been piecing together the story of the human/dolphin relationship, I have had the nagging feeling that somebody, somewhere, is manipulating the public to think less of dolphins than they deserve. Why would anyone want to do that? Who would be in the best position to do it?

On July 6, 1999, an article appeared on the front page of *The New York Times*, entitled "Evidence Puts Dolphins in New Light, as Killers," stating that dolphins are dangerous to swim with in the wild. Within five days I was overheard saying something about dolphins in public, and a seven-year-old boy approached to tell me that

I should be careful, because dolphins are dangerous. I asked him where he heard this, and he told me, "A program on Nickelodeon TV said so, just yesterday!" Within a week another program appeared on TV called "The Wild Side of Dolphins," portraying them as cold-blooded killers and wild, dangerous animals.

This was a most effective campaign. I was impressed with the distribution system employed to deliver this questionable message. I was not surprised to read that one of the lead researchers on the team that put the announcement into the public domain was a *"Dr. Dale J. Dunn, a veterinary pathologist at the Armed Forces Institute of Pathology."* No one seemed to question his role in this study, or why a veterinarian would be attached to a military institute, or why a pathologist (whose proper study is diseases) might be interested in the subject of dangerous wild dolphins. In the article we also read: "Experts say dolphins are smarter than dogs and similar in intelligence to chimpanzees." Oddly, one of the researchers interviewed said that although there haven't really been any injuries so far to humans, people need to be much more careful when near wild dolphins. Tame dolphins in captive situations are safe, but not wild ones.

The manipulation of information for a hidden agenda was transparent. The article mounts a frontal assault on the idea of swimming with dolphins in their natural habitat. Quotes were taken from the website of a woman who leads trips to do just that. In a snide tone the article goes on to say:

> The new-age dolphin operations go much further. In advertisements and tour promotions, they say dolphins are highly evolved spiritual beings. The dolphin's mere glance is enlightening, they say.
>
> "Dolphins reach deep into our souls, opening the door to our hearts," Marie-Helene Roussel said in an advertisement for her Delphines Center, on the Web (www.dolphinswim.com). Anyone with $1,600 can join her late this month on a six-day sail around Bimini in the Bahamas for "healing encounters" with dolphins.

Her partner, Swami Anand Buddha, a former Louisiana life-guard, says he found unconditional love, peace and bliss when he first looked into the eyes of a wild dolphin. "This," he says on the Website, "is why I am working with people who are interested in exploring the potential of being transformed by love and higher intelligence of the dolphins."

But now that image is being shattered as scientists document the grim slaughters....

What grim slaughters? Although odd behaviors of dolphins in the wild are described, no situations where humans were endangered are mentioned. This poor excuse for objective journalism appeared on the front page of *The New York Times*.[3] What can we learn from this?

Why would anyone want to discredit a dolphin? Is there anything that could be gained by doing so? When one looks closely, it is not hard to see where the culprits are. There are careers that require numbness toward the true nature of the cetaceans. Dolphins have proven to be useful to many people, for many reasons. They have provided meat for many years, from the table of Henry the Eighth to the rice bowls of the Japanese today. They have lubricated the finest watches and the transmissions of Rolls Royces and Toyotas, brought fish to hardworking fishermen, helped locate millions of tuna, paid for oceanographic institutes by performing for audiences, made television and movie studios large profits, and protected the Republicans at their national convention in San Diego.

Some of the people who have profited by dolphins in these instances have had real respect for them, knowing them to be special creatures. Most, however, were not willing to see them as different from any other animal.

There are reasonable suspicions that a purposeful dis-information campaign has been going on, initiated by the US military and delivered to the public by various private companies for the past thirty-five years.[4] In a biography of Dr. John Lilly titled *John Lilly, so far...*[5] is a description of a secret US Navy conference held in 1980 at which Dr. Forrest G. Wood and Dr. Robert Buhr urged their colleagues to oppose the ideas of Dr. Lilly in public: "Their complaint was that his efforts had established in the public mind a pervasive image of dolphins as intelligent beings."

By now, almost every American has spent time at one of the large ocean theme parks, being amused by the leaping dolphins and splashing orcas. And all of us have heard the subtle distortions of certain facts enough to doubt that these creatures are any more than how they are described: "about as smart as a bright dog."

One must give credit to these theme parks for providing millions of people the opportunity to see firsthand the amazing forms and abilities of dolphins and small whales. From the perspective of the Delphic Wave this has been, on balance, a good thing. It has provided a means for people otherwise landlocked to encounter the wise beings of the sea. Improvements in husbandry techniques have lengthened the lives of the orcas, belugas, and dolphins who live in these places. Much of the improvement has been motivated by the economics of their care. An untrained orca can be worth more than $250,000, a trained dolphin in the range of $25,000–$50,000. It only pays well to keep cetaceans if they are "religiously" well treated. Whatever the motivation, this has produced some valuable results. Our understanding of most of their mental capacities, their biological processes and needs, their ability to heal humans, to communicate with each other and with us, and to move gracefully through the water has come from studies conducted at these facilities. Despite the anguished cries of the animal liberationists, not all of the activities of the "captivity industry" have been bad.

And to avoid being labeled as naïve, one must be willing to give a hard look at the distortions promoted by this industry as well. To the person whose career depends on dolphins—as subjects of biomedical research; as wet clowns doing six shows a day for clapping tourists; as mine-sweepers locating dangerous weapons; or as an easily harvested food source—it is important that dolphins not be protected too much. Too much recognition of their special status, and somebody's job will be at risk.

When confronted with the realization that cetaceans feel pain, reflect on themselves and, by extension, on their families, and a great range of other subjects, one cannot go back to denying their rights.

Now That We Know That You Know, What's Next?

The high and complex intelligence of dolphins, their certain insights into more than survival, and the possibility of self-awareness in all cetaceans are now verified facts. It will take some time and the absorption of this dramatic realization before we will begin to see the effects. What changes might we look for?

Not only will the entire whaling industry—the proponents of industrial whaling and dolphin harvesting for meat and oils—have to be re-examined in this light, but the issues of subsistence whaling and dolphin "fisheries" will have to be opened up again as well. And of course the existence of the approximately 1,200 "domesticated dolphins" around the world in human-managed facilities will need to be evaluated in this light.

As Dr. Albert Schweitzer said, "The thinking man must oppose all cruel customs no matter how deeply rooted in tradition and surrounded by a halo."

Much of the enthusiasm for interspecies communications research has dwindled over the last two decades. This has been both surprising and disheartening to those of us who look forward to the recognition of the Cetacean Nation. There are very few research programs of this kind underway currently.

On the other hand, studies that do continue this line of exploration have contributed important proof of dolphins' intelligence, language abilities, cultural skills, and cognitive processes.

Dr. Louis Herman and Dr. Adam Pack, at the Dolphin Institute located in Kewalo Basin on the Hawaiian Island of Oahu, have been conducting the longest-running program of research into dolphin communications. They have contributed greatly to our base-line knowledge of a dolphin's ability to follow complex instructions, to assemble syntactically correct behaviors, to be able to correlate bio-sonar information with visual information, and a host of other details of a dolphin's communication skills.

This is paralleled by the wonderful work of Dr. Ken Marten, also on Oahu. He works with the dolphins of Sea Life Park, but is an outside researcher, working under the aegis of Earth Trust. He has been a leader in research into cognition, the ability to think. He has demonstrated many times over that dolphins have remarkable cognitive skills. He conducted his own mirror tests many years ago, with positive results. He has also shown that dolphins have a form of social culture, with the ability to teach each other, passing on special abilities. Today he is using a type of "touch screen" for the dolphins to interact with video and computer systems, going even further into demonstrating their range of abilities. His videotapes of dolphins playing with Bubble Rings are classics, a remarkable record of advanced behaviors that has furthered our understanding immeasurably.

In both these programs, we have increments of advance, but they are small when compared to the advances that are possible. Both show the mechanics of communication and thinking but not the contents.

This was one of the frustrations that bedeviled Dr. Lilly's research. His aims were to leap into the development of a dialog by quickly building a common language of whistles, mediated by a computer interface. He had hoped to be able to electronically translate a simple set of dolphin sounds into sounds that humans could understand and vice versa.

In the early 1980s, Apple Computer Co. donated the hardware for part of the interface he needed, and a custom-made signal analyzer was built by Hewlett-Packard, able to analyze twenty channels of sound signals simultaneously. In the end, little progress was made. Lack of funding—despite support by numerous celebrities (Robin Williams, Burgess Meredith, Olivia Newton-John, John Denver, Jeff Bridges, John Sebastian, Stephanie Zimbalist, Lee Majors,

Werner Erhard, Frank Herbert, Paul Winter, Laura Huxley, and others)—along with the slowness of the computers of that era kept John from attaining his goals.

Today, SETI (Search for Extra-Terrestrial Intelligence) uses a one-million-channel analyzer; affordable laptop computers are running at lightning speeds with enormous memory capacity; dolphins are being maintained in better and better conditions; and there is a large pool of experts available for the research.

The challenges are not to be taken lightly. The adjustment to entirely other paradigms of living has never been easy for humans. The colonial era demonstrated this to us, showing the ease with which people can disregard the humanity of others when ulterior goals are being pursued. If we can be so callous toward our fellow humans, with whom we share every aspect of biology and physical context, having only our cultural differences, how much more challenging is it to contact, communicate, and empathize with an alien life form? Explored by science-fiction authors for a long time, with Hollywood making its observations very graphically, from *Close Encounters of the Third Kind*, to *ET*, to *Contact*, we have almost come to terms with this challenge, but not yet.

Lilly suggested to the founding group of SETI that they dedicate 10 percent of their annual budget to dolphin communication research, to actually begin talking to a real "extraterrestrial." That way, at the end of each year, some success could be reported. To this date, no report from SETI has ever shown a single instance of interspecies or alien communication. Too bad, they should have listened to John....

To envision the challenges involved, imagine this:

You are walking across your yard toward your car to go to work. You glance down and see an earthworm in the grass. You pass on by.

If you had taken the time, you might have noticed that the worm was changing colors, from dark pink to a lighter shade of dark pink over a period of about two minutes.

The worm was talking to you, sending you a message as quickly as it could, in a visual medium. It was doing everything it could to approach you in the medium that you use most capably. But it was far too slow for you to notice, far too little information in the message for you to "take it seriously."

This is similar to the situation we face in communicating with dolphins via sound. We are too slow, with too little content, and their interest wanes quickly. They like the fact that you are there, making an attempt to play with them, but you just aren't very interesting.

And when they are trying to talk to you in ways you can hear, they must speak through their nostrils, slowly, in the deepest register of their voices, and, to top it off, in the air where they never normally speak. Try that yourself sometime....

A Dialog with a Dolphin

The challenges of interspecies communication are huge, both technical and intellectual. The breakthrough will change the course of history forever, and the field is wide open.But almost no one new is stepping into the field. It is professionally dangerous to take on the entrenched military and the theme-park/entertainment industry.

It does not show up on most intellectual radar systems, but another shot was fired in this hidden war of science paradigms by the release of Drs. Marino and Reiss's report on dolphin self-awareness.

In our re-evaluation of history, we have looked at the long story. In today's circumstances we might feel frustration at the slowness of change, the lack of support for the obvious. We can take heart in knowing that a great deal of time has had to pass to reach this moment, and that the day of a full and intelligent dialog with another kind of being is nearer than ever.

The battle goes on. The images in our minds of the dolphins are less obscure, and the need for understanding them and their messages has never been greater.

We are forced to ask ourselves whether native intelligence in another form than man's might be as high, or even higher than his own, yet be marked by no material monuments as man has placed on earth. At first glance we are alien to this idea, because man is particularly a creature who has turned the tables on his environment so that he is now engrossed in shaping it, rather than being shaped by it.

It is difficult for us to visualize another kind of lonely, almost disembodied intelligence floating in the wavering green fairyland of the sea—an intelligence possibly near or comparable to our own....

—Loren Eiseley[6]

If *we* are self-aware, we will recognize the "long loneliness" spoken of by Eiseley, the distance we feel deep inside ourselves as we look into the star fields at night, alone with our desire to know our true role in life.

If we allow ourselves to accept the self-awareness of the dolphins, we may begin to open the door we have hidden behind, to see the best friend we have longed for. The encounter with the Other, the long-lost friend, requires only the willingness to walk to the sea and stand waiting with an open heart and mind, or to visit the nearest pool where dolphins wait for us.

Look into their eyes, and see who looks back. *(See Plate 11.)*

CHAPTER SEVENTEEN

Captivity, Freedom, and the Future

Diviner than the dolphin is nothing yet created,
for indeed they were aforetime men
and lived in cities along with mortals.
They exchanged the land for the sea and put on the form of
    fishes.
But, even now, the righteousness of the spirit of men in
    them
preserves human thought & human deeds.
      —Oppian[1]

Our journey has brought us to the rockiest section of the road in the desert of our understanding. It is still not "paved," made easy for our passage. We have arrived at a battleground. The war between two armies of belief regarding the role of animals in our lives, human responsibility to them, and the question of captivity has hardened many people's minds into distinct camps. With all that we have examined in these pages, how are we to resolve the question of captivity? Are there more than two ways to see this challenging aspect of our lives with dolphins?

First, we will look at two distinct viewpoints—a utilitarian model that sees all animals as specimens and animated substance without souls, and another model that is inspired by the idea that animals have intrinsic worth and must be treated with some kind of respect, as yet undefined to everyone's satisfaction. To illustrate how I have come to my present position on this question, I will conclude this tour of ideas with a story of my "enlightenment" regarding this issue, the gift of understanding I was given by a dolphin.

Two Sides to the Coin: Some Background

From the study we have been making of how dolphins and whales contribute to the human experience, it is clear that we must give thought to the issues surrounding zoos, aquariums, and other types of managed animal environments. As mentioned, today this issue is hotly debated.

To the scientist and the theme park owner, captivity is not an issue. It is simply the word applied to the condition of an otherwise wild animal that is under our care. They require careful husbandry; they afford us opportunities for controlled research; and they can educate the paying public by demonstrating their trained behaviors. People on this side of the captivity issue consider it a necessary, if sometimes troubling, aspect of their work to gain knowledge and to earn a living.

This all seems correct and natural to a large segment of the population. The major religions and most philosophies of today place the animal kingdom outside the "circle of care," that arena inside of which only humans are found. In this paradigm, all else serves man. While enjoined to exercise kindness toward animals, man is free to use them as he deems necessary.

Economics is the primary shaper of pools, staff profiles, and trained performances in the ocean theme parks. The expense of building pools for cetaceans is enormous; the quality of staff that can be hired is limited by the budget for salaries; the amount of time spent on developing demonstrations of behaviors is determined by salaries as well. In university laboratories and military research programs, it is the pursuit of knowledge and its uses that shapes the working environment. Money and facts justify the captivity of cetaceans to the people in these fields. Ethical considerations are minimized. The possibility of pain in the lives of captive animals is ignored, denied, or considered to be a price they are willing to have the animals pay.

Millions of people share this view. But more millions of people have never given it a thought; animal captivity is simply part of the world they live in. "What is the problem with dolphins in pools?" they ask. "We keep tigers in zoos, don't we? What's the difference?"

There is another viewpoint, a diametrically opposed paradigm that has developed in recent years. The animal-rights movement has been growing since the 1800s, when the first anti-cruelty organizations were founded. Their original impetus was a kind-hearted attempt to halt the surgical exploration of animal bodies without anaesthetics. Science led the European mind to the horrors of vivisection, cutting open living animals, several hundred years ago. This created a response: the Royal Society for the Prevention of Cruelty to Animals was founded in England in 1824, the first organized action taken by any species of life on Earth solely for the benefit of other species. Since then, huge organizations have grown to prominence with all aspects of the lives of animals squarely in the center of their concerns. The work they have done has been excellent in most cases. Millions of animals owe their stress-free lives to this movement.

And, as with all movements, extremists have taken the original impetus further, building a citadel of righteousness at the far end of the spectrum of belief.

The "animal-liberation" movement, as it is called (which must be distinguished from "animal rights"), has achieved some success by bringing to public attention the plight of animals being unnecessarily tortured in the name of cosmetic testing, brain trauma studies, etc. Early successes in anti-fur campaigns and improving the lot of factory-grown animals emboldened the self-titled "freedom warriors" and led them to mount a fierce campaign to "liberate" dolphins and whales from enclosures of all kinds. Today the battles continue, rising and falling in intensity depending on the most recent situation someone has chosen to exploit.

The contention of the extremists regarding dolphin captivity is that no dolphin ever, anywhere, under any circumstances should be under human care. (And if one reads their literature closely, they do not condone any contact at all. In some very extreme situations, this has led to people being so misguided as to kill dolphins in pools, explaining that they feel it is better to be dead than alive in a pool.[2]) The oft-repeated refrain is that dolphins are "magnificent, sentient, free-ranging creatures that deserve to be left alone in the sea." No argument is allowed; no questions are accepted in regard to this position. Lawsuits are filed, protests are organized, media exposure is arranged, and massive information campaigns are waged, all in the name of an absolute that they call freedom.

To many people, this position seems somewhat reasonable, not extreme. Many thousands of people give generously, innocent of what they are actually supporting, to the organizations that take this stand.

To be fair, it must be acknowledged that some of their claims are correct, that there have been abuses, torturous conditions, misguided research programs, neglect, inadequate facilities, abandonment, and a host of other problems in the so-called "captivity industry."

And, also in fairness, one must condemn the extremes to which some have gone. The good work in the area of animal rights must not be confused with the actions of the extremists.

Fighting Against Nature: Dolphin Soldiers, Dolphin Guinea Pigs

One area of extreme behavior toward cetaceans is in the military use of dolphins. Much of the information necessary for a full disclosure of this subject is secret, and will remain secret for the foreseeable future. But we can poke around, looking to find a splinter off the "hologram," to peek inside this hidden area:

- It has been widely rumored that dolphins were surgically "lobotomized" by Navy veterinarians in Key West, Florida, in an attempt to make them docile and more trainable, less "willful." This is called psychosurgery, a practice now outlawed for use on humans.

- The body of a dolphin holds many secrets. One is the functioning of its skin. Navy research has attempted to replicate their skin to use on the outside of torpedoes, submarines, and ships. Hundreds of research projects have been carried out on their skin alone. The surface of a Trident submarine, the most deadly military vehicle in history, is covered with a rubbery coating simulating whale skin.

- The cetaceans' ultra-sonic echolocation system is called biosonar by the military,[3] and at least 580 research papers were published on this ability alone in the twelve years between 1966 and 1978. Much of this research was done by the Russian military.

- The research continues. In a single program under the Office of Special Warfare, the US Navy spent $2,398,000 on one dolphin sonar research project in the years 2000 and 2001. (Project Number: MMB1)[4]

- Publicly available information also shows that another secret research program using "marine biosystems" (dolphins) has been undertaken. The funds for the program in 2000 were $2,720,000. This program is also under the heading of Special Warfare. (Work

Security: Secret, Project Number: MM40) This may be a weapons system based on dolphin sonar.[5]

- There are currently several programs that have enlisted dolphins directly into the ranks of the US military. To quote from a Navy website:

  > The Mk 6* & 7* MMS were used to support waterside security at the 1996 Republican Convention in San Diego, CA.

  MMS stands for Marine Mammal System. This small paragraph and its footnote reveal many details to the trained eye. The Mk 6 project has been in use for more than thirty years; the two programs are available to be used within the United States at private functions or at any strategic location in the world; there were serious considerations that mines might have been in use in San Diego's harbor in 1996; Mk 6 is using dolphins to "mark" the location of an intruder; and the long-maintained position of the US Navy that dolphins were not in use in Vietnam is now revealed to be untrue.

- Most incredible is a project costing *$17,099,300*. It appears to be designed to develop electronic control of marine mammals. If this is in fact the case, the nightmare that Dr. Lilly faced may finally be coming true. Dolphins and whales may be used as weapon deliverers or unwitting soldiers under implanted electronic control of human operators. Remote-controlled dolphins. This particular project is called the *"DARPA CONTROLLED BIOLOGICAL SYSTEMS PROGRAM."* Project Number: MM88. Contract Number: DN308477. (DARPA stands for Defense Advanced Research Project Agency, a Pentagon office.)[7]

---

*Mk 6 is a dolphin swimmer and diver detection system that can detect and mark the location of an intruder. This system was used in Vietnam in 1970–71 and the Persian Gulf in 1987–88.

*Mk 7 is a dolphin mine-searching system that detects and marks the location of mines on the ocean bottom.[6] *(See Plate 12.)*

. . .

In total, a quick survey of 1,019 projects on a defense contractor's website *(http://rafiki.nosc.mil/projects/projfiles/)* reveals ten projects involving marine mammals for the years 2000–2002. The total budget for these ten projects as listed is *$29,070,600,* almost ten million dollars per year. (These figures do not reflect salary costs or overhead. They are direct project costs for supplies, equipment, software, maintenance, fuel, travel, and office expenses. The total costs are impossible to calculate from outside, in the civilian world.)

We can safely assume that the entire picture is not available for public scrutiny, that this is only a portion of the military interest in cetaceans. Not even the US Congress knows the full extent of the expenditures. As "black budget" projects, there may be research underway having to do with such advanced technologies that any mention of them would "compromise national security." *(See Plate 13.)*

For those people who still hang on to the old paradigm of fear, limitation, and the need for human control of the natural world, the military view of dolphins makes sense. And for those who have a less fear-dominated posture, it seems horrible and insensitive. All of us have viewpoints consistent with the assembled imprints and beliefs we hold. There are as many "reality tunnels" as there are people. However, there are those who endeavor to keep the windows open, to allow each day to shine a new light on their worldview. I like to think that the readers of this book are among them.

A Middle Path, a Change of Heart

Somewhere in the middle is most likely where we will find a healthy and sustainable attitude toward our sea friends. A scientific approach with a sensitive subjectivity seems a good way to go, or a well-informed and spiritually sensitive attitude. What does this look like? Where are we today in relation to the Delphic Wave?

After much deliberation, I have chosen to share a personal story to illustrate the path I have walked looking for the answer to our question. It lies along the odd track that a dolphin showed me.

I had gone to Florida to see my favorite dolphin, the one with whom I had swum first, and the one who initiated me into the world of the "other."

My human friend, Deena Hoagland, works with disabled children, sharing her gifts of therapy alongside my dolphin friend. She let me accompany her to work that day and allowed me to photograph a session of Dolphin-Assisted Therapy.

The quiet time of day had come, when the dolphins are given a few hours away from people. (In the wild, dolphins rest in the middle of the day, usually spending time in their odd sleep, floating among friends, from about 11 A.M. to 1 P.M.) Deena had seen that Squirt recognized me and wanted to spend time with me. I was delighted and a bit overwhelmed to think that Squirt could have remembered me. It had been several years since I had seen her, and she was so busy swimming with so many people. Could she really remember me? Deena was emphatic, so I was given special permission to spend time with Squirt during her rest time.

I walked out to the pool and sat on the edge, looking for her. She came up right in front of me, bobbing up, turning to one side so that she could look directly at me. She held still, took a breath then began to swim slowly along the side of the pool, turning lazily and swimming past me, again and again. She watched me steadily.

I had come to see Squirt to satisfy myself. I had set up an institute to study the interaction between humans and dolphins (and whales) and, while sorting through all the information I had gathered, discovered that I held two completely opposed points of view.

One was that having dolphins in captivity was an essential part of the education of millions of people who, today, are concerned for their well-being, rally around the campaigns to stop the killing of dolphins while fishing for tuna, and who are fascinated by the friendly smile of the dolphin wherever it might be found.

The other point of view holds that no dolphin should ever be confined in an enclosure of any kind, their life reduced to living in a small area, eating dead fish, and being made to do silly tricks for people. If a dolphin in the wild swims many miles in a day, using its exquisite ultrasound to explore an ever-changing world under the sea, and the dolphins who live in tanks have had to shut down their echo-location abilities to avoid being overwhelmed by the echoes from the bare walls, how can it be right? By having dolphins in captivity, we teach children that it is OK to do this, that animals are specimens for our use and pleasure. This is a wrong message, and not an element of good education.

And here before me was the dolphin I loved most, in a small enclosure, fenced off from a public canal through which boats passed, their smoking motors churning away. I was distressed, feeling a deep frustration at what I saw as the ugly setting and the painful captivity of my friend. I wanted to set her free.

There she was, three feet away, lying on one side to give me a good looking-over. She whistle/squeaked quietly, the pitch rising beyond my hearing, and dove under water, then came back to the same position. She looked calmly at me, her curving mouth suggesting a grin that I had to remind myself was not necessarily the image of her real feelings. She opened her mouth, showing me her perfect teeth. Chomping down on a mouthful of water, she squeaked again and dove.

This time she stayed under longer, then came up lying on her other side. Her other eye was going to do the looking this time. A scratch on her head made me think of the size of the pool and the rough coral bottom, and then I realized that the scratch pattern was that of dolphin teeth. Rough play leaves these marks often, but they heal quickly. At least she was playing with some other dolphins. She was breathing calmly, exhaling with a puff and filling her lungs quickly. She rolled onto her back, her tummy uppermost, arched toward me. Her genital slit was surrounded by beautiful white/blue skin, the inner folds growing dark pink as they disappeared into her. She seemed to be enjoying my close examination of her, so she rolled very slowly, watching me look at her. I stared at her tail a long time, memorizing its details. I had long since grown fond of cetacean tail flukes, the shape endlessly bewitching to my eyes.

She dove and I watched her arrow off, flying across the pool, eight feet beneath the surface. She surfaced by the trainer's platform and came to a stop. She looked toward me to be sure I was watching and put her head on the platform, resting her chin and then her entire head up on the carpeted deck. She was holding her head up on the platform by manuevering her tail to lift herself high out of the water. I watched intently. She let herself slide back into the water and came back to her station in front of me. I couldn't imagine at first what she was trying to tell me. I felt dumb, too slow to pick up an obvious message. Her head on the platform? Why?

Tired, I stretched out on my side. Squirt stretched herself out in front of me, an obvious mimic of my posture. She squeaked, whistled, and seemed to be chuckling. Then she turned and aimed her rostrum at my heart, half her body rising out of the water until she was six inches from me. She balanced there and I felt a burst of ultrasound tingling my chest. Then she slid backward into the water again.

Why?

Her large eye blinked at me, then slowly closed. She puffed and slid below the surface, gliding down and away. Smoothly, she swam to the other end and surfaced. She turned, stroked her tail once, and came gliding back, her body hardly creating ripples, the water line just below her eyes, which were still watching me.

I glanced at my watch and saw that I had only a few more minutes. How had the time gone so quickly? I looked at my camera and saw that I had shot my last photo on that roll of film. I jumped up and quickly got another from my backpack around the corner, and slipped the film in. I walked back to the edge of the pool and saw that she was under the stairs at the other end.

I raised the camera, focused the lens on the water surface in front of me, and said, in my mind, "Squirt, I need some good pictures of you. Would you come and let me take a few photos?" Before I finished the thought she appeared, exactly in the middle of the viewfinder, coming straight up at me out of the water. I pressed the shutter quickly and wound the film forward and snapped another shot as she fell to one side, splashing a wall of water away from me. *(See Plate 14.)*

She dove again, swam away, and disappeared.

Just then, Deena came out and said, "Has she been a good girl? I know she remembers you. I bet she's sad you're going."

I turned to look for Squirt as I walked out the gate and she was just visible, looking directly at me from forty yards away. I sent her a heartfelt thanks and a wave of love.

The Bouillon Cube Effect

Three days later I was driving through the forests and mountains of northern New Mexico on my way to my daughter's college graduation, and I began reflecting deeply on my visit with Squirt.

What had her movements meant? What was she trying to show me? What had I learned? How was I going to get her out of there?

Suddenly, as if an ocean wave were washing over me, I saw what had happened, my heart filling with surprise. I had gone there to find out how to help her be free. I had been intent on this, and yet I had not once during my visit felt her being anything other than free.

She had demonstrated to me that she was at home, happy and fulfilled. Somehow, her presence had penetrated me, keeping me focused on her, her quiet gestures, and her calm. No glimmer of frustration, no anger or display of anxiety at her confinement had marred our time together. It was clear that she was perfectly at peace with her life.

Despite a long tradition at Dolphins Plus, the dolphins there are no longer let out to swim in the canal. For years they had been encouraged to swim free several times a week, to get exercise, to catch fish, to have time to themselves. Then the Marine Mammal Protection Act (MMPA) began being enforced and the dolphins could no longer swim free.

Does this surprise you? The MMPA was enacted to protect dolphins and whales, to stop people who were doing dreadful and unkind things. However, it also stops good people from doing good things. Lloyd Borguss, owner of Dolphins Plus, had enjoyed the option he had to allow the dolphins to swim free. He was able to answer people concerned about captivity with a description of their "semi-captive" situation. Now, they can no longer go free. The conditions placed on anyone having a license to keep dolphins in the US include total, 24-hour, 7-days-per-week responsibility for their welfare. A dolphin not under the direct supervision of the licensed "owner" is breaking the law.

Although there was some relief to the Borgusses over this since the dolphins had become so valuable and were always a cause of concern to them while out swimming in the bay, it was a sad day when the gates swung shut the last time. Their family of dolphins had never abandoned them in all the years of "semi-captivity." After being let out into the canal they usually returned to their enclosures within a few hours. Only Fonzie, the famous male, had left for longer periods, once or twice overnight. He always returned, but those were worrisome nights for the Dolphins Plus staff.[8]

Squirt had shown me her level of comfort, her quiet spirit in her home among people. She had kept me from my own anxiety over her situation and had demonstrated her commitment to her work, her mission of helping humans. I realized that she had been working on me. It was as if a bouillon cube had been dropped into the boiling waters of my mind and had taken three days to reach that point when it suddenly dissolves. In computer language, her download was coming online.

I pulled the car off the road, my eyes filling with tears. Before me, I saw the Delphic Wave in recent times, re-establishing right relations between the two fully sentient races of Earth, uplifting humanity once again through the agency of the cetaceans. And I saw Squirt as an advanced soul, fully willing, completely dedicated to her service to this plan. She is a gifted healer, a wise partner in one of the most extraordinary efforts ever undertaken by humans, to work in an equal partnership with a dolphin in diagnosing and treating physical and emotional dysfunctions.

What foolishness I had held, thinking it to be wisdom. I thought I could help her out of her cage, only to realize that I was the one in a cage, a box of fixed ideas. My frustrations with my own life, the limits I always found against which I felt helpless, were being projected onto her and onto all dolphins in "captivity." How, if I thought of them as special beings embodying advanced qualities, could I think of them as victims? Do they not make their own choices? Could they know what they are doing when they are captured, allowing themselves to become partners with us?I had heard several stories from people involved in the capture business of days trying to catch dolphins, always feeling taunted, played with, until one day a dolphin simply swims up and places its head through the catcher's hoop, allowing itself to be lifted out of the water. Not all dolphins are taken from the sea this way certainly, but some are. Not all dolphins come willingly, but some do. Not all dolphins are suitable for human contact, but some are.

I was overwhelmed by the implications.

I saw the role of the Delphic Wave expanding before my inner eyes. The horror of whaling was being brought to a stop; dolphins were now popular, even loved by everyone. We were moving toward a new relationship, a horizon of experience that no one had anticipated. We were actually doing very well, improving ourselves and our relations with animals of all kinds over the last 150 years.

By visiting orcas in small pools and dolphins crowded into blue, featureless, concrete tanks, I had witnessed situations that were painfully inadequate. Tears flowed as I returned to some of those scenes, realizing once again the depth of compassion with which they must view us, as people who just don't understand. How stupid we must seem, so slow to comprehend what we used to know. How bad are our memories, to have forgotten our best friends, our benefactors? How crude we must appear, with such rough manners, treating them as animals that do tricks to amuse us.

Swept up onto another plane, I saw another vista open. I saw the millions of lives given freely, spent on enabling our awakening. I realized that it was we, the human side of the partnership, who had yet to come to terms with the reality, and the responsibilities, of this parallel destiny—how far we have yet to go. Where in the world is an appropriate embassy, a place for the cetaceans to represent themselves to us, as they wish?

I saw that it is time for us to accept them as Souls, evolved Beings entirely different than us, who have inalienable rights and whose differences cannot be allowed to make them second to us in any way.

It is human destiny to have hands, to be the Wise Apes who can make things, change environments, and understand and manipulate the hidden side of physical existence. If we are to be joined into a conscious partnership, it is human responsibility that must step up to the necessary standards and create healthy, safe, beautiful environments where both species can interact in comfort.

We are only partway there. We can now keep dolphins and whales alive for a very long time. Lolita, the orca who lives at the Miami Seaquarium, has been in her small pool, barely able to turn around, for almost thirty years, and despite the inadequacy of her home, is physically healthy. There are many dolphins who have been born and have thrived under human care. We can do the basic "husbandry." Now it is up to us to build places for them to live amongst us that fully support their needs.[9]

The revelation continued. I could see a future of interaction; a chain of interspecies villages along the coastlines of the world; huge floating islands, grown out of sea minerals with small cities on them, where a new kind of person who had been raised among cetaceans would live a lifestyle we cannot fully imagine.

Another panorama opened before me and I saw the entire oceanic globe of our planet. Australia was visible, its thousands of miles of beaches surrounding a group of lively humans, ones especially suited to interspecies contact. The Australian national character is more free, playful, and wise in its respect for nature than many others. The Delphic Wave had not only begun there and been re-identified there through the Legend of the Golden Dolphin, but was destined to complete its global movement on her eastern shores. Then a sad note entered the music of this vision.

I recalled that Australia is heavily influenced by England, where a dislike of animal abuse led to a recent total ban on dolphinariums in England. The rest of Europe followed suit, closing most sites where humans had been able to interact with the Sea People. And Australia, child of destiny, has also followed suit.

While the country was rising to the challenge of stopping its oldest commercial activity, whaling, in the late 1970s, it began looking into the public aquariums and dolphinariums. By the time Peter had his visions in 1976, Australia was well on its way to ending all cetacean display programs. Only two Australian "dolphinariums" exist today, their owners committed to making dolphins accessible to people.

The sadness of this insight into the Australian situation was palpable. I could see, however, that it was not a lost cause, that a concentrated effort in Australia to tap into public consciousness to re-orient it toward appropriate facilities, excellent natural lagoons along the coasts, and a new, enlightened relationship was still possible. It would take a miracle, but it was possible.

If not Australia now, where is the new Delphic focal point? The scene shifted again, and I saw the Caribbean Sea, the entire basin, from the northeast coast of South America to the Central American coast, Mexico, the southern US, the Bahamas, Cuba, and the outer islands. A new era is dawning there. All throughout the region dolphin swim facilities are destined to be built.

Back on Solid Ground

Gently, the images and thoughts swam away, receding into the waters of my mind. There I was, sitting in my car, my face wet with tears, looking at the dry northern plains of New Mexico sweeping to the west. My mind was spinning.

This revelation meant that I was going to be on the opposite side of an argument from almost everyone I knew. I was going to be an advocate of "captivity" in the eyes of many people. I was going to be hated, attacked, and banished by well-meaning friends; and my lifework, my commitment to serving the Delphic Wave, was going to be far more complex than I had ever imagined. I saw that I was going to be in hot water some times, defending my position by trying to lead people through some complicated ideas.

I had a heart-wrenching moment when I saw that I must now accept keeping dolphins amongst us, in "captivity" as I used to call it.

I now support *appropriate* facilities for humans and dolphins, perfect examples of which still do not exist.

There is much more to say about freedom and the captivity question. Another book will need to be written to explore it fully. It is beautiful for humans to be with dolphins. At sea or in pools, dolphins love to play with us. A dolphin I know has lived in the pool where he is for over thirty years. It is only eight feet deep and has smooth concrete walls. He is healthy, happy, playful, and well-adjusted. He uses his ultrasound more than any dolphin in the wild I have ever encountered. He is about to become a father. And, if he were not in his pool, he would have died long ago, having been rescued from a beach, ill and battered. His success has been possible because of the unwavering commitment among those who care for him to love him as an individual, and as a worthy companion on the path of life. He has something to teach us all.

Where Is Freedom?

If you or I were to live in an apartment in New York City it is not unreasonable to think we might have an experience of freedom there. It is also not unreasonable to imagine living in a house in the rainforest, near a beach where dolphins visit, feeling trapped in a dead-end place too isolated and rustic. The degree of freedom in our lives is a reflection of our attitudes, not our outer circumstances. A dolphin in a pool may be as free, or even freer than one at sea. No food worries, no need to swim all those miles each day searching. No sharks, no hammerheads, no spiny things. It can be an easier life and now, with all the children to explore and play with, an even more stimulating and wonderful home.

"Thanks, humans, I'm loving it!" I heard Squirt say inside my head, squeak/whistling. "There's no place like home.

"Feel free to write about all this, Scott. Let 'em know what I think. Feel free."

CHAPTER EIGHTEEN

The New Gift: Dolphin-Assisted Therapy

To the Dolphin alone nature has given that which the best philosophers seek: Friendship for no advantage. Though it has no need of help of any man, yet it is a genial friend to all, and has helped man.

    —Plutarch (A.D. 46-120), High Priest of the Dolphin Temple, Athens

At this juncture in the Tale, we have established that dolphins and whales have been somehow present and involved in many of the advances we regard as "humanizing." If we have been gradually "tamed and civilized" over the centuries, dolphins and whales have not only been observers of our progress, but have played consistent roles in the drama. As we draw closer to the present time, you have perhaps grown uncomfortable with our notion. Somehow, the suggestions of dolphins awakening the human heart and whales supporting our material advances are fine to imagine in the past, but as part of our everyday world ... well, it is a bit much.

The story of Beau and his mission with the Crystal Whales is both factual and fanciful. To assert that the peculiar act of a man following a mystical message and dropping a stone into the ocean had anything to do with the demise of Communism and the fall of the Berlin Wall is peculiar, if not laughable—if it were not for the facts.

Additionally, the increase in human awareness of not only whales and dolphins but the ecology of the entire planet is a fact of enormous importance. This change has arisen in part from fanciful sources and events, as I have shown. Fanciful and true.

We have followed the tale of the Wave westward, bringing it forward in time. We now place it within the Americas in the first decade of the twenty-first century. What is the latest news of this Wave? Where is it cresting today? Where will it be tomorrow? Is there any way, now that we know about this Wave of Light, that we can support it, work with it, be co-creators with it?

After all my years of research, travel, observation, swimming, and dreaming, I have come to one idea that foreshadows the next appearance of the Wave. It may allow us to surf its energy to a new shore, a better place for our children's children: Dolphin-Assisted Therapy (DAT).

Joey, Fonzie, and the Cultural Hologram

I have been collecting dolphin-related articles from magazines and newspapers for many years. One from 1991, which appeared in *Parade*, a Sunday newspaper supplement, particularly grabbed my imagination. Entitled "The Dolphin Didn't Let Him Down," it told the heartwarming story of a little boy named Joey Hoagland who had been befriended by a dolphin. At the age of three he required open-heart surgery and had a stroke during his third operation. His left side was affected, and he was unable to raise his arm, move his fingers, or sit without support. A dolphin named Fonzie had given him special attention, and before anyone could imagine it happening, Joey began to interact with the dolphin, learning rapidly how to use his left side again.

This story has found its way into the Hologram, the cultural body of ideas that inform our daily lives. I have found that many people around the world, in widely divergent lifestyles, have heard this story. In gas stations, at parties, in restaurants and waiting rooms, I find myself frequently asked what I know about "dolphins healing children."

Entering the Mysteries of Dolphin-Assisted Therapy

In 1995 I came upon an announcement on the internet for a Symposium on Dolphin-Assisted Therapy, sponsored by an organization calling itself AquaThought. I read all the promotional materials, and wished I could go, but it was in Mexico, and I had no means of getting there. The next year another symposium was announced. It was again to be held in Cancún, Mexico.

Having no funds to register or to buy a plane ticket frustrated me, but a gathering of friends was to prove fateful. We had come together to share our dreams and desires, a circle called to place our prayers for future projects into a common space, where we could support each other's dreams. When the time came for me to tell my desires, I decided to be very specific, and told about the symposium, even though it was to begin in only three days.

From across the circle came a question, "How much money would it cost to go?"

I answered quickly, "I believe $1,000 would do it."

The answer came back, "OK, you've got it. Who do I write the check to?"

I arrived at the hotel in Cancún just as the opening reception was concluding, and through an odd set of circumstances found myself being asked to deliver a keynote address to the Symposium. Something mysterious was going on.

The next morning the Second International Symposium on Dolphin-Assisted Therapy began. I was in my element, with speaker after speaker impressing me with their programs. Video was shown of dolphins swarming around children, spraying them with ultrasound, patients smiling as they came out of the water. A paper was presented that excited me, explaining the physics of dolphin ultrasound and the possibility that this was how healing was being stimulated.

As I sat there, I realized that there are many opinions about what DAT is, and how it should be done. There were many points of view being displayed among the speakers, and the audience was divided. A split was evident between the medical people present and the ones who were more interested in the spiritual, New Age ideas. There were engineers looking for effects to recreate with technology, dolphin trainers who were wary of the animal rights people, and several entrepreneurs in evidence. Each seemed to hold the other to be hopelessly out of touch with what was really happening.

I started to get nervous. I saw that what I had to say was not very scientific, yet my interests, my passions, led me to want to support all the science that could be brought to the issue. I found myself sweating, wondering when I might be called on to speak.

Dave Cole, the founder and principal investigator of AquaThought, who had asked me to speak, went to the podium and began, "Hello gang! I know most of you here, and you all know that I have a pretty large sense of the importance of Dolphin-Assisted Therapy. Well, last night I was introduced to someone who has an even bigger picture of this whole topic."

Laughter rose from the crowd. He continued, "I want to introduce to you a man with a Legend. Please welcome Scott Taylor."

Polite applause greeted me as I climbed the stairs to the stage. My sweat hadn't stopped. I said a little prayer and reminded myself that this is what I had said I wanted, and that any prepared speech would not be in touch with the situation in which I found myself. I tried to relax and enjoy the moment.

I took the microphone and began. All the years of workshops, teaching classes, and speaking to groups came back and I found my voice. I outlined my tale, telling of the mysterious Legend of the Golden Dolphin that had found me, and the work I had been doing to unfold more layers of its meaning.

I came to the DAT story and said how I had determined, as a well-educated guess, that the dolphins were supporting the work of everyone in the audience, if the Delphic Wave idea was credible at all. I added that the most important message the dolphins could give to humankind now was that of Dolphin-Assisted Therapy.

As I spoke I envisioned the Tale as an umbrella, spread over the people in the room, enfolding them into one group of many individuals. I told the audience that they were part of the Legend itself, playing critical roles in its unfolding. I thanked them, scientists, therapists, engineers, people of spirit, administrators, trainers and owners of facilities, for the roles they were playing so well.

It was silent while I spoke, and I watched several people go into a stunned space, their faces taking on a distant look, as ideas flashed through their minds. Several people had started out skeptical, their mouths set in a grim line as they endured another "spiritual rave by a New Ager," only to be grinning by the end.

When I came off the stage, I was surrounded by eager people, all wanting to tell me stories, ask questions, and offer ideas. I was fielding questions when a small woman came forward, obviously excited. She had dark hair, large glasses, and an intense look about her.

She said, "Excuse me! I don't usually force myself on people like this, but I just have to know more about this Legend you were talking about. I use legends and myths in my work with kids and I have never heard of this one."

I began a polite story about the origins of the tale, and she interrupted again. "You said we were all in the Legend. What does this mean? What does it say about us?"

I looked at her nametag, which simply said "Deena."

I paused a second to gather my wits and then said, "Are you Deena Hoagland?"

She leaned back, her jaw dropped, and she said, "How did you know that? Yes, I'm Deena Hoagland."

I smiled, thanked the Dolphin Gods, and said, "I've been wanting to meet you for a long time. If anyone here is inside the Legend, you and your son are." I had recognized her name as the mother of the little boy in the Sunday *Parade* magazine article, Joey.

Deena and I spent a lot of time talking during the remainder of the Symposium. She told me about her struggles with the facility she was working at, where she was doing volunteer work bringing disadvantaged kids into a program that included swimming with dolphins. She had been running the program for several years, raising all the money for it herself by having bake sales, asking companies for donations, and collecting funds wherever she could find support. I discovered that she is a Licensed Clinical Social Worker, a professional therapist who recognized the value of her son's experience and formed an idea of how to offer something similar to kids and their families. Up until this time, she was working for free, doing the group work for kids of the area where she lived in south Florida as a gift.

I was moved, hearing of her dedication, her commitment to this work. I could hardly imagine the daily heroism involved, the steady challenges of seeking out and then working for the kids whose lives were almost lost in our fractured and fast-paced society. We became friends then, and allies. I will return to her story later....

The Symposium went well. I met people there who have become close friends, whose lives and mine have now intertwined. I met people whose dedication to serving the needs of children with severe disabilities was being supported by university research programs; I met a man whose daughter had been healed by contact with dolphins and whose passion had become the building of the world's first Dolphin-Assisted Therapy healing facility, fully dedicated to research and therapy with Dolphins. (His quest continues today, with much forward movement to report.) I met a social worker from the hard streets of Chicago, where gangs were being taught how to learn from animals, how to survive in a way that didn't destroy. Her quest was to bring them to the dolphins as the best teachers imaginable. I met a dolphin trainer from one of the most well-known dolphin research programs who was almost ready to get up and walk away when she was first introduced to me, sensing that I might confront her for her role in working with captive dolphins. I was able to reassure her, and found a woman whose love of the dolphins was so profound that her heart ached. Her love, her passionate work, her meaningful focus in life was to enable dolphins to enjoy being with us, to provide for them the best companionship possible. She had fought for years to improve conditions for the dolphins she worked with, and continues to do so. She was exhausted and disheartened by the life she led, living, as it were, in the center of a bull's-eye, a target for people with emotional imbalances who could not accept that she loves dolphins more than they do. The animal-liberation activists had stolen much of the joy she deserved.

I saw videotape of a program in Mexico where hundreds of children with central nervous system challenges (birth defects, cerebral palsy, muscular dystrophy, stroke victims, injuries, paralysis, etc.) were being taken through a simple process, putting them in water with a facilitator or two for safety, allowing the dolphins to do anything they were inspired to do, and documenting the results. The statistics of the positive effects were impressive. (Later I met an ex-employee who told of serious questions about the statistics. I asked if the *overall* results were positive, and she said they were so positive that she was working with another group to open their own facility.)

I also heard the story of a little girl who had been born with a very serious condition: the plates in her skull were fused, unable to expand and grow. This condition is called micro-cephalia, and usually results in early death. The brain tries to grow into a space that does not expand, and idiocy and death follow. Her parents, after finding nothing else that would help, tried Dolphin-Assisted Therapy. Videotape of the sessions showed four dolphins doing the work. Two would position themselves on each side of her neck, another one behind her aimed at her lower skull, and one would position herself under her, aimed up at her spine. They flooded her with sound, pouring wave after wave into her, the water buzzing with the disappearing clicks and whines of ultrasound.

Results? Well, her father climbed on stage with her in his arms. When we all clapped she looked up at her father, laughed, and clapped back at us. The plates in her skull had unfused and were growing normally. (Oddly, the submitted paper to the symposium does not refer to the microcephalic condition. There may be several explanations for this. One is that the story told on stage by the introducer was mistaken; one is that the paper, which is not detailed, was prepared by someone other than the stage presenter and was not accurate; another may be that there were concerns to keep the facts of the situation off the public record. The symposium proceedings say only that she had "... a diagnosis of mild sub-cortical atrophy predominantly on the left side, resulting in mild retardation in the development of motor, adaptive and language areas...." In any case, this young girl was markedly different from the one on screen, who looked like a sad and lost cause.)

Then there was Deane-Paul, a Down's Syndrome child who the standard medical establishment predicted would never become outwardly directed, never able to show his emotions or to initiate contact with another person. His mother was told he would not live the normal span of years, and with that, she threw away all the papers his doctors gave her. Incensed that anyone would dare tell her how long her son would live, she set out to find a therapeutic model outside the normal medical model, something that would give Deane-Paul a fighting chance. She was determined and began her search once Deane-Paul was old enough to travel. She heard of the dolphin possibility and took her son to Florida, where he was to meet Dave Nathanson.

Nathanson is, to many people, the father of Dolphin-Assisted Therapy. He was a psychologist working with disabled kids, who in 1978 thought of a way to hold children's attention better. He reasoned that water calmed kids, and dolphins might be interesting to them, an enticement. Perhaps a reward might be made of them, as inducement to pay attention to therapeutic tasks. His early experiments went well. He found that children with Down's Syndrome learned four times faster, with much better retention when the learning sessions included dolphins.

Dr. Betsy Smith was working in south Florida at the same time, and heard of Nathanson's work. She set up an experiment in which autistic and disabled kids were given one of two experiences, either a day playing with dolphins at a facility, or a day at a similar beach, playing with inflatable dolphin-shaped toys. She monitored the pre- and post-interaction behaviors of both groups. The reaction of the kids who got to play with real dolphins was startling in its difference. They were calmer, more willing to take direction, more happy and communicative. As the experiment went on, it became more and more evident that the dolphins were having a real effect.

Enter Deane-Paul, whose response to Nathanson and the dolphins was profound. He paid attention. He learned quickly. He made it clear to everyone that he loved the dolphins. Deane-Paul's progress stunned everyone. He became as much a "poster child" for Dolphin-Assisted Therapy as Joey Hoagland. Images of Deane-Paul continue to flash around the world whenever DAT is discussed. *(See Plate 15.)*

(I have spent many hours with him, and I must confess, one of my favorite memories of our time together was when he suggested we play hide-and-seek in the airport in Cancún as we waited. He re-taught me about playfulness and reminded me that being an adult is no excuse for not playing silly games when you need to, a lesson I have also been taught several times by dolphins.)

Deane-Paul's learning curve normalized under DAT. This means that his *ability to learn* began to approach that of any child his age. He will always have the peculiar traits of Down's Syndrome. These people with an extra chromosome have been described as angels, people who seem to live in a world of gentleness, without malice. Their angers arise from frustrations that melt away quickly. They have far fewer social discomforts than we do, and can share startling insights.

When Deane-Paul was introduced to the Symposium, he strode on stage, took the microphone and proceeded to do a weird kind of rap song, which was almost unintelligible (which seems to be part of that musical idiom). It was a hit. His mom told the audience he had decided he wanted to do a dolphin rap song for us. He was very proud of all the applause.

By the end of the three-day gathering, I had seen and heard a long list of inspiring stories from dedicated people working with patients who are suffering and whose lives were greatly improved by Dolphin-Assisted Therapy.

A Theory About How DAT Works

To someone who is suffering, there can be little inducement to tell lies about relief. How does one doubt someone with tears of relief in their eyes? The many, many reports from individuals, including articulate adults, of pain relief and significant change produced by dolphin interaction beg for our serious attention.

There is a difficulty at the core of attempts to understand this new form of treatment: It is impossible to establish a baseline against which to measure effectiveness. Who is to say that Deane-Paul, the girl with the skull fusion, or even Joey would not have had the same recovery without ever meeting a dolphin? No one can be certain, within the wide, wide universe of possibility. And it would be foolish to ignore the evidence of effects caused by dolphin contact.

AquaThought, the brainchild of Dave Cole, has contributed much to this work. Dave not only conceived of IDATRA (International Dolphin-Assisted Therapy Research Association), which organized the symposiums (sadly, there were only two), but he suggested a peer-reviewed journal, publication of a set of standards and practices, and anything else that would make the field of DAT stand up to the scrutiny of the scientific and medical establishments.

At the second symposium Cole read a paper that is an excellent contribution to the science of this field. He suggests in his paper, entitled "Electroencephalographic Results of Human-Dolphin Interaction: A Sonophoresis Model,"[1] that the effects we see in human subjects could be brought about by the ultrasound of the dolphins. He points out that a bottlenose dolphin is capable of producing up to 8.3 watts per square centimeter of sound pressure, which is more than *four times the power used to shatter kidney stones with ultrasound*. The theory suggests that, since the ultrasound pulse can temporarily make cell walls permeable through a phenomenon called "cavitation," chemical changes can occur that otherwise would be impossible. Hormones could cross cell wall barriers, minerals could be flushed from cells, and deep cellular changes could be facilitated. Growth of cells could be either turned on or off.

In addition, Cole has found that an electro-encephalogram (EEG) reading of people who swim with dolphins is classifiable as the "Dolphin Effect," which is similar to the brain's response to anesthesia. The brain becomes deeply calm and balanced, both hemispheres operating at the same level. Combined with the stimulus associated with dolphin contact, and the increase of theta waves in the brain, dolphin contact has a unique set of produced reactions.

As has been found in other forms of animal-assisted therapy, human emotions are stimulated by contact with friendly creatures. The warm water where dolphins are found is a factor, creating a welcoming, weightless environment. The level of attention that a dolphin gives a person is far greater than any other animal. The gentleness, adaptability to personal limitations, curiosity, and general playfulness of dolphins are part of what a patient responds to as well. And as we are now discovering, dolphins participate in the process of therapy as not only rewards for the patient, as a puppy might be used, but as intelligent agents in the design and application of the therapy.

With all the attributes mentioned above and the fact that a dolphin can physically change cells, combined with their communication skills, we have come upon a fellow being in the universe who can be a partner in our efforts to improve lives and heal bodies.

Papers and Places: Where Is the Data?

Hard data is difficult to come by in the world of DAT. There are, to the best of my knowledge, only eleven papers on the subject that have been published under peer-review.[2] There is an additional number of unpublished papers in what is called the "gray literature" (student theses, un-reviewed research reports, etc.), several of which contain excellent work and important statistics regarding documented reactions to DAT.[3]

However, the situation is in a double bind. Scientists are hesitant to do research to prove DAT's effects. The medical field hesitates to prescribe it without the certainty that science could provide. Therapists are few and far between, and facilities will only occasionally make themselves available for research projects. There is no place in the western hemisphere that exists solely for DAT research or treatments. There are few places to go for treatment, if you can get on their schedules. They have been known to be booked in advance as far as seven years.

I have recently read reports of ex-navy dolphins in the former Soviet Union serving in DAT programs, but the reports are not clear as to the circumstances, or whether the dolphins are doing this only, or if they are also part of marine animal shows. If the claims are correct, the Russians are having astounding results. Deaf children, some of whom had never heard a sound, are being "taught to hear in a new way by the dolphins."

Dr. John Upledger, of the Upledger Institute in Florida (where the technique called cranio-sacral therapy has been developed and taught for many years), told me in a telephone interview of his experiences during cranio-sacral therapy sessions in water, with dolphins present. For five years, he and his student therapists experimented at Dolphin Research Center by having a patient float in water four feet deep (in which the therapist could stand). The dolphins were fascinated and became involved. Dr. Upledger reports a most unusual technique offered by one dolphin: he would swim up to Dr. Upledger and place his blowhole under one of his hands, while the other hand was on the patient. John reports feeling surges of energy coursing through his body, from hand to hand. The dolphin, A. J., did this unheard-of behavior many times. Patients rose from the water relieved of pain, better balanced, and more healthy. How did this happen? As Dr. Upledger says, "Who cares? It works. If we wait for science to approve of this, we will have wasted years." The

Upledger Institute is the first to evaluate an established physical therapy in the presence of dolphins.

The bottom line is this: a dedicated facility is needed, somewhere in the Caribbean region. It should be of exceptionally high standards, with very large areas for free swimming by the dolphins, as well as closed-off areas where therapy sessions can occur. There should be an onsite clinic, a hotel, an excellent restaurant, and a very healthy environment, affording the therapists, patients, their families, and the researchers high-quality facilities. (Recent developments suggest that a dedicated DAT facility may become a reality in the near future. A man whose daughter was helped dramatically by dolphins has purchased a former oceanarium. He intends to develop a DAT program, with research facilities.)

As Dave Cole says in a filmed interview, "We don't know whether dolphins can cure people, but until we do, we know they can help a lot of people."[4]

Island Dolphin Care, Inc., a Model DAT Program

After the conference, Deena and I kept up a correspondence. She had been given the space and support for her own Dolphin-Assisted Therapy business at Dolphins Plus, and she was excited about running her own programs.

I arranged to visit Deena and arrived in the Florida Keys hoping to see her in action. I was not disappointed. She has set up a non-profit foundation called Island Dolphin Care. This allows her to receive tax-deductible donations to support her work and to continue to charge modest fees for her services.

Her methods of going about the mysterious business of Dolphin-Assisted Therapy are a model for others. She takes pains to describe in detail to potential clients what to expect, and what not to expect. She insists on a complete set of patient's records to evaluate. Then, based on the reports, a questionnaire the parents fill out, and phone conversations, Deena designs a program of activities for the patient.

Rarely are two programs the same. One may involve a speech therapist working with her after the dolphin swims, and a physical therapist to work on atrophied muscles. Another patient's needs may bring in a counselor to work with the parents, siblings, and the patient about family issues. The sessions are one week long, but many families opt for more than one week. They come as a family, as many members as possible. The child is part of the dynamic of the whole family, and everyone is affected, so everyone is part of the work that will be done. They stay in a nearby motel and come to the sessions together.

The patient is treated in a special classroom Deena has set up, filled with games and puzzles and pictures and toys, all of a dolphin or ocean theme. The class is private, one on one, and the parents are part of it. The actual dolphin swim is later, usually taking about thirty to forty-five minutes. A trainer is on hand, Deena is there and sometimes another therapist, as well as the patient, and of course the dolphin. (It is Squirt who has worked the most with Deena, a masterful healer with whom I had my first in-water encounter years ago.)

The dolphin plays an important role in developing the actual therapy in the water. Example: perhaps the goal is to engage the child's attention, with the aim of acquiring language. Letter boards are at poolside as well as, say, a ball and a hoop. The activity calls for the child to touch the letter board when a question is asked. If the response is the desired one, the child gets to toss the ball to the dolphin, who brings it back.

Squirt may decide this is not working right. She might whistle, grab the ball and race away, causing huge waves to splash up the sides of the enclosure, tossing the ball in the air. The child squeals with delight and claps her hands. When asked to identify a letter, she does it flawlessly again and again. Squirt has just changed the protocol, and it worked.

Deena and the trainer have learned to watch and listen for Squirt's suggestions.

At the end of the session there is always some kind of special interaction with a dolphin, like a dorsal fin tow, a game of catch, or just squirted water in the face. After the swim a slow-down time is taken. Then classroom work begins. Sometimes it will be two therapists and one parent all working with the one child, a very good teacher-to-student ratio. I am not a therapist of this sort, and not qualified to describe Deena's methods in detail, but the results and the dolphin interaction I have witnessed have been well worth further research.

Witness to a "Miracle"

I was invited to watch a series of sessions that Island Dolphin Care provided for a young girl who was profoundly autistic. At eleven years old, she looked no more than eight. She was thin, pale, and limp in her movement. Her parents had tried many therapies, but had never achieved one of the most important goals when working with an autistic person, which is direct communication.

K had never spoken a word, nor had she ever intentionally looked anyone in the eyes. She had no gestures or signals that she used to communicate. Hers was a small and apparently scary world.

Her parents chose to try the Island Dolphin Care approach, and decided on three weeks of sessions. From the start K had no problems getting in the water, and she seemed to recognize the presence of Squirt. She was not responsive, but time would tell....

After a week, working in the classroom and in the pool with Squirt, K began to watch Squirt closely and took a ball from Deena's hand to toss to her. She seemed to be responding just as Nathanson's research has suggested, which is to say that her desire to play with Squirt overcame her painfully shy manner. She was beginning to pay attention. *(See Plate 16.)*

By the end of the second week, K was speaking. She was using sounds to indicate her desires, both in the classroom and in the pool. Smiles began to be a regular expression. She looked into Deena's eyes and asked for a ball.

By the end of the sessions, the parents were overcome with emotions as they said their farewells. They had worked very hard through the three weeks, attending classes with K, working on the poolside platform, and taking her on jaunts with her brother in the afternoons. I was invited to step into the classroom for the last session. As I entered, K turned to me and smiled. She looked at me, saw my camera, and watched as I raised it to my eye. She looked into the lens and smiled. Then she turned to Deena and asked who I was. *(See Plate 17.)*

I wiped the tears from my eyes and watched her point to pictures and name them, and answer questions about swimming, about Squirt and about herself. Her words were halting, shortened, and not clearly spoken, but were understandable nonetheless.

Deena's assessment of K showed her to have gained almost thirty words or verbal sounds and over twenty gestures. And her eye contact had gone from none at all to intermittent direct contact.

The parents were leaving with an entire regimen of classwork prepared for them to follow in the coming months including work with flashcards, puzzles, books, and pictures. The excitement they showed, knowing that they were now going to be able to converse, to hear her needs, to ask her to respond to what they were giving her, was contagious. I wanted to check up on them to get a follow-up report, but realized this was impractical. They had come from what had been East Germany, and were returning there to carry on the program begun by Deena and Squirt.

Life changed forever for that family over those three short weeks. Nothing had opened the door to K's life before; no therapy, drug program, or course of education had made any progress for her. In three weeks, Squirt and Deena found a way past the barriers, gently offered a way out, and were met by a little girl who had smiles to share with us all.

Does Dolphin-Assisted Therapy Work?

Yes, it does. Its results depend on the therapist, the setting, and the larger context, and the situation the patient is in. One cannot reasonably expect physical changes to occur, even though there are stories of this happening. One can hope for a breakthrough, a magical moment of new and delightful change, but this is also not always the case.

But somehow, people's lives are improved. Sometimes, a new responsiveness is brought out of children who were not expected to grow and improve at all. And in some rare cases, the patient finds a new life, a rich and exciting adventure with their newly contacted family and friends.

Research into Dolphin-Assisted Therapy is slowly progressing. As more facilities become available and as more competent therapists and scientists do the work, we will see more and more clearly the correct application of this kind of therapy.

It appears that the ultrasound that dolphins produce can have beneficial effects. In a recent conversation with Dave Cole, he reports that a senior researcher in the field of ultrasound has verified his suggestion that sono-phoresis could be the mechanism creating physical changes. A thorough analysis of this will require a massive effort to replicate the conditions under which dolphins have caused these results, because so many factors are at play. And we must consider how important it is to remove the dolphin from the process. It is likely that the living presence of the dolphin is a crucial component that can't be replaced.

Assuming DAT becomes well established, what will we think of creatures who offer to heal us of various afflictions and systemic malfunctions? When we accept that dolphins can do this, and are very willing to give freely of their ability, what will we have learned about the world around us?

Will we be able to tolerate abuse of any of the creatures that share the world with us? Will we see them as inferior creatures whose bodies can be processed into cheap products for our throwaway lifestyles? Or will we awaken one day to a world full of friends, companions, and experts in special ways of living, all of whom have lessons for us? If and when this day comes, we will have made a giant step forward, toward the destiny of humanity.

As the Dogon people put it, we will have re-organized the universe, and brought peace back to life.

.   .   .

Dolphin miracle boy speaks for first time
By Mike Brownhill, PA News
April 2001

A boy of eight who had never uttered a word has spoken for the first time—after swimming with dolphins. Nikki Brice was locked in his own world all his life after being starved of oxygen at birth, although he had the physical ability to speak.

His family from Weston-super-Mare, North Somerset, turned in desperation to a dolphin therapy centre in Florida—and within days he said his first word.

From the Human-Dolphin Therapy Centre in Miami, Nikki's mother Tabitha told of her joy at hearing her son speak for the first time. Mrs Brice said: "It is a miracle. It is a dream come true. Coming here was a make-or-break situation and I didn't expect Nikki to make such good progress."

His mother said: "We flew out last week and quickly got into a routine at the therapy centre in which Nikki is undergoing daily intensive therapy and 40 minutes swimming with dolphins. We hadn't been there long when Nikki was told to get out of the water at the end of a dolphin swimming session and he stood very quietly at the side of the tank. He must have thought that he wasn't going to be allowed to go swimming with the dolphins again because he suddenly pointed at the water and said, 'In.' He was telling us that he wanted to get back in the water. We all just stood there in shock because it was so unexpected, but once we got over it we quickly told him that he could go in again and he soon cheered up."

His mother, who managed to raise $10,500 to fund the therapy, added: "I have hoped for years to hear Nikki speak and I really didn't mind what his first word was. I am chuffed to bits with what has happened —the dolphins really have helped him to speak. Coming here was a fairy tale come true for us. We just heard stories about children getting better before, now we are actually seeing it before our eyes.

"It is like seeing magic happening before your eyes—even more so because nobody can explain why all these wonderful things are happening. There is something magical that happens between children and dolphins, something that I don't think we will ever fully understand. We feel like we will come down to earth at some time or wake up and find it was a dream."

Scientists are baffled by the therapeutic effect dolphins can have on people suffering from depression or people with learning difficulties. It is thought the underwater sounds made by the creatures to communicate may play a part.

Chris Connell, spokeswoman for the Miami centre, which has a 97 percent success rate, said: "Swimming with dolphins is an essential part of treatment because this not only provides a therapeutic benefit but is also a motivational tool. The 40-minute swimming sessions are run in conjunction with conventional speech and physical therapy and encourage the children to do well."

Dr. David Nathanson, who is instructing Nikki during a three-week intensive therapy session at the centre, said: "I am very pleased with Nikki. He is doing very well and we are delighted that he has spoken for the first time. Obviously it is early days and a great deal needs to be done yet, but Nikki has finally broken out of his world of silence."

PART THREE

Human Destiny

The Garden of the Golden Dolphin

"WE ARE NOMMO
WE COME IN PEACE
TO SPEAK TRUTH
AND DECLARE IMAGE WAR
ON OGO, ANIMAL MAN."

Scattered among the OGOs are the resurrected souls
of an invasion force of NOMMO Image Warriors,
sacrificed in the holocaust OGO wrought upon the planet
in his quest for power and possessions
... reincarnated now in OGO-form to infiltrate and guide
the barbarous OGO masses into the Oceanic future ...
—Peter Shenstone, *Legend of the Golden Dolphin*

A Lie We Love, A Life We Cannot Live

An interesting fact: the first television series syndicated around the world was *Flipper*. It was not until the 1980s that another series found wider distribution. This program was called *Dynasty*. It told the story of self-absorbed rich Texans and their lifestyle. From the innocence and interspecies possibilities of dolphins, the world's attention was turned to glamour and opulence and venal behavior. The '80s became known as the *me* decade. (Now the most widely distributed program is *Baywatch*.)

For the impoverished native in a developing country who trekked into town once a week to see the only local TV set, the story of dysfunctional Texan lifestyles was a poison, loosed upon his innocent desires. *Dynasty* was the epitome of the unsustainable desires being created by the global entertainment and advertising corporations. Images of a slim, fancifully coifed woman in a hand-made gown glowing with pearls, holding a cut-crystal glass of $1,000-per-bottle champagne, standing in front of windows that open onto expansive lawns and manicured gardens ... all this looked desirable to anyone. This heaven-like image embodied the shared dreams of hundreds of millions of people.

This and many other images have been shown to the world as an achievable lifestyle—a distant goal, admittedly, but one with a path beginning outside one's door, from school to commerce to monetary rewards and independent wealth. It is an unsustainable lie.

When we say we want a world of abundance for everyone, we are saying something we may feel, but we aren't clear about how it can happen. There are huge challenges to be met in giving the basics to the teeming billions with whom we share this planet. For instance, it will require a totally new type of refrigeration to provide the most health-improving appliance of all to the hundreds of millions who still live without it. The world economy and ecologies would collapse under the demands on the steel industry alone if we were to simply replicate the inefficient designs we now use. This is not about "having a cold one" after mowing the lawn; it is about being able to preserve food long enough to think of something other than the single goal of acquiring that day's meal—such as education for one's children.

We are a great distance from sustainable living for everyone. There is a lot to be done, and it must be done quickly.

The first stage of the needed change will occur when we find limits to our desires. Humans are the only living things that intentionally take more than they can use, then pollute the waters and soil with the discarded waste. Humans are a major source of the suffering we all deplore.

All of this is inspired and supported by the images we absorb. Our collective "desire body" is being fed a steady diet of fantasy and false promise, which creates a craving for the products that accompany the imagined lifestyle. The chains of discount stores that cater to the low-income, poorly educated, and sadly misinformed do well selling cheap reproductions of the hand-made gown, plastic champagne glasses, and lawn care products for that perfect green status symbol.

This is not the product, in my estimation, of a conscious conspiracy of evil minds committed to enslavement of the masses. It is instead the consequence of a failure to maintain right relations with our biological selves. In a careful examination of the underlying causes of greed, selfishness, small-mindedness and abuse, we find one fundamental issue that lies at the foundation. It is the nightmare of Separation.

We find ourselves separated from the world, our desires, and especially from our selves. This sense of separation generates anger, a systemic anger that in turn creates all our aberrant behaviors. Greed, selfishness, abuse, and deceit are products of our anger at the division within us. Karl Marx called it alienation, the condition of being separated from one's world. Our anger stems from the frustration that we really do know better, but can't find the way to do it right. We are angry because we find ourselves cut off from the nurturing we used to receive in the laps of our mothers and fathers, or we are furious because we never did receive it. We have a burning anger inside at the circumstances of our lives that keep us apart from what we require to succeed, to be loved, to give our love, and to find meaningful existence. This anger is the root cause of our selfish behavior, our disregard for the needs of others, and our abuse of the world.

We suffer from a sense of separation and cause more of it as a result. Why else would we torture or abuse our fellow humans, unless we felt no connection to them, no compassion for their all-too-similar lives? Why does the term "man*kind*" ring false to those who carefully observe the relations we maintain with each other and the rest of Earth's animals?

The Mental Health of Dolphins

It is in the eye of the dolphin that we see the understanding gaze of creatures who are not separated from life or from each other.

This is not a mystical claim or a wish-fulfilling fantasy. It is a simple and readily observable truth. Even if we disregard the extra sense they have with their sonic imaging and their built-in wholistic awareness, we still know dolphins to be well integrated into their surroundings.

We may find examples of dolphin behavior that appall us, such as the killing of infants by males, the apparent forcefulness of sexual relations sometimes reported, or the intentional violence that has been observed between individuals of different species, but this does not add up to a picture of brute ignorance or an unconscious distance from life such as we suffer from. It simply demonstrates the range of natural behavior that can arise in an organic life form that is part of the living world.

To early humans the dolphins demonstrated traits that stimulated friendliness and compassion. They seemed magical, fearless, from another realm entirely. They were seen as demi-gods, divine beings who live partly in this world, partly in another.

To us, when we gaze into the eye of the dolphin—or, wonder upon wonder, into the eye of a living whale—we see a consciousness that surpasses our own experiences and we see a marvelous self-awareness that understands its role in the ocean world.

Neither the forms of ancient worship nor contemporary affection are misplaced. Both ages have seen something in the dolphin that has inspired us, has lifted our eyes to other possibilities. In gazing into the cetacean eye, we sense directly the life of a being who is not separated from its own true nature.

It is self-awareness we crave in our quest to end the long separation. It is a clear understanding of the meaning of our lives, the tasks we can do to find the goal of satisfaction, the lives we can lead that will end our feeling of futility.

And it is the dolphin who has embodied that spirit of self-awareness since before the era of Apollo's temple at Delphi, where the lesson of "Know Thy Self" was written on the wall.

How do we see ourselves today? Less and less do the majority consider themselves to be part of the biological system from which we have emerged. We are far from an awareness of the sources of our food in Western culture. Children today too often think that milk comes from factories and meat comes bloodless on plastic trays, with no connection to the cows alongside the rural highway. Losing the sense of the biological self has led us into a dire fantasy, a deluded nightmare of exploding consequences.

We are not comfortable with the suggestion that we each must find an appropriate limit to our acquisitiveness. How does it make you feel to have me say you ought to have a cap on your income, say, $50,000 per year? We can go into details about how much should be allowed for couples, how much per child, the elderly, etc., but the question is this: Are we willing to accept limits on what we are taking from the world?

Without those limits, we find ourselves in a free-for-all where nothing is free for anyone, and everyone must act like a shark to have his or her desires met. While not everyone who has the means does this, advantaged people around the world continue to exploit industrial opportunities to produce useless items that might return a tidy profit. Such people are not evil; they are part of a system they have never adequately questioned. They are not attempting to live within the organic limits of their own true nature, along with the rest of their kind, because no such image lives in their minds.

Image Warriors: The Nommo Human/Dolphin

What does the Human/Dolphin look like? Those of us who have, by whatever means, awakened to our own true nature could be classified as Dolphins in Human guise (or Nommo, if you prefer the Dogon/Zulu version). If you have discovered the false assumptions and mistaken concepts of the world that we live in and found some success in advancing the "feminine traits" of gentleness and sensitivity to all nearby beings, you are a Nommo. If you have emotional intelligence, the power of yielding, and a deep love for children and their world, you are one of the Dolphin Clan.

We are self-aware, yet tuned in to the world of cars, houses, food stores, electricity bills, and television programs. We see ourselves as "in the world" but not "of the world." We often rise to another level of ourselves, to that inner quiet place where we see how perfect the world can be, where creative forces generate solutions to problems, where gentle and kind relations exist. It is as if we rise to breathe the air of another realm. Like a dolphin, we leave the normal world for a moment to breathe in, to absorb the fiery element of spirit and change.

Then we dive back in. We swim among the ones who do not realize they are in water. These people keep their heads down, watching for the patterns in the carpet that covers the floor of their life. The patterns lead them from childhood to school, from there to a job, a family, children, work, insurance, birthdays, an old folks' home and death. Change does not enter here, without deep fear. Few creative dreams disturb their sleep.

For me, it was tough awakening to the fact that not everyone is self-aware or likely to become so anytime soon. I often find myself observing with astonishment the unaware, the "drowned church" of the modern world, where no thought is given to one's personal impact on the delicate life system, and no limits are accepted.

The world has been made idiot-proof. The "shallow end of the gene pool" is not self-selecting for disappearance. The Nommo are crowded and engulfed by teeming schools of fish.

Like weavers, we who are among the Delphic Tribes are laying new patterns among the old, gradually replacing the worn path that is followed by the benighted so that it no longer leads to an end in the desert, but to an abundant garden or the wide-open sea, the limitless ocean of life.

Closing the Sacred Hoop: Permaculture

Our tale finds its end where it began. In Australia is a new dream, one of practical application, one that can manifest the healing of our own forgiveness. It is called Permaculture.

Bill Mollison must be regarded as the father of Permaculture. The word was compounded from Permanence, Agriculture, and Culture and is meant to describe a set of design tools that can be used to create sustainable systems for humans to live in harmony with the natural world. It is a practical, easily learned system, drawing on any and all sources that are healthy and helpful in creating sustainable living.

Bruce Mace introduced me to the ideas of permaculture on the same day that I heard the Legend of the Golden Dolphin for the first time. It interested me, but the dolphin story was my first love. Then permaculture re-entered my life many years later. I decided to take the Permaculture Designer's Certification Course. One was being offered in Northern California that year, and Mollison was going to teach it. It was one of his last classes, and I realized I should not miss the opportunity to learn directly from the Master.

Sixty-five of us spent two weeks camping in a damp field, soaked with fog and rain, about an hour north of San Francisco. We hardly noticed the weather. We were swept up into the grandeur of the visions of Mollison, grandeur built upon a starkly un-blinkered view of the disastrous condition of the world and fired by an unquenchable passion to meet the challenges head on.

We learned that if we knew the world was going to end tomorrow, the best response would be to plant a tree.

We were shown system after system of elegant, simple solutions to enormous problems. We were taught techniques for redesigning water flow across the landscape using two sticks, a piece of string, and a beer bottle. We were told stories of ice-making in the desert, homebuilding that children can do, heating and cooling systems for any climate, kitchen garden design, village design, systems for local commerce, farming techniques that create more and better soil, and a seemingly endless list of means to create a better world.

Mollison's teaching technique was amazing. We were all entertained, challenged, provoked into thinking, and deeply inspired. An image came to my mind of us as a mob being ushered onto the low end of a spiral ramp. As the days went by, we were ascending the ramp, becoming more and more orderly in our thinking. By the end of the two weeks, we were lifting off, flying from the top of the incline we had climbed together. We were inspired to see the world as a wonderful assortment of problems for us to chose among, to bring solutions to. Our main challenge was going to be choosing which solutions to apply.

Permaculture is a gift from Australia to the world, a golden key to taking a species-wide initiation into functional self-awareness. To save this world from human destruction, humans must find a sustainable path. Permaculture offers this, as a sort of magic bag, endlessly pouring out solutions for the challenges we face.

> Here, in the arena of the ImagiNation, we shall engage OGO-Man in unarmed combat to The Bitter End ... and build The Palace of Freedom for the KINGDOM COME!
> —Peter Shenstone, *Legend of the Golden Dolphin*

At the end of the Designer's Course, I sat on a cliff, looking out to sea. I contemplated the path I had walked following the dolphins and realized that a merging of the secret story of man's origins with the practical wisdom of permaculture could make a lasting difference. If there was to be a "new dawn," a positive step forward for us into an era of healthy spirituality, healthy bodies, hearts, and minds, there would have to be a corresponding advance in our ability to design sustainable living systems.

Sustainability is an issue of both time and wisdom. For something to be sustained, it must be supported by life itself. It is only in the 4.5 billion years of organic life on the planet that we can find patterns of action that have withstood the tests of time. Permaculture is a huge collection of practices gathered from around the world that have proven to work, to be non-destructive and to support life.

More than anything, permaculture teaches one how to read patterns, the timeless forms of nature. By seeing them, one sees the place where one stands and what can be arranged so as to build a path into a healthy future. Through patterns, one accesses the natural mirror in which we come to know ourselves.

What a revelation: Nommo are permaculture designers. To be an image warrior is to be a person who creates living images of sustainable systems for himself and the world.[1]

The Dawn of the Golden Dolphin

The Human Story has just begun. We are almost past the worst stage. We are awakening to the reign of the dragons of fear and are now banishing them forever. We are in the dawning of a new day, the time when the Dolphin of Peace reappears. *(See Plate 18.)*

She is coming to live beside us, in the waters of life surrounding our island homes. It is time for us to plant gardens, build homes to last for a thousand years, and set up living systems that will support us. We have much to do in the new world, much which is outside our dreams today. We will go beyond our imagination; we will live as new beings, full of wisdom and ability. Our future is not visible to us now. It lies just the other side of our immediate task. It awaits the completion of the night of the singular Self, separated and lost in the desert, wandering far from home. In embracing permaculture, not as a movement but as a path through life, we awaken to the larger Self, that of all life. In that moment is the dawning of our destiny.

. . .

The dolphins hold the Dreams, we hold the Means.

It is the Time of the End of the System of Things,
the Great Tribulation ... the cusp of AQUARIUS!

The beautiful blue-water world of Oceania is
dominated by the two space races:
The NOMMO, "Master-of-the-Waters,"
And OGO-Man who subjugates the islands
which dot a quarter of the planet's surface.

OGO has discovered the god-energy
of destruction ... and seems intent
upon destroying the water-world
he arrogantly calls Earth!

The amphibious NOMMO came to
Oceania from the star system SIRIUS
many millions of years ago.

They then evolved fingers and feet into
flippers and flukes, the better to appreciate
their new watery paradise ...

OGO, arch-killer, has unleashed a
merciless attack on the NOMMO,
driving them towards extinction!
Now they have only their minds and their music,
the power of their Dreaming, with which to combat
OGO's terminal threat to the planet's existence.

But their Dream-plan is daringly simple:
To reCreate Heaven on Earth
before OGO vaporizes Her!

And build a new New World
under the new Aquarian heaven.

Mankind is an unbalanced, spiritually
immature race dominated by its brute,
killer nature. The only way NOMMO
can save themselves and their beautiful
blue-water world (and indeed Mankind itself!)
is to tap Man's loving feminine potential,
and liberate the human Spirit.

Time and time again for thousands of years, the
    NOMMO
connected with OGO, planting the seed of civilization,
a process intended to "conquer the beast in OGO-
    Man."
In India and Sumeria, the so-called Cradle of
    Civilization,
contact was made, and was repeated throughout the
    lands
bordering the Great Sea.
Each time the NOMMO simply offered themselves in
    loving
friendship, leaving behind nothing but an image of
    goodness in
the myths and legends of OGO-Man.
And the promise of things to come!
"WE ARE NOMMO
WE COME IN PEACE TO SPEAK TRUTH.
AND DECLARE IMAGE WAR ON OGO, Animal
    Man."

Scattered among the OGOs
    are the resurrected souls of
    an invasion force of NOMMO
    Image Warriors, sacrificed in the
    holocaust OGO wrought upon
    the planet in his quest for power
    and possessions ... reincarnated now

in OGO-form to infiltrate and
guide the barbarous OGO masses
into the Oceanic future ...

The Time draws near for the
gathering of these Freedom-loving
NOMMO-souls..., in preparation
for the final battle of the Image War
between NOMMO's Dream and OGO's Nightmare.
Australia ... Island of Dreamers and Dreams,
Green-and-Gold jewel, never quite what it seems.
Set in the midst of an ocean of Space,
Aquarian Ark for the whole human race.
On the Boomerang tip ancient Mount Warning
Is first to reflect the light of the dawning.[2]
Outback in the Centre, Ayer's Rock of Ages,
The hub of the world is calling the sages.
Australia ... an Isle where The Spirit can roam
Free as The Wind to the wild dolphins' home.
To Monkey Mia at The End of the Earth,
Where the promised Family will find its rebirth.

Here in Australia at The Time of the End
Awaits welcome reunion with a long-lost friend.
For the Great ancient Whales are NOMMO of old,
And Freedom lies in a Dolphin of Gold.

—Peter Shenstone, *Legend of the Golden Dolphin*

CHAPTER TWENTY

"Build a Boat of Pleasing Proportions ..."

We, as relative newcomers, may be asking too much of ourselves to communicate meaningfully with minds as ancient as
those of the whales and dolphins ... the whales and dolphins
may have more to teach us than we have to teach them.
—Dr. John Lilly[1]

Our historical journey has led us from the pre-history of Australia, to India, Sumeria, Egypt, North and South Africa,
Greece, Palestine, Rome, and then across Europe. We went to the
Americas and watched the whales and dolphins become part of modern global culture. In the end, we saw how the long trail led back
to Australia, where human wisdom has accumulated a set of design
tools to respond to the difficult challenges we face. Permaculture
provides us with an opportunity to work cooperatively with the long
wave of history, the Delphic Wave.

We have also looked at a political imperative—a new nation that
has the cetaceans as its citizens. This is a revolutionary recognition
of the rights of whales and dolphins, and it creates a mandate to
care for the water of the world.

. . .

The mysterious truth we have pursued has been somewhat revealed, yet remains partially shrouded. We have lifted only one of the veils of Isis. We know more about the long history we share with the cetacean families, and we know the responsibility we bear for our centuries of unconscious abuse of them. But the questions remain: "Who are the dolphins? Who are the whales?"

> The Mock Turtle said: "No wise fish would go anywhere without a porpoise."
> "Wouldn't it really?" asked Alice, in a tone of great surprise.
> "Of course not," said the Mock Turtle. "Why, if a fish came to me and told me he was going on a journey, I should say 'With what porpoise?'"
> —Lewis Carroll, *Alice's Adventures in Wonderland*

As we have seen, the lives and deaths of whales have played important roles in human history. The lessons we have learned from dolphins have shaped our lives. There is something deeply important about the cetacean family. We may not yet know all the reasons, the facts of the matter, the why or how, but the evidence of history and of personal experience shows us that we must treat them with the utmost respect.

For the Norwegians, the Japanese, and the pirates who still insist on killing whales and defying the desires of humanity, the arguments to stop fall on deaf ears. They consider anything other than the science of population estimates and the profitability of whale-meat delicacies to be emotional rhetoric, unworthy of consideration. Harvesting the protein resources of the sea is paramount to them, and our cetacean friends are easy targets.

For the Faroese, the Makah, and to a lesser extent the Japanese and Norwegians, the idea of cultural independence is more important than any suggestion that these are intelligent beings or that larger issues are at stake. All such suggestions are tossed aside, casually ignored as "mere emotional arguments."

Esoteric tales alone won't change their actions, nor will statements about cetacean intelligence or beauty or friendliness. These move the hearts and minds of most people but leave us unable to enter into a dialog with the market-driven world of today. If these are the only ways we have learned to speak about the cetaceans, we cannot hope to change the minds of those who cannot hear such "unscientific" facts. To overcome the bias against "emotional arguments," we who love the whales and dolphins must find ways to demonstrate their value in the global ecosystem. The complex relationship between the whales and the ozone layer must be investigated fully.

Science can help by finding ways to measure their other qualities. Well-supported research must be carried out in two areas: cetacean self-awareness, which has already been demonstrated and can be made more evident; and scientific proof of the efficacy of Dolphin-Assisted Therapy. Both are vital necessities in this war of values. These areas must be delved into as never before. The Japanese are notoriously intractable and the Norwegians are determined to retain their position, held for centuries, at the top of the hierarchy of whalers. It will require compelling evidence to change their ways.

To save the whales and dolphins we must, in the end, combine science and spirit, fact and feeling. Neither will do it alone. We must dissolve old boundaries and find ways to demonstrate the exceptional status of the dolphins and whales, with scientific proof of their esoteric nature. In doing so, we will open the door to hidden worlds.

If we are led by the cetaceans to cross another threshold, to bring into the light of day the intuitive factor, the inner voice that has always guided human progress, it will be a real achievement. It is this inner voice that I have tried to bring into our shared awareness with this book. I have risked using science as a support for mythology; I have brought personal experiences of my own into a historic scenario spanning centuries; and I have made allusions to facts I cannot verify. These are truths we can prove if we strive to do so. I am confident that you, the reader, will have had flashes of intuition while reading this book. You will have had a moment or two when a vista opened up, a light blazed, and a deeper knowing was yours. It is this that we must find ways to express alongside the facts of science.

The ancient dolphin-inspired key of self-knowledge unlocks the gate onto the path of the greater Self, the interdependent Whole. The intuitive voice, the inner kingdom, the divine spirit in humankind—this is the gift the cetaceans offer us, and we have had it all along.

When humans express the desire for healthy oceans, abundant fish and seas filled again with the songs of whales, and they take actions to ensure that these conditions return, we have answered a call. From out of our past comes that song. From out of the depths of the ocean comes that song, and it sings to us of the future.

It is now, in our post-modern world, in which empty hearts embrace terror as communication, that the great challenge has arrived.

In the simplest terms, it all comes down to marks on paper. Our agreements as to who is entitled to all of the elements of a decent life are only that, and we are the authors. Life itself has opened the universe of possibilities, and we live now in the mansions of our own design. We have chosen pain and suffering as the price for most to pay in the hopes that the few might live well enough that they will find a way to end all suffering. In ancient times, this was the idea behind the aristocracy, the supremely advantaged few. Today this applies to the highly developed countries, who owe so much to the "two-thirds world." Until those who have been given so much live up to their responsibility the pain will continue.

Will we prove to be more than a provisional species, an experiment in the laboratory of organic life that could not tame itself, toilet-train itself, or balance its desires with its abilities? Will we find and embrace our limits, grateful for the limitless world around us? Will we find comfort and satisfaction when we draw the final arc of the circle of life around ourselves, defining where we will and will not go? Today is the day. Now is the time.

> Our task is not to be humanitarians, not so much to participate in conservation of species as to be willing, positive participants

in the future evolution of all species, including man, upon the planet Earth. Man must come down from his throne and realize that his future is coextensive with the future of all species. Instead of functioning as a reluctant caretaker, the zookeeper of Earth, it is time for man to change his beliefs and become what he is, another species that desires survival not at the expense of, but in concert with the other organisms of the planet.
    —Dr. John Lilly[2]

The Delphic Spirit has become restless, and it has begun to move again. It is seeking a final resolution of its sojourn on Earth, to establish and nurture a kind and self-aware consciousness on this planet. Across the Pacific Ocean in Australia, the Delphic Spirit is moving and the sacred Story of the Dolphin has been coming to the surface.

We can envision this as a hoop, the Sacred Hoop of Life, as it is often called in Native American stories. The Sacred Hoop of Life is now being made complete, like Ouroborus, the rainbow-colored, globe-girdling snake of the ancients, biting its tail, reconnecting with itself, closing the circuit. This circuit is connecting the vitality of America, the intelligence of Europe, the passions of South America, the fertility of Africa, and the wisdom of Asia to the point of origin, where the Dream Time lives, a Rainbow Bridge around the world that will enable the children of the future to gather the fruits of every land.

On the eastern shore of Australia, where the sun shines first on that great island continent, stands a mountain. To the Aboriginal people, this mountain is called *Wollumbin*, the Cloud Gatherer. It is here that the Rainbow Serpent (the iridescent star whale, Jiderra, in his terrestrial form) is said to begin and end. His head and tail meet at Wollumbin, after circling the whole of Australia. And it is here that the Legends of the Dolphins tell us that the Rainbow Spirit, made of all races and colors, has come to complete its circuit of the whole Earth. The Dolphin Spirit is coming back to its place of beginning.

Each river system flows into the ocean. Each watershed has its own magic, its own cultural truths. Some of the truths are universal, some are local. At this time we are being called to discover the golden threads within each magic system, each way of mastery, to weave them into a new pattern for humankind. This is the calling of the Nommo, the Ogo Titiyayne, the Rainbow People at the end of time. It is our task to create a universal magic, a worldwide system of human behavior that will stand the test of time, that will lift humanity into a new realm of life. Permaculture is part of this, and so are the trends toward world-music, eclectic spirituality, diverse culinary styles, and the availability of the hidden traditions of all cultures. These are outer signs, indicating a global inclusiveness that is struggling to be born. We can do this. We are already doing this. We can be conscious participants, if we want to be. As George Harrison said, "Within you or without you."

The Hopi elders of North America have reportedly said to all of us: "We are the ones we have been waiting for." It is not someone else, or in some other time that this task is to be accomplished. It is now.

In a time scale we do not often sense, this is occurring. We are experiencing a completion. At each of the sites we have visited the Delphic Wave has left us a message of hope that one day Jiderra, Vatea, Vishnu, Oannes, Apollo, Nommo Dié, Dag, and others would return. The linking of this message of return to the recent upsurge in contact with whales and dolphins is obvious. These are momentous days.

The Two Spirits Within Us: Dragon and Dolphin

We are of two spirits, we humans, and our polarization is reflected in the world. One spirit is contracted and fearful, arming itself, driven to build fortresses to defend possessions, and the other is free, living in the abundance of a limitless Earth that is only kept from perfection by our smallness of spirit. Part of us is Male in expression, penetrating the surrounding world with desire and the will-to-possess. And part of us is Female in expression, yielding to the greater Will of Life, providing a womb for the generation of the children of Love. Part of us is rather Dragon-like, with a fierce territoriality, living within a world-view of fear and force. The other part of us is Dolphin-like, gentle and playful, while secretly powerful and deeply wise.

The events of September 2001 marked a moment in history when ancient antagonisms within the human breast came out, manifested in the ironic use of fear in an effort to create a world of justice and love. The Dragon is thrashing his tail.

This is the time of the Return. The Dolphin is revealed now, and she is swimming peacefully, with a smile, in all of our hearts. She has shown us the way to become a success in life, to fit ourselves into the scheme of living. She shows us the way, by diving in. She immerses herself, having shaped herself to fit the world as it is. She does not force the world to fit her needs, but instead has become beautiful by adapting to fit the world in which she lives. *(See Plate 19.)*

Although stories tell of ancestors from the stars, the dolphins we swim with today are from our world. They show us that we can do as they have done, here on Earth, making ourselves into joyous participants in the play of life.

There are dreams in the oceans, plans and stories for us all, that will take us into a new time, a world of fulfillment and joy beyond our human dreams. The dolphins are waiting for us....

Tear Down the House of Your Old Beliefs and Be Free

History, science, and personal experiences by the tens of thousands lead us to an irreducible conclusion, that dolphins and whales are highly evolved creatures with attributes that place them in a special category. These attributes indicate the presence of an embodied soul, aware of itself in its limited biological form, a rare and precious state. On our planet this advanced state is shared by humans and cetaceans alone. All other life forms are still advancing toward self-awareness and the full appearance of the soul. It is this self-awareness that brings the divine, the spiritual essence of a being, into the realm of living, breathing, and organic life. Throughout history, as we have shown, the idea of self-awareness has been associated with the dolphin. Matsya Avatar, Oannes, Apollo, Jesus, and many indigenous traditions point to the path of enlightened self-awareness as the way to attain the promise of human destiny.

Every cultural tradition says that light is our final heritage. To be enlightened, to rise into the celestial heavens, to overcome darkness, to wear a halo of divine radiance, all these speak to us of our future, when we will have mastered the challenges of our dark beginnings. Today, our highest technologies are systems of light, from hydroponics to solar power systems, from computer technologies to laser scalpels. We are well suited to being masters of light, with our eyes, hands, and brains so closely linked.

Dolphins and whales are masters of sound, living in a realm of sonic waves that they know in detail, shaping pings and bongs, creaks and squeals into meaning, understanding, and all of the essentials for life beneath the waters.

If we accomplish our task to master light, and we meet them at the shore with their mastery, we will find that the combination of sound and light, wielded by wise and compassionate beings in coordinated harmony, will produce marvels.

Perhaps our shared destiny will be among the stars, or we may find new realms of life and experience here on our shared planet.

> Tear down your house and build a boat, abandon possessions and look for life, despise worldly goods and save your soul.... Tear down your house, I say, and build a boat with her dimensions in proportion—her width and length in harmony. Put

aboard the seed of all living things, into the boat.
—The God EA, *The Epic of Gilgamesh*, Sumeria,
7000 B.C.

Taking up this challenge calls for a choice to be made. It is made in the stillness and silence of our inner cathedral, the temple where the throne of the Self stands. This is the place where we stand in awe of life, where we yield to brilliance beyond our capacity to see. It stands upon the shore of the future. We are called to know our real selves, our limits and our abilities. Banishing the fogs of delusion, we stand revealed. From that shore, we can set out on the next adventure of the human legend. The dolphins and whales will once again give us their best, leading us into this new realm. In choosing, we will redeem ourselves, empowering humankind to take up our roles as welcome companions of the souls in the sea.

A Whale and Dolphin Primer

A detailed description of the physical characteristics of dolphins and whales is beyond the scope of this book, but some of the special traits of their bodies are useful to keep in mind when thinking about the roles they have played in our human drama. The following description may seem exhaustive, but it is quite elementary.

Stereo Dolphins

According to Dr. John Lilly, pioneer brain researcher and the most widely known dolphin expert, dolphins have three distinct mechanisms for generating sound. Two are within the blowhole structure in the top of the head, and one is located in the throat.[1]

Beneath the muscular flap that naturally rests across a dolphin's blowhole are their nasal passages, not unlike our two nostrils. The passages each have a pair of balloon-like sacs opening off of them. These are filled with air when a dolphin inhales and can be squeezed by surrounding muscles. Not unlike balloons, the "neck" of each sac can be stretched taut, regulating the escape of air. This produces an infinitely variable range of sounds under extremely fine control. The air can be circulated from one sac to another, so air is not necessarily lost when "vocalizing," And, as Dr. Lilly has pointed out, the two separate structures allow the dolphin to "speak" in stereo.

These two sources of sound, side-by-side and less than two inches apart, create an omni-directional, expanding "ball" of sound. The sounds can be varied in frequency in less than one-thousandth of a second, in a range that reaches at least ten times as high as human hearing. And each side can operate independently. This enables the dolphin to both "whistle" and "squeak" at the same time. It is as if they can speak in two languages at once.

This omni-directional field of sound is broadcast from the center of the head of the dolphin, in an invisible, expanding sphere. The dolphin listens to the returning echoes to gain a sense of the location of everything in its vicinity. The sounds can be heard by other dolphins, of course. It is part of the dynamic of their culture to be made aware of the world by each other.

A full scientific exploration of the capacity of the dolphin to create this expanding sphere in stereo has yet to be done. Although this differs somewhat from the traditional concepts of holography, which uses light in a single beam that is split in two, there are some similarities. The two separate yet nearly identical sources of sound, off-set by a known distance, could give the dolphin a kind of stereoscopic sonic "sight," part of a "holographic" auditory "vision" system.

The returning waves of sound are, of course, picked up by the ears. However, the outer structure of the ear plays less of a part in their hearing than in ours. Their ear openings are tiny, the eardrum far inside. The auditory nerve, however, is very large, capable of accepting sonic information of many kinds.

A dolphin's skin is taut, a smooth wet layer on a base of hard blubber. The soft outer layers quiver sensitively. Their skin is somewhat like wet rubber or chamois leather laid over marble. The entire hard body of a dolphin rings with the returning sounds of its clicks and whistles.

And, amazingly, the teeth act as transceiver antennas. Each tooth in a dolphin's mouth is nearly identical, shaped like an upside down ice-cream cone. Inside are micro-tubes, radiating out from the center of the tooth. This structure is ideal for transmitting and picking up high-frequency sound, much like a radio antenna. In addition, the spacing of the teeth is very regular. Dr. Lilly discovered that the spacing of dolphin teeth is exactly matched by the primary wavelengths of their echo-locating signals.[2] Their teeth act as pickups for their returning sounds, conducting them through the jaw bone directly to the auditory nerves at the corner of the mouth, behind the ear. The teeth also act as transmitters for some of the highest frequencies the dolphins use. This is only one of the systems of sound they use. The other is perhaps even more amazing.

Somehow (it is still not conclusively determined how it is done) a dolphin can produce long trains of clicks in its throat. Dolphins do not have vocal cords as we do, they do not breathe through their mouths, and the effect is not produced by air movement, but instruments show the clicks originating from the throat. These sounds are channeled upward through the skull and out by way of the bulging forehead.

The large forehead and the smile are almost the definition of the face of a dolphin. It is commonly assumed that behind that forehead lies the large brain of the dolphin. This is not correct.

Inside the forehead is a sack of oil, surrounded by a net of muscles. This flexible sack can be shaped, stretched, squeezed, and moved around by the dolphin or whale to change the form of the sound-beam it is emitting. The sack is called the melon and is, in fact, an acoustic lens. It is an organ for shaping sound waves. By the use of the melon, the dolphin can send out a precise beam of sound, either wide or as narrow as three degrees. This is a separate mechanism by which a dolphin examines its surroundings. It is this system that enables them to see details. Not location alone, as in the stereo field of sound coming from inside her blowhole, but such fine detail it can be said that dolphins experience a wholistic reality so complete and accurate that they live in an "ocean of truth."

Dolphins have been tested exhaustively in regard to their sense of sound. Many times over, indicating the disbelief that it could be so precise, dolphins have been tested to determine the degree of detail they are capable of perceiving. Biosonar, or ultrasonic imaging, is their specialty. It has been shown that a dolphin can reliably "see" the difference between otherwise identical metal disks or balls, polished to create the same reflectivity, and machined to be precisely the same size. In 97 out of 100 trials, a dolphin has been able to tell the difference between these disks without being able to see them with her eyes. This means that a dolphin is somehow able to tell the difference between two kinds of metal via its biosonar alone.

This is astounding. It implies that dolphins can see into matter and can detect the molecular differences between substances. We have long known that they can sense the speed of our heartbeats, the filling and emptying of our lungs, and even "see" metal rods in mended limbs. We have watched them catch fish easily in perpetually muddy water using their sonar alone. Now we know they "see" a world we do not see, that they are aware of not only the surfaces of things, but the inner physical nature of that thing. A dolphin approaching you will wag its head back and forth a few times, scanning you. Like an x-ray machine, it can see right through you. It can examine the finest detail of your physical form—bones, air spaces, even the flow of hormones from your endocrine system. It knows the physical components of your emotions, as well as the condition of all your organs and muscles....

In contrast, humans are primarily visual creatures, dependent upon the reflected light that bounces off objects to identify them. We are dependent on the light that is not absorbed by the object, thus actually seeing what the object is not. From this, we must *interpret* our visual sensory input, rather than having direct perception of the nature of objects.

The range of dolphin sounds is extensive. Human hearing reaches as high as 22,000 cycles per second in young healthy ears. Dolphins hear frequencies more than ten times this high. This is well within the segment of the electromagnetic spectrum we call radio waves. A dolphin could be described as a biological radio station, broadcasting and receiving. Even the low end of their sonic awareness is exceptional, as they are capable of hearing into the sub-sonic range, well below our hearing.

The power output of a dolphin's biosonar is impressive. Surgeons sometimes use ultrasound to shatter kidney stones and dissolve cataracts in living people. A bottlenose dolphin can produce over four times the power used to do this, from within its head. We explore this in more detail in another part of this book as we look into the phenomenon of Dolphin-Assisted Therapy.

Several scientists have considered whether dolphins and whales might have a sort of onboard theater in their heads. Perhaps the melon can hold temporary images, created by other cetaceans by the use of their biosonar. Perhaps communication between them takes place as literal transmissions of virtual realities, internal "images" formed of oil. Imagine, then, a sperm whale, with a head over twenty feet long and a melon full of oil and spermaceti, more than eight hundred gallons of it, perceiving a series of images as they appear in the fluid, projected there by another whale. Like a 3-D holographic theater inside their heads....

Could the odd behavior of the sperm whales, when they form a "marguerite" in the Arctic Sea, be some kind of exchange of theater performances? Sperm whales have been observed floating together in groups with their heads touching, breathing synchronously for hours on end. No convincing biological explanation has yet been put forward to explain this behavior. It appears to be part of their culture, a social activity which has values we do not know.

Imagine You Are a Dolphin

All of these attributes add up to a very odd combination. For a moment, imagine yourself with eyes that work very well underwater. Try to imagine yourself with eyes that can be bulged outward to give you a larger field of vision; eyes that can be temporarily coated with an oil, by blinking, that changes the effective curvature of the lens, enabling you to see perfectly well both under water and above; and eyes that operate independently of one another. In addition, each iris is constructed to enable stereo vision in each eye. (Instead of a circular iris opening, it forms a "u" shape, with rounded openings at the ends of the "u".) Now add a sense we don't have. Use your imagination to create an ability that helps you to place yourself in your surroundings and to sense the pulsing, flowing, pumping movements of every living thing around you by means of sound waves. You are also able to see the turbulence in the water itself, the vortices and swirls and waves of energy passing through it (for us, this would be analogous to seeing the wind).

Your sense of taste has replaced your sense of smell, and you can analyze the contents of the water in fine detail, tasting the fear or tranquility of fish, the state of the pregnancy of your pod mate, the nearness of land, and the exotic flavors of currents from afar.

Now add in an awareness of magnetism. Somehow, cetaceans navigate by following magnetic patterns. (Inside their heads is a small deposit of magnetite, sensitive to magnetism. The Earth has a variable magnetic field, and its fluctuations have been used to explain some whale and dolphin strandings, when normal patterns are disrupted temporarily and the invisible magnetic "path" they are following leads them ashore.)

As this imaginary self, you are also a master of weightlessness, moving in three dimensions of space with ease and grace. Some of the somersaults and twisting turns of dolphins defy description, and their delight in launching themselves into the air is legendary. It has been theorized that the leaps of a dolphin or a whale may be for the experience of gravity, which is attenuated underwater. Perhaps the huge whales, weighing fifty tons or more, are savoring gravity like wine when they vault high into the air, enjoying the odd sensation of being pulled back down to the water. Those who have been documented doing this over two hundred times in a row may be quite drunk on the sensation.

Do we and cetaceans share the same world? Perhaps not. By recognizing the three-to-one ratio of water to land, and adding in the depth of the sea, we realize that the planet they experience is much, much larger than the one we experience. It has been estimated that whales and dolphins have greater than nine thousand times the useable space to explore and inhabit that humans have. By this calculation we discover that we are minor players on a fraction of the inhabitable space of this world. Why then do we call it "Earth"? Probably for the same reasons we say the sun rises, when we know it does not....

Weightless Love in Perfect Bodies

As a consequence of the floating weightlessness of their lives, cetaceans do not experience some of our most normal sensations. Let me illustrate: if we lean forward and touch another person from our chair, we mostly move in two dimensions and depend upon the weight of our body to keep us in place and to provide the resistance that keeps us in place, not floating away from the person we touched.

To a dolphin, full contact as we know it almost cannot happen. Any amount of pressure they place on anything outside themselves pushes them away from that thing. There is little resistance.

Given the above, we realize that two whale lovers must be very creative, cooperative, and committed to pro-create. In some species, it takes a third whale to serve as the "couch" on which the female whale reclines while she is being impregnated. (To compensate for some of the difficulties of oceanic lovemaking, the cetacean penis is prehensile, capable of independent movement, exploring the body of the female, seeking entrance.)

Each caress between dolphins moves them apart. To stay in contact, forward motion is maintained, which enables steering toward one another. Cetaceans live in nearly constant motion. Paradoxically, this enables them to stay together.

A few more details: The reproductive organs of cetaceans have many uses. The penis is under the complete control of the male cetacean. It is erected by muscular action and can be erected, in the dolphin, in as little as five seconds. It has been observed to be an organ of reproduction, of pleasure, and of exploration. Males have been seen to pick objects up with the penis, to examine textures, and to hook unsuspecting human swimmers behind the knees with it. Females have been known to carry items in their vaginas as well. Whale penises can be as long as twelve feet and are virtually prehensile, capable of searching for and entering the vagina of the female as if independent. Mating between all cetaceans is an act of delicacy, despite their size and the fluid medium in which they live.

And, there is the awesome power of their muscles. This enables them to do things we consider miraculous. For example, tail-walking: think of the control and power it takes to stir your tail hard enough and in the right pattern to extend more than 300 pounds of dolphin body upright, almost entirely out of the water, while making backward progress across the surface of the water. No one yet has been able to describe the physics of this natural talent.

All cetaceans are endowed with very powerful bodies, capable of living well in the endlessly tumbling sea. Their size and strength can be awesome:

> An eighty-foot female blue whale held fast by a modern harpoon head attached to three thousand fathoms of line once towed a ninety-foot, twin screw steam chaser, with its engines going full speed astern, for seven hours at a steady eight knots, covering over fifty miles without letup.[3]

If we squeeze a grapefruit seed between the thumb and the side of our forefinger, we can send this small organic projectile a long distance with little effort. This is largely due to the tapering shape of the seed exactly matching the exertion of pressure by the thumb, great at first and tapering off. If we see the body of a dolphin like this, with water-like curvature that is hard yet slippery, we can begin to think of them being moved by the water itself. This is a startling thought—that their use of the properties of water may be quite different than ours, almost opposite our most basic ideas of resistance and physics. If a dolphin can reduce the resistance of the water in front of itself, using ultrasonic stimulation of the water molecules, perhaps it is able to swim with less effort than we have thought, as effortlessly as it does in front of boats that are providing a propulsive force in the form of a pressure wave. We know that the rapidity with which cetacean skin replaces itself is a factor in their speed. A dolphin can accelerate so fast it literally jumps out of its skin. This has been witnessed thousands of times in dolphinariums, where a drifting cloud of skin particles will be left behind when a performing dolphin speeds for the surface to do one of its prodigious jumps twenty feet into the air.

After years of study of the hydrodynamic efficiency of the dolphin body, the US Navy designed its fastest ships, the nuclear-powered frigates, to have a row of small holes along the knife-edge of the bow, through which high-pressure steam is pumped. This creates a coating of minute bubbles, flowing along the sides of the ship, decreasing the resistance of the water. The bubbles are effectively "floating" the ship so that it is only partly in contact with the surrounding sea. It is well known that the most advanced torpedoes and submarines are covered with an imitation of whale skin as a result of these studies, so one is led to wonder whether this bubble sheath is another of the many inventions derived from the study of our friends.

Brain Power

Brains are constructed along similar lines in all creatures. They are usually divided into two halves with a core inside them. Advanced brains have more dense structures and more surrounding layers.

Dolphins have been shown to have the ability to manage their brains in a manner far superior to humans. They can shut down half the brain for rest and reawaken it in an instant. This level of control allows them to use their brains with very high efficiency. The average human's brain has waves of activity, with each side operating at high capacity for about twenty minutes, then switching sides. We operate at much less than full capacity most of the time. Dolphins, on the other flipper, are capable of using both sides at once, one side, or each side independently. This produces many times the efficiency of the human brain.

The sperm whale brain is the largest brain in the known Universe, at about twenty-two pounds (ten kilos). Our brains weigh, on average, about three and a half pounds (one and a half kilos). The bottlenose dolphin, the one most of us are familiar with and which has had the most testing done on it, has a brain far larger than one would expect. It is approximately 40 percent larger than an average human brain.

There are many issues still inconclusively discussed among neuroanatomists regarding the quality of cetacean brains. Despite clear data showing the high density of neurons, the complex folds on the surface, and the microscopic similarity of its structures to the human brain, some scientists have suggested that the large brains of cetaceans are explained by their need to control their large bodies and complex sound mechanisms. They then equate the quality of the brains of dolphins to those of apes or dogs. They leave out one crucial factor. The physical environment of the ocean provides dolphins and whales with virtual weightlessness. At whatever depth they are, they do not rise toward the surface unless they want to. It might at first seem that large brains would be needed to control their large bodies, but the weightlessness factor suggests otherwise. Their brains are available for much more than body control, and we find ourselves wondering again how they use their magnificent mental organs.

Masters of the Breath

Living in an environment where they cannot breathe, eternal visitors beneath the waves, all whales and dolphins are masters of the breath. They must be completely aware of every breath. They must calculate the distance to the surface of the ocean in an equation that balances the amount of air left in their lungs, the time to get to the surface, and the condition of the surface itself.

A speeding dolphin may begin expelling its exhausted air just before reaching the surface, blowing a hole in the water, into which it rises. The air can be expelled at nearly 200 miles an hour, exploding out, emptying virtually 100% of the air from the lungs. The dolphin breathes in immediately, often finishing the breath after submerging.... The body, as it plunges downward, creates another hole in the sea for a split second, during which the breath can be completed. The inbreath can be accomplished in six-tenths of a second.

Some cetaceans have been observed to breathe *out* all their air before deep dives, depending totally on the absorption of oxygen into their muscle tissues to sustain them, sometimes for over an hour and a half of submergence.

From the perspective of the ancient spiritual science of breath control called Pranayama, whales and dolphins, who hold their breath most of the time, are practicing what is called a "dying breath," one that is gradually consuming its oxygen, growing less and less rich with the vital "fuel" of prana. This contrasts with most breathing, which is rhythmic, constantly replacing a portion of a constant volume of air. For a yogi, the mastery of the breath is one of the paths to mental stillness, the goal of yoga. Normal breathing induces a rhythm that stimulates the movements of thought, according to the yogic philosophers. Breath retention enables the higher perceptions that naturally occur when the mind is alert and without thoughts. Added to the fact that the oceanic dwellers are entirely conscious breathers, perhaps this is another clue to the apparent calm and depth of insight of the cetacean mind.

What does this imply from a human perspective? All religious traditions teach techniques of breath control as a means for changing one's mental state, from the simple quietude of prayer to the formal practices of Pranayama. As the breath is slowed we experience withdrawal. When we slow down enough, by withdrawing our attention from outer stimulus, we find a rhythm that pulses through the body. Beneath the heartbeat, which changes speed, is a steady beat. This is the breath of cellular life, sometimes called the sidereal pulse. All living things have this pulse. It is an obstacle to consciousness expansion. Going beyond it is the goal of meditation, and it is rarely achieved. Only by complete alignment with this pulse, so that there is no difference between one's being and the pulse, can it be transcended. This is not possible to fully describe in words, and must be discovered experientially. The near-weightlessness of floating in water aids the process, as validated by Dr. John Lilly in his float tank experiments. It seems unreasonable to assume anything less than an awareness of this state by cetaceans, who bring so much attention to breathing while suspended in virtual weightlessness.

This transcendental state, beyond the sidereal pulse, engenders a unified consciousness in which life is directly known as interdependent. This is a goal pursued by many disciplines, and is not often experienced. We can imagine a fifty-ton whale plunging down into the sea, its body slowly arcing up and down at the speed of the sidereal pulse, tail flukes propelling it into the dark. It is fading its singularity into a torus of unity consciousness, to cruise the bottom in perfect self-induced absorption in one-ness. They have been doing this for at least 30 million years. It must be worth doing.

The muscle tissue of dolphins and whales is very dark in color, a result of the presence of high amounts of *myoglobin*. Myoglobin allows the cetacean to take dissolved oxygen directly into its muscle tissue. This is one way it avoids the bends as its lungs are squashed flat and its air compressed at the great depths to which it can dive.

Sperm whales may take full advantage of this compression of their bodies when they dive more than 4,000 feet to the sea floor, hunting the enormous squid. They cruise along the bottom, squeezed down to a skinny version of their topside selves, attracting giant squid to them with imitation mating sounds and their waving, white bottom jaw, which can move sideways as well as hanging straight down. When the squid wraps its forty-plus feet of tentacles around the whale and starts to chew into its skin, the whale races for the surface, pumping its tail powerfully so that it rockets upward. It rises so fast that as its body expands, the squid is torn limb from limb by the inexorable increase in size. Once the squid is torn apart, the whale simply circles around and swallows the floating remains. Circular bite marks on the sides of adult sperm whales indicate that squid of enormous size are sometimes encountered and presumably eaten in this way.

We live at the bottom of a well of atmosphere. At sea level, every square inch of our skin is under fourteen pounds of air. Dolphins and whales live in a dense ocean, 800 times denser than air. At a depth of one mile, reached by several species, the pressure is an astonishing 2,600 pounds per square inch.

When a dolphin dives to 1,000 feet, its lungs collapse, all the air squeezed out of the inner spaces, dissolved into muscle tissue, and it becomes a smaller version of itself. Rising, the small amount of air remaining does not contain enough nitrogen to be dissolved into the bloodstream to create bubbles, a factor in the ability of a dolphin to avoid "the bends" upon rapid ascent.

Organs and Systems

The blubber layer surrounding the bodies of cetaceans serves to retain their mammalian body heat in the colder water. Whalers discovered long ago that the bodies of whales must be processed quickly to prevent the inner heat of their decomposing stomach contents, unable to escape through the blubber blanket, from literally cooking the flesh of the whale. Some even took advantage of this, taking meat for their supper that had cooked itself from whales used as fenders between catcher ships and the factory ship. It has been accepted under International Whaling Commission rules that a whale must be processed within thirty-three hours of its death to avoid processing meat that has cooked itself, decomposing too far for use and producing rancid oil.

A unique bloodstream is woven through every cetacean body. To improve the efficiency of their heartbeats, some veins are wrapped around arteries, so that as the blood is pumped away from the heart, the energy is transferred directly into the returning veins. This has the effect of nearly halving the pressure needed to pump a cetacean's blood supply, thereby increasing its energy efficiency for prolonged dives and the rigors of ocean life.

Sperm whales have a singular arrangement no other cetacean possesses. In the sperm whale, the blowhole is placed not on top of the head, but at the front. The air passages in the skull can be as much as twenty feet from the blowhole. The skull has two air passages, but the "nose" has only one opening. The sperm whale's left airway is connected directly to the blowhole, but its right airway does not connect, instead ending in a chamber at the front of the head. There is a theory that the whale may fill its right airway with warm air to melt the adjacent spermaceti, creating a sort of on-board floatation chamber filled with liquid wax. When it wants to dive, it may cool the wax with sea water, drawn into a chamber beneath its left nostril, increasing the specific gravity of the spermaceti. No one knows for sure....

Returning to our *visual*ization (note how we use this word to describe the inner creation of an alternate awareness), we can now add several more cetacean body qualities to our image: clear, calm minds in weightless bodies that ring like a bell, singing songs that range from the voice of stones to the rarity of radio waves; with eyes that adapt to a multitude of conditions, an ability to see the invisible as well as the hidden, strength and agility nearing the unlimited, skin that is ultra-smooth, and a sleekness of form that seems the epitome of liquid perfection—theirs is a life especially graced with the signs of climaxed evolution. Their physical vehicles are as near perfect as bodies can be.

The human body pales in comparison. Ours is a much shorter evolution, with current hypotheses placing our "humanness" between 180,000 and 100,000 years (measured by the ability to speak). The cetaceans have been living as they are today for approximately thirty million years. Ours is a story that has only its first part told, and which may yet prove to be a tragically short story. Will we honor the gift of cetacean friendship? Will we listen closely to the songs in the sea?

> How do humpback whales remember the changes in their songs? One possibility is that whales, like human bards, sometimes use rhymes to help recall their lines in a long oral performance. Analysis of the songs shows that when they contain many themes, they also include rhyme-like material, phrases with similar-sounding endings that link dissimilar but adjacent themes. When songs contain few themes and are presumably not so hard to remember, we do not hear this sort of material.
> —Katherine B. Payne, "A Change of Tune,"
> from *Natural History*, March 1991

On the Souls of Dolphins

The dolphin, closer to us than any species in the natural universe, made a decision as to what needed to be reshaped.... By reshaping themselves to fit their world instead of the world to fit them, as man is attempting to do, they have reached a state of grace that fits our concept of Utopia ahead of us. Their lack of aggression, intelligent interest, friendship for no reward and magnificent creative play are a reflection of Utopia that we may all recognize.

To destroy them may well be the same as killing the only angel that knows the way to heaven....[1]

I've attempted to show that humans and dolphins share a unique quality, which I call the presence of an advanced soul. What do we mean when we speak of the soul? Can we be specific and accurate?

There are many definitions of the soul. For some, it is the spark of divinity within. For others it is the knowing, deciding self. For others it is the immortal essence of one's being. And there are those who cannot accept the soul as a constituent part of living beings, insisting that the soul cannot be within a rational dimension, but rather is an ineffable quality that is necessarily mysterious. While parts of these definitions seem correct, none is wholly satisfying.

Experience has shown me that an answer to this most basic question can be found. It need not be a mystery.

I do not claim authority on this important subject, but after thirty-five years of study, I have developed a working definition of the soul that I have used as the basis for some of the ideas in this book.

My studies have not all been in books, or at the feet of a teacher. My exploration of the nature of the soul has been disciplined during some stages of my life and free-form and eclectic during other times. The early years were devoted to gaining some measure of control over my mind by disciplined exercises in concentration, which many teachers now call meditation.[2]

It was meditation that led me to the empty mind, the charged and capable vessel awaiting the soul's command. It was my open mind that received the gift of the Legend of the Golden Dolphin, and it was my soul that heard it and commanded me to respond. It was in meditation that Peter Shenstone first encountered the Legend, and it was while floating in warm salt water that Dr. John Lilly first began his research into the possibilities of the mind, which led him to the dolphins. Floating minds, strange minds, they have been meditating for millions of years, calling out to our souls.

My soul was guiding the path I walked, revealing itself gradually to me. By the time I set out to encounter the dolphins, I was well prepared for their teachings. To truly know the dolphins, one must have mental health and stability, as Dr. Lilly points out. He begins his second book, *The Mind of the Dolphin*, with a chapter on the need for well-adjusted humans to be the ones to engage in interspecies communication research.

Fundamental to a study of the soul is knowledge of the constitution of a human, the "parts" of us that are working together. For our purpose, which is to understand the souls of humans and dolphins, I will offer an expanded framework of definition that owes much to Paramahansa Yogananda and to the works of Djwhal Khul, who used Alice Bailey as his scribe.

Some Definitions

The **Spirit** is the essential life itself, the spark of fire that animates the living form, which makes of the elements and molecules a living creation. It is not knowable, due to its very nature. It is the motivating energy of our existence, the tide of life.

The **Soul** is the first level of embodiment, the point at which the spirit takes on its first, most refined form. It is the cause of the repeating cycle of living forms, referred to as inhabiting the "causal" level of existence. It is the record of progress from disorder to order, the history of an individual being as it undertakes the processes of becoming more and more fit for demonstrating perfection, and it is where the karmic forces make their most important claims, causing the re-iteration of life, the return to form for the purpose of refinement and final coherent existence (usually called reincarnation).

The soul is the state of being that precipitates the body into existence. As the body sheds its limitations it is made more and more suitable for enabling the soul to express and experience itself. It is the soul that causes the breath to arise, and it is the soul that continues to exist after the breath ceases. The life we live is a movement of breath, the rhythm of the soul.

The soul itself is a temporary and finite creation, facing a final dissolution at the end of the larger cycles of existence, with only spirit existing outside as well as inside creation.

We feel the soul when we feel purpose. It is present when we feel the special goodness that comes with helping others. The soul is said to concern itself only with the whole—the group of beings with whom we are most deeply associated and the larger community of beings—and not the details of daily living.

When we create and contemplate beauty, we are looking through the eyes of the soul. When we find a natural knowledge of right behavior, and know to avoid the wrong, we are listening to the voice of the soul. And when we feel love, embracing the lives of others, or feel the embrace that other souls offer us, we are in the heart of the soul.

In the end, it is the soul that observes and is aware of itself, through the mechanisms of biological life. Our constantly changing feelings, perceptions, and thoughts are transient, the surface phenomena of our lives. There is an inner "observer" who witnesses life, and that is the soul. This presence allows us, and dolphins, to be instinctual, intuitive or counter-intuitive, as we choose.

Every type of creature has a soul as its point of origin but few types have developed their vehicles enough to enable the soul to be fully present, aware of its life through the entire spectrum of its bio-systems, coordinating those systems for uses other than survival. In the case of humans, we aspire to artistic, sensual, or philosophic endeavors, while the cetaceans seem to focus on sheer joyous experience as the texture of the life of their souls. We do not know their aspirations, but it appears that the pursuit of joy is a big part of them.

And finally, the **Personality** is the three-part body that we are most familiar with. The personality consists of the physical body, the collection of feelings and sensations called the emotional body, and the mental processes we call the mind. The personality is made up of the parts of ourselves over which we have the most direct control. Sensations, feelings, and thoughts are the three worlds we live in, the worlds of the personality.

We are spirit, soul, and personality, all functioning together. Each aspect depends on the others for biological life to exist. We have no reason to think of cetaceans as being any different in this regard, and their self-awareness puts them in the rare category that we occupy—they are the only other beings on Earth who do not live by instinct, but are guided by their reflective minds.

Self-Awareness, the Mind, and the Soul

One more level of detail will help us work out an understanding of the soul: the mind has two levels. The lower mind is anchored in the physical brain and controls the functions of the physical body. It has a limited range and is concerned with the singular life in which it finds itself. We do not easily notice all the operations of the lower mind, some of its functions having dropped below the threshold of normal awareness. Only by the practice of special techniques can we re-engage with the control of some body functions. The higher mind has abstract concerns, processing creative impulses and language, contemplating life and death, meaning, purpose, wholeness, beauty, love, and joy. It is through the higher mind that intuition comes, that source-less inflow of direct knowledge that lends us brilliance.

With these definitions "in mind," when we say that dolphins have souls, we are saying that they are, like humans, aware of their selves and in conscious contact with their bodies, emotions, and mental processes. I believe that this is unique to cetaceans and humans.

There is a condition of self-observation that is evident in both humans and cetaceans. I am not suggesting that a chimpanzee is unaware of its feelings, but that it is not as able to contemplate the importance of those feelings. The chimp is focalized primarily in its lower mind, with few higher-mind functions. The soul we are trying to illuminate is demonstrated through a fully functioning personality, with the higher aspects of the mind accessible and involved.[3]

Science and spiritual views agree—if a person is highly developed, he or she demonstrates qualities such as altruism, compassion, service to others, joyousness, and brilliance. This condition of development is often measurable in body fitness, emotional stability, mental acuity, and balanced actions. Physical fitness is the least necessary component in this regard, oddly enough.

A well-developed and integrated human is not immune to the emotions of human experience, but has discovered balance while having intense feelings. An advanced soul does not feel less, it feels more, with a better system of understanding and appropriate boundaries. Through the lives of brilliant souls we see the possibilities for advanced and "perfect" Human-ness. It is perfection of a suitable soul vehicle that we see in the lives of saints, avatars, and the wise heroes of all cultures. And here we find the dolphins, exemplary models of soul development. Their bodies are efficient, under conscious control, and ultra-sensitive. Their minds are self-reflective and they control their reactions to stimuli. Dr. Lilly discovered that a dolphin will limit itself, not over-stimulate itself even if given the opportunity. Only humans are known to do this as well.

The condition of "radiance" is that in which something's inner qualities cannot be contained within the physical form. Awakened humans are radiant, shining a mental and spiritual light in all directions. Dolphins, even average dolphins, shine with an energy that calls us to them, that enlightens our senses and stimulates our souls. It is the radiant dolphin soul that calls us to our own radiant destiny.

Two Souls, One World

As simple as this description of the soul may seem, I believe it can help us lift another of the veils of Nature. I do not accept the idea that the soul is beyond knowing. The intellectuals and academics who debate endlessly about the soul have simply lost themselves in thickets of words, tangles of nonsense. They have forgotten that as we approach Spirit, truths get simpler, less complex. Words may give us safety by insulating us from direct experience, which many of us equate with unpleasant feelings, but they cannot replace gnosis.

For most creatures, life is direct experience. Responding to instinct is direct, unmediated life. Hunger rises, feeding follows. Patterns cross the retina, interest rises, movement follows. Muscles ache, food is digesting, sleep follows. These actions are the outworking of biologically sophisticated systems, responding to the requirements for sustained life.

And at the end of the process of development of living systems and mental sophistication, as far as we know it on this Earth, is the condition of self-awareness. This reflective process enables us to combine sensory information, memory, desire, and an odd new factor—intuition. This mysterious ability, to know without having to go through a process of mentation, is unique to those who have left instinct behind.

No other creatures besides humans and cetaceans have intuitive abilities. We can evaluate a situation, not only bringing into play the simple mathematics of what will improve or make more difficult the situation, but tapping into another source of knowledge, one that synthesizes information and non-local awareness into a more effective response.

To investigate this, swimming among dolphins is the best way I know. For those of us who have played with dolphins in the water, this is where we easily see the intuitive brilliance they carry. Beyond playful, they seem to bring another quality to the encounter. Taking into account our clumsiness in the water, dolphins will adjust to our level, slowing their boisterous rough-and-tumble style of play to match our limits. They have taught thousands of people lessons in overcoming fears, in re-opening the gates of possibility, in creative freedom. And somehow, the lessons are always appropriate for the person receiving them. How do they know how to do this? What insights does a dolphin have into us? They live in the ocean, swimming all night long, feeding on swarms of fish they herd together with their friends, exploring hidden terrain, breathing carefully each breath from a world they can only briefly enter, yet are totally dependent upon—their life is so different from ours, it is astounding that they can find ways to teach us and to play with us that match our individual conditions. It really is fun to play with a dolphin. They actually have taught lessons to thousands of people. How?

I am satisfied, after ten years of swimming with dolphins in all kinds of conditions—from wild populations that may have never seen a human before, to dolphins whose mothers were born in man-made pools—that all of them have the same ability to understand my needs, my state of mind, of heart, of soul. I can only conclude that they are insightful beings, with access to intuition. They know without having to study the situation, without having to know me personally.

I hope you will find an opportunity to join a dolphin in the water one day. I hope you find there, as I have, a friendly soul who is eager to explore the possibilities of life. They are calling us to join them in living the one way that works, that is supported by all of life—the way of Joy.

Drop the complications that fill your head, soothe and balance your emotions, keep your body fit, and leap into the water. Receive the gifts the dolphins offer. They are our elder sisters, the pure and playful souls in the sea.

On the Nature of
the Delphic Wave

I have used the term "Delphic Wave" throughout this book as a general description of the influence of cetaceans over human development. I would like to take this subject a bit deeper. I offer here some thoughts on the questions of where the Wave has brought us, and to where we might proceed.

The human family is not yet divine. We hold the deep patterns of divinity within us, but we are not yet mature. The exemplary lives of women and men in all countries and in all ages—those who joyously serve their fellow humans with effective dedication—are but indicators of our possibilities. The challenge we face is great.

Until we pass over the threshold that lies ahead, we are free to choose our destiny—life or death. We can end our journey on the path toward awakening. It is all too clear how we might do this. Assuming we do not choose to have the human story be a short story, we can move into a life that is beyond the cyclic processes of death and rebirth. By doing so, we can go beyond the inevitability of death. We can enter the realms of the eternal, the self-sustained.

The Delphic Wave is preparing us to move on to the next level of life. It is a level we cannot see from where we are, and we can only catch glimpses of it in the lives of our radiant sisters and brothers. In an active visualization of a harmonious and environmentally healthy world, we can catch a glint shining off the possible future that lies ahead. But, until we shift into mastery of life, we are facing the death that is the natural outcome of ignorance.

The cycles of life, the ups and downs, the expansions and contractions we have examined in this short book, are a record of our efforts to become Master Surfers, riding the Wave. In this metaphor, we are riding a wave of consciousness, a wave that is teaching us. What lessons are we being taught? Perhaps if we play on this mysterious wave a bit more, improving our stance and learning to ride it with more confidence, we can more effectively apply ourselves.

Life is not easy. Not at the highest levels of affluence and not at the levels of abject poverty. Often, the human spirit finds a form of freedom when there is little left to lose, and happy smiles will follow you down a street in the poorest parts of a city. Despite the smiles, life in the slums is filled with misery and futile yearning. And in the boardrooms and country clubs of the elite, there are empty smiles, dark dreams, and tortured consciences. This well-padded world has its own demons who do not yield to luxuries, demons whose hungers cannot be satisfied. Life is not easy.

The Wave is creating higher sensitivity in us all. We all are learning to yearn. Our yearning, our aspirations are rising and we are finding our inner voice so that we can call out for new forms of living, new ways of being.

After some years studying this, I feel that there are five principles through which we are being sensitized by the Delphic Wave:

1. Conflict—when divergent energies come into contact, tension results. Tension seeks resolution. Resolution of differences generates new conditions. Conflict is negative if it does not produce resolution. Conflict is positive if it generates new orders of cooperation.
2. Newness—we are being constantly exposed to new ideas. We are living in an age of ever-increasing floods of images and infor-

mation, exposed to cultures of all kinds, from all ages. This is stimulating our intuition, enabling us to navigate unerringly at higher and higher speeds.

3. Detachment—we are assimilating the lessons of our difficult planet-side lives, learning to recognize the universal challenges we face as separated selves, as personalities, while gaining insight into another dimension of ourselves, the unitary self, the interdependent whole of which we are a part. This is enabling us to rise above our immediate time and condition.

4. Creativity—the newness of our lives, exposed to so many influences, stimulates us to amalgamate energies in new ways, to develop new habits, new ways of working. We are responding to life in ways never imagined before.

5. Healing—we are being asked to recognize that health is an issue of the soul. Our physical condition cannot be separated from our emotional lives, our mental balance, and the conditions under which we grow to adulthood. All of the conditions of our lives are in need of care, to enable us to be fully awake and capable of responding to our needs and those of the world.

As we respond to these influences, we move into a style of life that produces harmlessness. We creatively respond to the inherent conflict in the joining of new energies, which calls on us to be detached from our limited points of view, so that we might heal our relationship with the greater life in which we are taking part. In so doing, we overcome the harm we have done and we do no more harm.

Simple mathematics shows us that if each of us is able to take good care of ourselves and just a little bit more, the world becomes not only tolerable, but joyful. Each of us only needs the means to take care of our own corner of the world—the food, clothing, shelter, education, medical care, tools, and inspiration people have always needed. This is so simple we have overlooked it.

And equally obvious is the simple, profound, and omnipresent story of the love we have been shown by the whales and dolphins. We do not need for them to talk, to directly heal us, or to project images into our heads. If these fantasies prove to be possible, and we receive these gifts soon, we will have been given more than we need to overcome our current challenges. All we need is to recognize the presence of Earth beings who have become harmless, unified in mind and heart, living lives of joyous celebration of our beautiful world. By modelling this basic truth, they present us with the undeniable possibility of our own destiny. They prove it can be done.

Behind the dolphin's smile is satisfaction, a contentment we do not know. Yearning, striving, and the endless pursuit of a success that we cannot define has left us sceptical that anything other than stressful desires leading to temporary satisfaction is possible. We feel no certainly that such a state as theirs would satisfy us.

Who can we ask, if we do not trust the messages of the dolphins or the songs of the whales? Ask any of your wise elders what life is all about. They will tell you that the struggles are not the point, that life is pure and whole in its simplicity. The small joys of gardens, walks with friends, playing with children and animals, dancing and singing and looking at the stars are not limited experiences, but are instead among the richest treasures life has to offer.

And, as dynamic humans, rest assured that horizons undreamt of await us. Other dimensions of life, totally unknown to us, lie ahead. Once we achieve our destiny, which is to climb up beyond the world of today, into realms of true sustainability, we will find that all of our hard-won and well-developed skills, so necessary here, are the means by which we will make our way.

I have called this gentle, nurturing, challenging, and powerful process, whereby life leads us toward greater life, the Delphic Wave. It is not limited to the influence of dolphins, but is delightfully easy to present to people everywhere in this guise. Don't let the name fool you. It is not happening to us, it is happening within us.

The Delphic Wave ... Come on in, the water's fine....

Notes

Preface:

1) The idea that there has been a wave of Dolphin-inspiration washing its way around the world comes from a study done by a man in Australia. Peter Shenstone experienced a flood of insights one night in 1976 while sitting in meditation in his home in Sydney. A spirit of Dolphin-ness soaked into his fertile imagination, leaving a huge tale, a living legend.

An inner voice told him how humanity has benefited from the guidance of dolphins, outlining a scenario that leads into an exciting future of health, harmony, passion, and creativity. Peter made a twelve-year study of this idea and created a set of hand-written and illustrated books called The Legend of the Golden Dolphin. He is still working with the ideas in private, but has gone on to other work (www.planetark.org). Until 1988, he actively shared his dolphin insights with many hundreds of people.

It has been my pleasure to study some of these materials, and to meet dozens of people in all parts of the world who have been inspired by his work. Some of the best scientific work being done today in regard to whales and dolphins was directly inspired by this legend, and many artists, activists, film makers, and therapists acknowledge the Golden Dolphin for its role in leading them to their life's work.

Very little has ever appeared in print about the Legend of the Golden Dolphin. It is now time to share it with the world.

2) Credo Mutwa to Kim Kindersley, Mafeking, South Africa, January 1995:
> "More and more people are feeling and crying for no reason. Their
> tears connect them to the sadness of the world. We have stopped

worshipping nature and devised gods in our own image, we gave glamour to destruction and beauty to death. But there is a great change coming over all people. There is a movement of sanctity in the world. The dolphin is the symbol to us of humanity's reconnection with nature and therefore with God."

Introduction: Who Are the Dolphins and Whales?

1) *Humans and Dolphins Have Similar Genetics*

For years, marine biologists have told us that dolphins and humans share many traits including intelligence and friendliness.

"The extent of the genetic similarities came as a real surprise to us," said David Busbee of Texas A&M University, who published his results in Cytogenetics and Cell Genetics.

Researchers at Texas A&M University applied "paints," or fluorescently labeled human chromosomes, to dolphin chromosomes and found that 13 of 22 dolphin chromosomes are exactly the same as human chromosomes. Of the remaining nine dolphin chromosomes, many were found to be combinations or rearrangements of their human counterparts. The researchers also identified three dolphin genes that are similar to human genes.

"Dolphins are marine mammals that swim in the oceans, and it was astonishing to learn *that we have more in common with the dolphin than with land mammals*," commented Horst Hameister, Professor of Medical Genetics at the University of Ulm in Germany.

Source: Seema Kumar, Discovery Channel Online News, www.discovery.com.

2) Hoyt, E., *Whale Watching 2000: Worldwide Tourism Numbers, Expenditures, and Expanding Socioeconomic Benefits* (Crowborough, UK: International Fund for Animal Welfare, 2000).

3) Jane Nowak, in *Encounters With Whales and Dolphins*, by Wade Doak (Auckland, New Zealand: Hodder and Stoughton, 1988), pp. 190–191.

Chapter One: A Telling of Legends, Part I, Australia, India, and Sumeria

1) Iris Yumadoo Kachallalya Burgoyne, *The Mirning: We are the Whales* (Broome, Western Australia: Magabala Books, 2000).

2) In a wonderful transcultural parallel, a group of educators and conserva-

tionists in South Africa found a whale whose body had washed up on shore. She had been struck and killed by a ship. Her bones were carefully preserved and reconstructed to hang from the ceiling of the Diversity Hall of the Two Oceans Aquarium.

One of the preparers wrote a poem in memory of her, asking forgiveness:

Oh, Mighty Whales,

For millions of years you visited our coastline,

to give birth in our shallows, to give Hope to those who heard your songs.

How can we begin to justify our reasons for the harpoons and factory ships,

Grinning sailors, bloody knives, blood on our hands and empty hearts.

Oh Mighty Whales, to those that survived, come, come to the edge of the sea,

We have homage to pay to thee.

We have built a monument, a beacon of hope, a gesture of peace and harmony.

Out of the rotting carcass has come, piece by piece,

the bones that will unite those that live to hear your song.

Oh Mighty Whales, we stand on the shore and wait.

Our thoughts are with you as you begin your pilgrimage once more.

Take care, for the seas are full of monsters of steel, that loom up out of the fog.

As you draw close, oh mighty ones, you will see the whale and hear its song,

Of peace and freedom.

We ask for forgiveness in this era of reconciliation and hope.

Come, come Oh Mighty Whales, come to the edge of the sea,

as you have for millions of years before.

Sing us your songs, Oh Mighty Whales, we have homage to pay to thee.

—Terry Corr, Capetown, South Africa

3) To us, it is unsettling to think of sacrificing someone considered to be the High Chief. Yet, to many cultures, this is the actual role of one's leaders — to sacrifice themselves in order to sustain the people.

It seems foreign to us to eat those we know to be our benefactors. But in our day the idea of transubstantiation, that the wine and wafers of the Church have been literally transformed into the blood and body of Christ, is a remnant of the same belief.

4) Many people acknowledge the existence of telepathic communication with dolphins, but science has not been able to satisfactorily explain this.

From Dolphinariums around the world come tales of trainers being trained themselves by the dolphins. Marineland of New Zealand used to have strict rules against handlers using whistles or hand gestures, relying solely on mind-to-mind communication to spur dolphins to do dozens of behaviors on cue. (Frank Robson, *Pictures in the Dolphin Mind*, Dobbs Ferry, New York: Sheridan House,1988).

If 30 million years of high intelligence combined with tight social structures *didn't* develop exquisitely refined methods of information exchange, it would be surprising.

It is worth taking seriously the idea that dolphins have not only provided examples of bio-wise behavior for centuries, but in some cases may have communed directly with humans.

5) Cornelia Dimmit and J.A.B. Van Buitenen, eds., *Classical Hindu Mythology: A Reader in the Sanskrit Puranas* (Philadelphia: Temple University Press, 1978).

6) A digression on the Indian subcontinent:

One of the oldest cities of man, known as Mohenjo-Daro, in Pakistan, was built almost four thousand years ago. It had extensive, even sophisticated water features, including a "swimming pool" built beside the Indus River. While there can be no certainty about this pool having anything to do with humans interacting with dolphins, it is a curious fact that it is in the Indus River that we still find the Bhulan, or Indus River Dolphin.

A freshwater dolphin, living in a heavily silted, polluted, dammed, and trafficked river, the Bhulan is now under severe environmental threat. It is estimated that only seven hundred remain.

In Varanasi, a city in India famed for its musicians, the Ganges River Dolphin lives. A man I met in America spent seven years living there, studying the ancient art of Indian classical drumming. He told me that each afternoon, when the students would practice on the veranda of his teacher's home on the shore of the Ganges, the dolphins would gather in the river below to listen....

To many marine biologists, the freshwater dolphins of India, China, and South America are the most ancient living forms of cetaceans. To those of us brought up on images of Flipper, the river dolphin is truly an alien-looking creature. Their eyes have almost atrophied to non-existence from living in perpetually silt-laden waters and are functionally blind, with no lens. They have very flexible spines, enabling them to touch their own tails, and their teeth are snaggly and needle-like, showing outside their mouths when closed. They are a muddy brownish- gray color, much like the water in which they live. Their heads are oddly shaped, with bulbous foreheads and pronounced "smiles." They often swim on their sides, scanning for fish with their excellent biosonar.

Modern fossil studies have finally located the bridging creatures, the "missing link" between land-dwelling and ocean-going mammals, on the Indian subcontinent. The fossils of "whales with feet" have been found in Pakistan, demonstrating conclusively that the odd story of whales and dolphins having formerly been land dwellers who gave up their terrestrial lives to become "extra-terrestrial" is substantially true.

This would have occurred approximately fifty million years ago, when the Tethys Sea surrounded the moving landmass of what is now India and Pakistan. Near that era, another type of whale was evolving in the area we now know as Australia and New Zealand. There, the baleen whales were appearing.

7) Berosus, from a fragment of Alexander Polyhistor as quoted in Robert Temple's *The Sirius Mystery: New Scientific Evidence of Alien Contact 5,000 Years Ago* (Rochester, Vermont: Destiny Books, 1998), p. 367.

8) *Scientific American*, July 1999, "Earliest Zoos and Gardens," p. 69.

9) Samuel Noah Kramer, *Sumerian Mythology* (New York: Harper Torchbooks, 1961), p. 198.

Chapter Two: A Telling of Legends, Part II: Tales from Egypt and Africa

1) "Thou shalt see the Ant Fish in his transformations in the depths of the waters of turquoise. Thou shalt see the Abtu Fish in his time. "... From Chapter XV, *The Papyrus of Ani*, translated by E.A. Wallis Budge, in *The Egyptian Book of the Dead*, p. 502 (New Hyde Park, New York: University Books, 1960).

2) The mythical Ant and Abtu are representations of what does occur in nature: In the perilous straits between the North and South islands of New Zealand, a dolphin named Pelorus Jack guided ships for over 26 years in the 1800s. He led the way through dangerous shoals, and his fame drew Rudyard Kipling, Mark Twain, and other prominent people of the day to comment on his life-saving service.

3) "The earthly king, on his demise, was also borne to the grave in the same

way as the divine being. The mummy of such a royal personage, who was regarded, on his death, as resembling or having actually become Osiris, was sometimes presented in the form of a local fish, swathed in burial wrappings. The 'brother' of this fish was Horus, the morning star, who led the Fish of Abydos into the Beyond and promised him resurrection." Erich Zehren, *The Bull and the Crescent*, p. 276.

4) Plutarch, in J. Gwyn Griffiths' *Plutarch's De Iside Et Osiride* (Cambridge: University of Wales Press, 1970), p. 243.

> The robes of Isis are variegated in colour...; the robe of Osiris, however, has nothing dark or variegated about it, but is one simple colour, the colour of light.... He is actually very far removed from earth.... The souls of men ... hav[e] no association with the god save for the dim vision of his presence ... then is this god their leader and king, for depending on him, they behold insatiably and desire the beauty which is, to men, ineffable and unutterable. This beauty, as the ancient story shows, Isis ever loves, and she pursues it and unites with it, filling this our world with all the beautiful and good qualities which have a part in creation.

5) Ibid, pp. 217–218.

> ... his limbs grew stuck together so that he could not walk and passed the time in solitude; and Isis, having cut and separated these parts of his body, provided him with easy movement.

6) Ibid, p. 205.

7) Ibid, p. 147.

8) In four different cultures, separated by thousands of years and miles, there is an identical mythical tale of Nine Gods coming across the sea in a canoe, who stayed a while, got things going, inspired and educated the population, then left. This tale was told in Egypt, in the Pacific Island cultures, among the pre-Incans of Peru, and among the Maya of Central America. Always nine gods depicted in a long canoe arriving from afar, then departing back across the sea....

9) G.R.S. Mead, *Thrice Greatest Hermes* (London: Theosophical Publishing, 1906).

10) Marcel Griaule and Germaine Dieterlen, *The Pale Fox* (Chino Valley, Arizona: Continuum Foundation, 1986).

11) Credo Mutwa to Kim Kindersley, for the film "Eyes of the Soul," Mafeking, South Africa, 1995.

12) Credo Mutwa, *Song of the Stars: The Lore of a Zulu Shaman* (Barrytown, New York: Barrytown, Ltd., 1996).

Chapter Three: A Telling of Legends, Part III: The Delphic World of Greece

1) Strangely, the site of Delphi and the temple of Apollo do not have a place where poisonous fumes could come from the earth. The geology of the area does not match this idea. There have been major earthquakes there, several times destroying the temples. This may have buried a chasm, but it seems unlikely. It is not known how this story came to be so widely accepted, that a Priestess would sit on a tripod, chewing her laurel leaves.

2) Eleanore Divine and Martha Clark, *The Dolphin's Smile: Twenty-Nine Centuries of Dolphin Lore* (New York: Macmillan, 1967), translated by F. L. Lucas.

3) Peter Jay, *The Greek Anthology: and other ancient epigrams* (England: Penguin Books, 1981).

4) Robert Graves, *The Greek Myths, Volume II* (Baltimore, Maryland: Penguin Books, 1955), p. 261.

5) Pontiff is a title used in the Roman Catholic Church, denoting someone who is a member of the *Pontifical College*, the inner governing body of the church. In Latin, *pontiff* means bridge, a structure for crossing over water. In Greek, however, it refers to the Greek God of the Sea, Pontos. Catholic secrets reveal a deep connection to the oceans and their mysteries.

6) Robert Graves, *The Greek Myths, Volume I* (Baltimore, Maryland: Penguin Books, 1955), p. 290.

Chapter Four: From Mystery to History: Why God Disappeared

1) Robert Temple, *The Sirius Mystery: New Scientific Evidence of Alien Contact 5,000 Years Ago* (Rochester, Vermont: Destiny Books, 1998), p. 164.

2) 1 Chronicles 10:10.

3) Judges 16:1-30.

4) 1 Samuel 5:2–4. The Ark of the Covenant was sheathed in the skin of dolphins. This was the chest in which was kept the most powerful object in Judaic history, a mysterious thing that seemed to be, by turns, radioactive, explosive, infectious, and blindingly brilliant.

For centuries the lists of the materials used in the construction of the

Ark and the Tabernacle included items made of badger skin. However, badgers didn't exist in this region. The word had been mistranslated and was, in fact, "dolphin."

Anything having to do with dolphins was sacred, an idea held by all Mediterranean cultures. Only the sanctified artisans of the Dolphin Temples were allowed to handle dolphin bodies, to make sacred objects from their bones, oils, and skin. In the metaphorical world of religious phenomena, if dolphin skin were on the outside of the Ark, Dagon could have been showing respect by "falling on his face" before the dolphin-god.

5) Robert Graves, *The White Goddess: A Historical Grammar of Poetic Myth* (New York: Noonday Press, 1948), p. 294.

6) The people of Nineveh, almost three hundred miles inland, believed in a divinity who sent messages to them via a person who rose out of the sea, part fish and part man, and they would have been very receptive to Jonah's ministry if he had been delivered to them by a "fish."

H. Clay Trumbull ("Jonah In Nineveh," *Journal of Biblical Literature 11* (1892): 10–12) wrote:

> What better heralding, as a divinely sent messenger to Nineveh, could Jonah have had, than to be thrown up out of the mouth of a great fish, in the presence of witnesses, say, on the coast of Phoenicia, where the fish-god (Dagon) was a favorite object of worship?
>
> The recorded sudden and profound alarm of the people of an entire city at his warning was most natural, as a result of the coincidence of this miracle with their religious beliefs and expectations.

7) In February of 1891, several hundred miles east of the Falkland Islands in the South Atlantic, the *Star of the East*, a whaler out of London, spotted a sperm whale. When he was harpooned, he dove deep then struck the tiny whaleboat as he struggled to the surface. Several men were missing when the sailors were picked up by another whaleboat. Once the whale was dead and being butchered, the innards were hauled aboard and the stomach was noticed to have a large lump in it that seemed to move. When it was cut open one of the missing sailors was found, still alive.

His name was James Bartley. He had been thrown into the air and inadvertently swallowed by the whale. Bartley could remember sliding over the teeth and down the throat, then nothing more until awakening a month later on board the ship. He had been in and out of consciousness, and barely recovered. He had been in the stomach of the whale for fifteen hours. He lost all the hair on his body, his skin was bleached very white, and he was almost blind for the rest of his life.

This story was attested to by the ship's doctor and all of his shipmates. James Bartley lived another 18 years, and died in his hometown of Gloucester, England, in 1909.

8) Paul William Roberts, *In Search of the Birth of Jesus: The Real Journey of the Magi* (New York: Riverhead Books, 1995), p. 152.

Chapter Five: Jesus the Dolphin

1) At the beginning of the Third Millennium, many people are now looking beyond their religion for answers to life's questions. For some, the inner voice speaks clearly, and they hear a different story about Jesus and his life. In my research, I have come upon several sources that say that Jesus is an Avatar who came from Sirius, an adept of the Blue Ray of Love and Wisdom. He is described as a Blue Dolphin, like the Nommo creatures from Sirius, sent as a teacher to begin a new chapter in the Earth story. He came as an Initiate and an Initiator. He is still with us, and his task now is to restore the world by working with humans to help the ecosystems regain health, and to act in concert with advanced students, opening up new dimensions of spirit. He is said to be available through the portal of self-awareness.

2) Andrew Harvey, *Son of Man: The Mystical Path to Christ* (New York: Jeremy P. Tarcher/Putnam, 1998).

3) Roland Schaer, Gregory Claeys, Lyman Tower Sargent, *Utopia: The Search for the Ideal Society in the Western World* (New York: The New York Public Library/Oxford Press, 2000).

4) Helena Petrovna Blavatsky, *The Secret Doctrine: The Synthesis of Science, Religion, and Philosophy, Vol. II, Anthropogenesis* (Pasadena, California: Theosophical University Press, 1875), p.313.

Chapter Six: Faith and the Gnostic Star

1) Alice Bailey, *A Treatise on Cosmic Fire* (New York: Lucis Publishing, 1925).

2) I want to be perfectly clear: The first stage of self-awareness is pure narcissism, a self-consciousness that is selfish. From that develops selflessness, a refocusing of self-awareness on an outside, transcendental object, usually by means of devotion to a master. Once this is accomplished, the capacity for focus and compassion is used to reclaim one's Self, fully aware of the

interconnectedness of all things, and the responsibility that goes with being self-aware.

3) Hekhalot Rabbat, in Dan Merkur, *Gnosis: An Esoteric Tradition of Mystical Visions and Unions* (Albany: State University of New York Press, 1993), p. 167.

4) I have extensive experience with this latter-day phenomenon, having been the first person taught the meditation called "The Flower of Life" by its most famous promoter, Bernard Perona (Drunvalo Melchizedek), in 1986.

Subsequently, a partner and I helped to start a Mystery School in Northern New Mexico where Drunvalo began teaching his version of the ancient Sumerian techniques of the Merkabah meditations.

As the Director of the school, I became increasingly aware of confusion arising within the students. A few found excellent results in their lives, coming to understand the "language of form," commonly called Sacred Geometry. Some found increasing discomfort, overwhelmed by the nature of the phenomena produced by these practices. The lack of rigor in their preparation for this powerful encounter with Spirit was the cause of this disturbance. Serious personality distortion can be the result of this inner work if undertaken prior to its natural timing.

The Naakal Mystery School closed in 1990. The author continues to counsel former students of the Flower of Life teachings. (See Chapter Seventeen.)

Chapter Seven: The Four Elements: Whale Oil, Coffee, Chocolate, and Tobacco

1) Coffee apparently originated in the highlands of Ethiopia and was brought into Arabia in A.D. 500. It was used as a food until the 1400s, when it was first made into a drink.

Coffee first appeared in England in 1601. Baillol College, part of Oxford, opened its first coffee house, The Angel, in 1650. It reached Paris in 1643 and was instantly popular. There were 250 coffee houses by 1690, and by 1782 there were over 1,800! The first coffee house in America was in Boston in 1689.

Chocolate first came to the attentions of Europe when Cortez landed in Mexico in 1519. It appeared in France and Italy in 1605 and was popular as both a drink and a solid bar by the 1650s.

Tobacco was first brought to Europe in 1556. It was sent as a commercial cargo in 1565, and by 1627 over one half million pounds of it was being produced in Virginia per year. It was controversial from the beginning, accepted in court by Queen Elizabeth and widely promoted by Sir Walter Raleigh.

When James the First was enthroned in 1603, he blasted the practice, banning it from court.

The *tabagies*, or smoking houses of London, were places where soldiers, who had begun their habits in foreign lands, would encounter the upper class, who could better afford tobacco. The clay pipes of the time were always very small, due to the cost of the tobacco. Snuff was first developed as a method of ingesting plant preparations in the Americas, and tobacco was mixed with spices and made into snuff to deal with the high cost of the plant in Europe.

2) Dictionaries define *Philadelphia* as a combination of the words *philos* (to love) and *adelphos* (brother). If adelphos means brother, the word must be referring to the brother-like quality of the dolphins, which is reflected in the word itself.

The earliest use of the word Philadelphia I have found is from Egypt. A Pharoah in the last years of the fourth and the first half of the third centuries B.C. was named *Ptolemy II, Philadelphus*. He occupied the Osiris Throne, which "rests upon the water."

Chapter Eight: Blood on the Waters: The Plunge into the Deep Dark Sea

1) Henry David Thoreau, *The Maine Woods* (Boston: Ticknor and Fields, 1864).

2) The orca, sometimes called the killer whale, does hunt and eat other whales. This is a part of the natural cycle of life, in which the orca acts as the culling agent, the eco-policeman who removes the sick and injured from the group. This does not compare to the brutal assault of humans.

3) The plankton cycle is complex and critical to life on Earth. First, the cold waters of the southern hemisphere collide with warmer currents, creating an upwelling of ocean-bottom nutrients. This feeds the phytoplankton, a simple form of plant life. It is the phytoplankton that sequesters the carbon atom, through the magic of photosynthesis.

The phytoplankton feeds the krill, a form of small shrimp that is the principal food of many whale families. Too few whales leaves too many krill. These eat too much of the plankton, then starve once the plankton are gone. Without balanced harvesting of the krill, their populations rage out of control, either over-consuming the plankton or not eating enough of it. When either goes uneaten, rotting as it floats in vast blankets on the sea, methane gas is released during decomposition, destroying ozone.

4) Robert McNally, *So Remorseless a Havoc: Of Dolphins, Whales and Men* (Boston: Little, Brown, 1981).

5) David Day, *The Whale War* (San Francisco: Sierra Club Books, 1987).

Chapter Nine: A Sublime Brain: The Sperm Whale

1) Edward O. Wilson, *Sociobiology: The New Synthesis* (Cambridge, Massachusetts: Harvard University Press, 1975).

2) Herman Melville, *Moby Dick or The Whale* (New York: Random House, 1930).

3) Ibid.

4) Ibid.

5) Ibid.

6) John Allegro, *The Sacred Mushroom and the Cross: A Study of the Nature and Origins of Christianity Within the Fertility Cults of the Ancient Near East* (New York: Doubleday and Company, 1970).

7) In a bizarre twist of fate, in 1978 the pirate whaling ship *Tonna* was returning from a successful hunt in the South Atlantic, loaded to near capacity with 450 tons of whale meat, when it spied a large fin whale. The captain yielded to greed and ordered his harpooner to fire on it. The whale was hit. The seas began to rise as the whale struggled, then finally died. As the whale was being brought to the rear entry ramp, the ship was caught sideways in the huge swells, pulled by the weight of the whale.

The fifty-ton weight of the whale was too much, and the *Tonna* capsized. Open portholes and hatches allowed the sea to pour into the engine rooms, blowing out the electric generators. The crew could not release the whale from the steel cables attaching it to the ship, and they ran for the lifeboats.

Forty-two men were rescued hours later by a ship responding to their distress calls. Only one man was lost, the captain, who defied every attempt to get him into the lifeboats. He waved to the departing crew from the bridge, a beer bottle in his hand, as the ship was dragged to the bottom by the whale.

Chapter Ten: Waves of Spirit: European Exploration
and the Return of Remembrance

1) Chia Gawain, *The Dolphin's Gift* (Mill Valley, California: Whatever Publishing, 1981), p. 173.

Chapter Eleven: "How Might We Seem to Them?"

1) Paula Underwood, *The Walking People: A Native American Oral History* (Buffalo, New York: Tribe of Two Press, The LearningWay Company, 1994).

Chapter Twelve: Dr. John Lilly and the Cetacean Nation

1) Dr. John C. Lilly, *Communication between Man and Dolphin: The Possibilities of Talking with Other Species* (New York: Crown Publishers, 1978).

2) In Florida, in the 1950s, a man named John H. Hurlbut built a unique aquarium, attached to his home. He had a pool constructed adjoining his own living quarters, so that, in effect, he lived side by side with a dolphin named Paddy. For seven years, these two "people" lived together, under almost constant observation of each other. Paddy was renowned for his sophisticated understanding of humans and his cooperative and friendly attitude. He assisted in a number of research projects.

This is the most extended shared living arrangement known. The experiment of Dr. Lilly and Margaret Howe took the idea further, but was not nearly as lengthy.

Paddy was a male bottlenose dolphin, approximately one year old at the time of his capture. His adult weight was estimated at 300 pounds, and he grew to 7 feet, 10 inches long.

His pool was 34 feet long, 21 feet wide, and just over 8 feet deep.

I have been unable to find records of how long Paddy lived with Mr. Hurlbut, but the reports on the experiments conducted there that I have read indicate at least seven years.

Reported in Kenneth Norris, ed., *Whales, Dolphins and Porpoises* (Berkeley: University of California Press, 1966).

3) Carl Sagan invited Dr. Lilly to attend a gathering that was to create the organization today called SETI (Search for Extra-Terrestrial Intelligence). As the only man on Earth who was actively engaged in attempting communication with another species, John was a good resource for this group

to interview. John's reputation preceded him, and the group playfully decided to create a mock "order" for themselves, with no rules, no dues, and no responsibilities. They even had someone cast little golden tie pins as membership badges. They chose to call themselves the *Order of the Golden Dolphin*.

4) Dolphin hearing has been tested successfully to 300,000 cycles per second (300khz). Radio frequencies by definition begin at 3,000 cycles per second. These lower levels are used for radio beacons and maritime mobile radiotelephones. AM radio frequencies begin at 535khz. Human hearing extends only to a high of 22khz.

5) Dr. J. C. Lilly, *Productive and Creative Research with Man and Dolphin* (Archives of General Psychiatry, Vol VIII, American Medical Association, 1963).

6) One dolphin, Sissy, was especially cranky before her LSD session. Afterwards, she was friendly and easy to be around, becoming a favorite among visitors. Another, Pam, had suffered three wounds by spearfishermen and was justifiably wary of all humans. After her LSD experience she was completely at ease with people.

7) Ronald M. Lockley, *Whales, Dolphins and Porpoises* (Sydney, Australia: Methuen, 1979), p. 83.

8) Current terms more accurately describe the substances that Dr. Lilly experimented with. They are now widely referred to as "entheogenic," which means "god revealing." The earlier term, psychedelic, means "mind-manifesting." Researchers feel this limits our understanding of these promising substances.

9) "Earth Coincidence Control Office" is one of Lilly's most charming ideas. He says that there are unidentified Beings who oversee the progress of a hidden plan that is being worked out on Earth. They arrange for intersections of lives and activities among Humans, through what we think of as coincidences. The notion that someone with an odd sense of humor is scripting one's life is explained by ECCO. This has been one of John's most widely accepted ideas.

10) As documented by *National Geographic* magazine, Joe and Rosie were eventually ignored so consistently in their floating pen that they began to look at release as a better option. Dolphins, like humans, crave contact with their loved ones. Once the object of their affections began to consistently ignore and avoid them, they lost heart. They chased live fish and began eat-

ing them again as their supply of hand-fed fish was withheld gradually. Finally, the gate was lowered amidst tears and farewell wishes, and they swam away.

Not shown in the program aired by National Geographic was their return, twice, to the enclosure, swimming among their former friends, who were instructed to ignore them, to not engage with them.

Who knows the thoughts and feelings of these two Delphic Heroes, as they swam down the channel to the ocean? Who knows how they felt about having been such close friends with humans, only to be sent back to the sea? (Both were given freeze brands on their dorsal fins so they could be identified easily at sea. For a short time after their departure they were each sighted in the company of other dolphins. Rosie was never seen to be in the company of a calf.)

11) Just as this book was being finished, my good friend and mentor left this world. Dr. John C. Lilly passed away in Los Angeles on September 30th, 2001. He was 86 years old.

12) The 6th International Cetacean Education and Research Centre Whale and Dolphin Conference, in Hervey Bay, Australia, 1997.

13) "Gilding the Lilly" was an interactive event broadcast over the internet. It was produced by many friends and associates of Dr. Lilly's, and it brought John to California for a week in 2000. He was hosted in a studio in San Francisco, where each day was filled with friends paying tribute to him from a different part of his life and work.

There was a day devoted to mind research, one to his dolphin work, one to float tanks, one to psychedelic research, one to physics. Tapes of the event are available at: http://sound.photosynthesis.com/John_Lilly.html

14) Several people have been working on this initiative, developing aspects of a serious appeal to the world to recognize the rights of cetaceans. In this effort, a draft declaration has been written. It is modeled on the Declaration of Independence of the United States of America, since it is intended to be readily understandable by humans, and represents a united effort of the approximately 80 species of the Cetacean Nation. (See www.dolphintale.com)

15) One of Dr. Lilly's continuing concerns, written about in several of his books, is the need for good mental health among those who interact with aliens of any kind. The challenge to one's sense of self is immense in this work, and relationships between whole species can be set back by the inappropriate behavior of a few people.

16) *Communication Between Man and Dolphin*, by Dr. Lilly, is recommended for many details about the legal structures that will need to be in place, answers to frequently asked questions, and Dr. Lilly's many ideas about not only the founding, but the on-going status of the Cetacean Nation and its representation.

17) Dr. John C. Lilly, MD, *The Mind of the Dolphin: A Nonhuman Intelligence* (New York: Doubleday, 1967).

Chapter Thirteen: Songs from the Sea:
Humpback Whales and the Birth of Environmental Activism

1) Chris Newbert, *Within a Rainbowed Sea* (Honolulu: Island Heritage, 1984).

2) In December 2000, in the waters surrounding Australia, a change was documented in their song over a very short period of time, when a wandering whale from the Indian Ocean came to visit whales from the Pacific. Researchers compared this to a new pop song suddenly climbing to the top of the charts.

3) By 1979, interest in whale songs had reached such a height that *National Geographic* magazine inserted a floppy record of their music into every one of the 10,500,000 copies of their January issue. It has been noted that this was the largest number of copies of any single recording in history.

4) The interception of and response to this space message was the subject of the first *Star Trek* movie. The "V'ger" referred to by the aliens is the *Voyager* spacecraft, and the voices of the whales have intrigued them to trace its origins.

A subsequent *Star Trek* movie also concerned itself with the plight of the whales, requiring the *Enterprise* to bring two whales from our present time to the future, to re-establish them on Earth after their extinction, to save the planet.

5) Roger Payne, *Among Whales* (New York: Scribner, 1995).

6) I have had the honor of meeting two of the men who attempted to protect the whales that day. Both still bear the invisible marks of one whose soul was scalded by the blood of the whales.

One is Paul Watson, the leader of Sea Shepherd, the self-appointed "Navy of the Cetacean Nation," which has been defending the whales and dolphins in dramatic ways, sinking ships, harassing illegal whalers, and causing important disruptions in the assumptions of arrogant humans.

The other is Michael Bailey, one of the foremost eco-warriors of our times. He has been present at the slaughter of the dolphins in Japan more times than he likes to recall, always trying to bring sense to the fishermen and the government officials. He is tireless, and more than dedicated. His life has never been at rest since he was bathed in the blood of the whale.

7) Peter Shenstone, *Legend of the Golden Dolphin* (Blackheath, Australia: Unpublished, 1976–1988).

8) From an interview with Dr. Urmas Kaldveer, Ph.D., Director of the Pelagikos Foundation, 1997, telling of his experience as the binocular man.

Chapter Fourteen: Dolphins in the Net

1) Mary George, "Aurora Schools Boycott Tuna Fish" (*Denver Post*, January 20, 1989).

2) It is not adequately recognized today that there is no international protection for "small-type cetaceans." The International Whaling Commission (IWC), supported by the United Nations (and whose laws are enforced by the privately funded and self-appointed Sea Shepherd Society), is the global organization with jurisdiction over whales. The IWC has been in existence since 1948, and has changed from a commission empowered to manage the stocks of whales to ensure that there are enough for commercial exploitation, to an organization dedicated to protecting them completely.

The Norwegians, Japanese, Canadians, and several small countries object to the controls exercised by the IWC, and long-standing arguments continue about the legality of the change that came over the IWC. For the moment the whales are protected, but efforts are currently being made to return to commercial whaling.

A "revised management scheme," or RMS, was put forward in 2002, which, if passed, would have instituted quotas of each species that may be "harvested" without threatening the regeneration of that species' population. In short, it would say how many of each kind of whale can be killed.

This proposal, defeated in 2002, will be resubmitted. If it ever passes, it will effectively open the door again for commercial whaling. We currently endure the regular slaughter of over one thousand whales per year. If the RMS is accepted, we may see many thousands killed per year. For the moment, only the IWC stands in the way, although it is very weak.

There is no parallel organization that protects dolphins, or any of the other smaller whales. Tens of thousands are still killed each year, most of them "harvested" by the Japanese or caught and killed as a bycatch of commercial fishing.

In the Faroe Islands of the North Atlantic, more than 860 pilot whales were killed between January and September of 2001, and this was a normal year. Although the Faroese claim a cultural tradition of killing the pilot whale and a need for the meat in their diet, it has been shown that as each slaughter happens, thousands of pounds of meat are dumped to make room for the fresh kill in their freezers. And the meat is laced with the heavy-metal poisons of the North Atlantic, making it very dangerous to eat.

Attempts are being made to extend the protection of the IWC to smaller cetaceans, but this effort is seen by the Japanese and other countries as a gross attack on their sovereign rights as a nation. The Japanese currently give themselves permission to "harvest" 17,700 Dall's porpoises each year, and uncounted thousands of other cetaceans species. They claim total control of this "resource" and have threatened to leave the IWC if moves are made to include dolphins, porpoises, or the smaller whales under the regulations.

In a careful analysis done by the author for the Global Whale Alliance, it was discovered that the Japanese Small-Type Whaling Association, in an attempt to counteract the criticisms of its call for legal whaling, posted a website detailing the impact of the ban on whaling on the four small towns whose traditions were affected. The shocking statistics are:

- It turns out that sixty-five people were affected directly.
- The religious ramifications of the end of whaling were that their traditional ceremonies, to absolve themselves of the guilt they incurred by killing whales and dolphins, were no longer being practiced.
- The cultural impact they bemoan is the end of happy parties where they exchange chunks of whale meat, and the loss of esteem this produces.
- The local economic impact is the loss of revenue of the restaurants in the towns which host the whale meat parties, and the impossibility of having whale on the menu for tourists who are curious about these out-of-the-way villages.

The sixty-five people who own the boats, own the licenses (which are in abeyance), and crew the boats claim hardship in direct financial losses. However, since they have been successfully maintaining their boats and engaging in other kinds of fishing for eleven years, it is hard to take seriously the losses they claim.

In Norway, the situation is similar. A very small number of people are the owners and operators of a small fleet of vessels that do the whaling. Since Norway receives over US$6 billion per year in revenues from its oil field leasing, and at least $4 billion from its direct oil field ownership, and is constantly looking for appropriate places to put its steady windfall of oil profits, it can well afford to subsidize a re-education and re-employment program for the few affected whalers and their families. Their argument is the same as the Japanese: it is a cultural tradition, and is not to be questioned.

Both nations accuse the rest of the world of *cultural imperialism*. Instead of embracing the changes that have come about over the last fifty years, when mankind began to realize the enormity of the gifts the Cetacean Nation has given us and stopped exploiting their benign nature, they insist on continuing what the rest of the world condemns. Their claim of arrogance and cultural imperialism on the part of others can only be viewed as a confused image they must see in the mirror. It is their attempt to keep outdated traditions alive that is the act of cultural domination, an arrogant defiance of the human family.

3) http://www.earthtrust.com/martentestimony.html

Chapter Fifteen: The Crystal Whales

1) Interspecies Inc., 301 Hidden Meadow, Friday Harbor, WA 98250, USA (http://www.interspecies.com/).

2) On June 8, 2001, Iceland rejoined the International Whaling Commission, specifically to pursue discussions in hopes of resuming commercial whaling. They had quit years before, declaring that the IWC was no longer a commission that managed the stocks of whales for sustainable use, but had become an anti-whaling commission.

They were right, but this is under attack again as I write. Commercial whaling could return in the near future. Perhaps our awareness of the extraordinary history we share with the Cetacean Nation can assist in preventing this.

Chapter Sixteen: The Challenge of Self-Awareness in Dolphins

1) Karen Pryor, *Lads Before the Wind: Adventures in Porpoise Training* (New York: Harper and Row, 1975), pp.234–253.

2) The Mirror Test seeks to ascertain whether a creature has a concept of self. By placing a mark on the body of an animal where it cannot see it, the animal is presented with the opportunity to demonstrate its self-awareness by being given a mirror. If the animal uses the mirror to see the mark, it can

be assumed that the animal realized it is represented in the mirror, that the image it sees is itself.

Only humans and some other primates had previously passed the mirror test. Dolphins have now proven for the first time that a non-primate species has self-awareness.

3) It so happens that I have led a trip to Bimini with Marie-Helene and her husband Buddha. We had an exciting, moving, fun, and profound journey. I shared tales and legends of the dolphins, they shared their many years of experience interacting with dolphins, and the people who came with us had a wonderful time.

Marie-Helene is a highly qualified therapist, with numerous certified skills. She caters to a clientele that has a spiritual inclination, and who are looking for changes in their lives, which dolphins can certainly stimulate. Their statements had been taken out of context, and Buddha had been described in demeaning terms as "a former lifeguard," ignoring his many years as an international businessman.

4) I have in my archives a copy of the original report submitted by Dr. Wayne Batteau's associate entitled: *Man/Dolphin Communication: Final Report, 15 December 1966–13 December 1967. Prepared for US Naval Ordnance Test Section, China Lake, California, Contract No. N00123–67-C–1103, Dwight W. Batteau and Peter R. Markey, Listening, Incorporated, 6 Garden St., Arlington, Massachusetts.*

This report authenticates the possibility of a human/dolphin communication system, providing the schematics for building electronic gear designed by Dr. Patrick Flanagan. Upon receipt of this report, all further research with dolphins became classified as secret by the US Navy. It is not possible to obtain this report in its original form by using the Freedom of Information system due to large portions being removed. I have provided copies of this report to at least thirty researchers around the world over the last seven years.

5) Francis Jeffrey and John C. Lilly, MD, *John Lilly, so far...* (Los Angeles: Jeremy Tarcher, 1990).

6) Loren Eiseley, "The Long Loneliness" (*The American Scholar*, Winter 1960–61).

Chapter Seventeen: Captivity, Freedom, and the Future

1) Oppian of Silica, Greek poet ca. A.D. 200.

2) At the Coff's Harbour Pet Porpoise Pool in Australia, a visitor in 1986 identified himself as "Bill." He badgered the staff for hours, haranguing them about the issue of captivity. He would not listen to the patient description of the circumstances of the dolphins under their care. All dolphins at the Porpoise Pool are rescued animals who would have been dead if they had not been taken in. Bill would have none of it. He said that the dolphins would be better off dead.

The next morning one of the female dolphins was found dead. She had a fractured skull, the obvious result of having her head bashed in. From the moment she was discovered, suspicion centered on Bill. When he was picked up for questioning, he was with others who protected him by insisting that he had been with them all night. No charges could be filed. Her murder went unpunished.

3) "BIOSONAR: Research has shown that dolphin biosonar is better than any current hardware system available for finding objects in shallow water. Unfortunately, we do not fully understand dolphin biological sonar and search strategies."

"In a project called ALTER (DN303032), we are exploring dolphin biological sonar to learn more about it. We hope to use this knowledge to develop new technologies that will improve current and future Fleet systems. The program is developing a computational model of the dolphin biosonar system which incorporates the animal's hearing system, search strategies, and classification capabilities for underwater targets. We also are measuring the animal's hearing system for development of new transducer models which mimic the animal's signal production and receiving capabilities."

Both quotes from a US Navy website: http://www.spawar.navy.mil/sandiego/technology/mammals/history.html

4) http://rafiki.nosc.mil/projects/projfiles/

5) http://www.spawar.navy.mil/sandiego/technology/mammals/history.html

6) Ibid.

7) http://rafiki.nosc.mil/projects/projfiles/

8) During Hurricane Andrew that devastated south Florida in 1998, the dolphins at Dolphin Research Center, on another of the Florida Keys, had been freed, urged to escape to safety, somewhere away from all the flying debris. The normal evacuation plans had gone awry, and the best the handlers could do was to open the pens, point out to sea, and yell directions to the dol-

phins. The rain lashed, the winds whipped, and the water was coming over the docks and still the people stayed on, their own lives in peril. Finally the last of the dolphins swam out into the approaching storm.

When the storm ended, the handlers, several of whom had refused to leave the Keys from concern for the dolphins, returned. They kept a watchful eye on the channel, hoping the dolphins would all come home and be uninjured. They all returned, most with no injury and only slight wounds on the others. Several of the dolphins returned with wild friends, bringing them back with them to their safe haven. None of these wild dolphins were allowed to stay but it certainly says something about the level of care, the shared love, and the sense of satisfaction that must exist for the dolphins, in their lives among humans.

In Mexico in August 2002, at the Dolphin Discovery facility on Isla Mujeres, a wild dolphin showed up one day, begging for food. It was malnourished and injured, apparently an outcast. When the dolphin handlers took a stretcher into the water, it calmly swam onto it, waiting to be lifted up, into a holding pen where it could be looked after.

9) The ultimate solution to the human desire to be near whales is for us to value the experience so highly that we spend whatever is necessary to give them homes equal to their majesty. Until then, the problem is painful for everyone.

The following is an excerpt from a letter I wrote to a journalist, commenting on her article about how Keiko, the whale in the *Free Willy* movies, shunned the freedom offered him:

> How shameful it is that Keiko is being used in ways that undermine the serious need for humans to re-think their relationship with animals. His story was a good one when he was rescued from the inappropriate Mexican facility, where warm water and inadequate care had left him with skin infections and stunted growth. He thrived in Oregon in the tank built especially for him. From the perspective of today's situation, it would have been far better for Keiko to have lived out his days as an Ambassador in Oregon.
>
> Instead, he is being forced to accept that humans do not want him to live among them anymore.
>
> This is the sad tale of Keiko: He is being carefully "told" that all his life has been of no consequence, that the relationships he has enjoyed with his human companions are of no lasting value, and that it is preferred that he "just leave, just go out into the ocean and fend for yourself." By ignoring him, more and more, Keiko is being asked to forget his friendships, to stop enjoying his relationships with peo-

ple, to take on the fearsome challenge of living wild in waters he does not remember.

This is a sentence of death....

As Ms. Donner [a producer of the *Free Willy* movies and supporter of the program under which Keiko is being "released"] says, "My personal dream is that they would just leave him out there to see if he rejoins his whale pod instead of his human pod."

To my ears, to my heart, this attitude is cruel. It is a betrayal.

He likes people. Why make him leave?

(As this book is going to press, Keiko has swum from Iceland to Norway, where he sought out human children to play with. He wants to be involved with humans.)

Chapter Eighteen: The New Gift: Dolphin-Assisted Therapy

1) "Sono-Chemistry is the interaction of sound with matter through the process of cavitation. Chemists induce cavitation by generating intense sound waves, creating alternating regions of compression and expansion that can form bubbles 100 microns in diameter. The bubbles implode violently in less than a microsecond, heating their contents to 5,500 degrees Celsius, approximately the temperature of the sun's surface."

Kenneth S. Suslick, "The Chemical Effects of Ultrasound," *Scientific American*, Vol.260, No.2 (Feb. 1989): 80.

2) S.B. Birch, "Dolphin-Human Interaction Effects," Doctoral dissertation, Monash University, Melbourne, Australia (1997).

Ryan De Mares, Ph.D., "Human Peak Experience Triggered by Encounters with Cetaceans," *Anthrozoos*, Vol.13, No.2 (2000).

D.E. Nathanson, "Using Atlantic bottlenose dolphins to increase cognition of mentally retarded children" in P. Lovibond and P. Wilson, eds., *Clinical and Abnormal Psychology*. Elsevier Science Publishers B.V., North Holland (1989): 233–242.

D.E. Nathanson and S.D Faria, "Cognitive improvement of children in water with and without dolphins," *Anthrozoos* Vol.6, No.1 (1993): 17–29.

D.E. Nathanson et al., "Effectiveness of short-term dolphin-assisted therapy for children with severe disabilities," *Anthrozoos* Vol.10, Nos.2–3 (1997): 90–100.

D.E. Nathanson, "Dolphins and kids: A communication experiment," *Congress Proceedings of the XVI World Assembly of the World Organization for*

Preschool Education (1980): 447–451.

B. Smith, "Project Inreach: A program to explore the ability of Atlantic Bottlenose dolphins to elicit communication responses from autistic children," *New Perspectives on Our Lives with Companion Animals* (Philadelphia: University of Pennsylvania Press, 1983).

B. Smith, "Dolphins Plus and autistic children," *Psychological Perspectives* Vol.18, No.2(1987): 386–393.

B.A. Smith, "Using dolphins to elicit communication from an autistic child," in R.K. Anderson, B.L. Hart, and L.A. Hart, eds., *The Pet Connection: Its Influence on Our Health and Quality of Life* (Minneapolis: Center to Study Human-Animal Relationships and Environments,1987),pp. 154–161.

B.A. Smith, "The autistic person experiences Atlantic bottlenose dolphins as therapy," *National Aquatics Journal* Vol.4, No.1 (1988):5–7.

Lorna Webb, "Impact of Semi-Captive and Wild Bottle-nosed Dolphin Interactions on Increased Well-Being and Anxiety Reduction." In press (2000).

3) Examples:
Vanessa Dyane Hoegel, *Perceptions of Dolphin Therapists and Dolphin Researchers on Using Dolphin-Assisted Therapy with Symptomatic HIV Disease.* Master's degree thesis, Pacific Oaks College, Pasadena, California (1997).

Ilanit Tof, *Psychophysiological Mechanisms of Therapeutic Dolphin-Human Interactions.* Submitted for BA in Psychology and Psychophysiology, Swinburne University, Melbourne, Australia (1998).

4) *And Then There is Hope…*, television documentary for Dutch TV. Production credits missing.

Chapter Nineteen: The Garden of the Golden Dolphin

1) Search your local region for a permaculture designer. Talk to him or her. Find a local designer's course to take. One such course is given each year by Bill Mollison's number-one teaching partner, Scott Pittman, at Hummingbird Ranch in northern New Mexico.
If you are in the US: Contact them through www.globalfamily.net.
Phone: 1-800-336-3493
Office address: 11689 Lowhills Rd., Nevada City, CA 95959, USA

2) It is a curious fact that Bill Mollison built his Permaculture Institute on the flanks of Mt. Warning, New South Wales, Australia. From there he taught the world how to design the future. In poor health, he has now retired to the wilds of Tasmania, leaving his beloved farm. Now defunct as a school, it served for many years as a model teaching center, launching pad for guerrilla gardeners, and revolutionary headquarters for a literal grass-roots movement to change the face of the world. The barren dairy farm that he bought to demonstrate his practical wisdom on is now a forest, with dozens of lakes and abundant wildlife, a wild garden full of food.

Just as the Legend predicted, Mt. Warning reflects the light of the Dawning. It is the highest peak on the eastern shore of Australia, the first point of land to receive the morning light, on the first continent to be lit by each new day.

Chapter Twenty: "Build a boat of pleasing proportions..."

1) John C. Lilly, MD, *The Mind of the Dolphin: A Nonhuman Intelligence* (New York: Doubleday, 1967).

2) John C. Lilly, MD, *The Scientist: A Metaphysical Autobiography* (Berkeley, California: Ronin Publishing, 1997), p. 205.

Appendix One: A Whale and Dolphin Primer

1) John C. Lilly, MD, *The Dyadic Cyclone* (New York: Simon and Schuster, 1976), in the chapter titled "The Dolphins Revisited," p. 198.

2) Ibid., p. 197.

3) Ivan T. Sanderson, *Follow the Whale*, quoted in *Whale Nation*, by Heathcote Williams. (New York: Harmony Books, 1988), p. 130.

Appendix Two: An Afterword: The Soul of a Dolphin

1) Robin Brown, *The Lure of the Dolphin* (New York: Avon, 1979), p. 200.

2) I feel that the traditional framework is correct, which places concentration (one-pointed attention) first, then meditation (sustained attention on a transcendental object) and then the goal, which is contemplation (absorp-

tion into the object of one's meditation). For me, the negative effects from weakening these distinctions between stages of mental development are issues of real importance, affecting the adequacy of preparation for soul embodiment.

3) Along with our adaptability has come a curious lack of certainty, however. We require guidance in every climate to survive. Either cultural transmission gives us the special knowledge of what plants are edible and how to find water, or we study books of this knowledge and hope it can be recalled when we are hard pressed.

Animals do not require this. Human infants must be placed at the nipple to begin suckling, but a newborn horse struggles to its feet and wobbles its way around until it can nuzzle its mother for milk, entirely unaided. There is in the horse and all other animals a mysterious ability that is innate, a set of knowledge that comes "pre-installed" in the bio-computer of animals.

Along with our human flexibility has come a kind of dependence, a sort of permanent childish need to be led, to be shown how to perform. Our ability to learn is unmatched as a result. And baby dolphins also must be shown where the teats are and how to breastfeed, and even must be taught to breathe.

Index

The Cetacean Studies Institute

"Enhancing the Relationship Between Humans and Whales and Dolphins"

The Cetacean Studies Institute maintains a large archive. CSI also conducts original research, especially in the areas of Dolphin-Assisted Therapy and interspecies communication. The resources of CSI are used to design educational programs for schools, nature centers, dolphin swim facilities, and study groups.

If you have gifts to contribute to the archive, whether it be funding, a library of books and papers, a record of personal experiences, recordings, films, photos, or artifacts relating to our mission, please contact us.

If you have relevant research to share, or an experience with dolphins or whales that ought to be part of our database, please consider sending it to us. Donations to CSI for its operations and projects are tax-deductible in the US.

CSI occasionally offers guided tours to sites where the Dolphin-Human Story can be explored. This may include visits to swim facilities, aquariums, live-aboard boat excursions among wild dolphins and whales, or tours of ancient cultural sites. Please contact us for a current schedule.

For more information:

www.dolphintale.com
or
Cetacean Studies Institute
PO Box 2116
Byron Bay, New South Wales
2481
Australia